SONORA

A UNIVERSITY OF ARIZONA SOUTHWEST CENTER BOOK

JOSEPH C. WILDER, SERIES EDITOR

David Yetman

SONORA
An Intimate Geography

PHOTOGRAPHS BY *Virgil Hancock*
MAPS AND DRAWINGS BY *Paul Mirocha*

Published in cooperation with the
University of Arizona Southwest Center

UNIVERSITY OF NEW MEXICO PRESS
ALBUQUERQUE

All color photographs are reproduced by permission of
the photographer, Virgil Hancock.

Book design by Christopher Kuntze.

LIBRARY OF CONGRESS CATALOGING-IN-PUBLICATION DATA

Yetman, David, 1941–
   Sonora : an intimate geography / David Yetman.—1st ed.
       p.   cm.
   "A University of Arizona Southwest Center Book."
   Includes bibliographical references and index.
   ISBN 0–8263–1701–4
   1. Sonora (Mexico : State)—Description and travel. 2. Yetman,
David, 1941–   —Journeys—Mexico—Sonora (State) I. Title
F1346.Y47   1996
972'.17—dc20   95–32463
                                                       CIP

For

VICENTE TAJIA & ALBERTO BÚRQUEZ

Sonorans whose love and knowledge of their land has

made my life immeasurably richer

and for the late

DOÑA CAROLINA VALENZUELA

whose indomitable courage and resourcefulness are

an inspiration to all who knew her

CONTENTS

MAPS

COLOR PLATES   *(following page 144)*

ENTRADA

I made my first trip to Sonora in 1961. At Nogales I crossed
the border, a nervous, excited, expectant youth heading for the
South, to Mazatlán, jungle, exotic beaches and peoples. I was
stopped by a uniformed border guard, his eyes concealed by dark
green sunglasses made darker by the visor of his cap. He pointed
efficiently to the customs office, an ancient, yellow building with
sagging doorways and an air of cold bureaucracy about it. A sign
above the crowded opening read *Aduana* (customs). I shut off
Odin's engine uneasily and glanced around, irritated by the blaring horns, the smoking diesel buses, the coldly curious stares of
vendors, ragged shoe shine boys, and athletic youths with quick-
footed appearance. Silent men in uniforms looked on menac-
ingly as I tightened the cinch on Odin, my Cushman motor
scooter, to protect my meager belongings—a tired old bulky
brown sleeping bag, a lumpy duffel, a dented boy scout canteen,
and a battered tool box. A boy no more than seven, with dark,
hopeful eyes approached me with a shoe shine box. "*¿Bola?*" he
asked, looking up. This was well beyond my sorry vocabulary,
limited at the time to numbers and a few phrases gleaned from
Berlitz Self-Teaching Spanish. I shrugged my shoulders and gave him
a peso.

So this was Nogales. I had heard stories from friends who had
made frantic trips here from Tucson in search of the fast plea-
sures of youth, hustling vintage taxis to whisk them to the zone
of spirits and perfume and a mythical powder called Spanish Fly.
Here I found myself in April of 1961, setting out for the fabled
land south of the border, alone, untutored in Spanish, lacking in
maps and appallingly unlettered in street wisdom, fearful of the
vague, rumored dangers of Mexico—an alien land of strange
customs, unfamiliar landscapes, banana politics, and disoriented
history: Sonora. That was the name of the state south of Arizona. Rumors abounded of spreading ranches, Indians, undis-
covered minerals, vast mountain ranges, uncharted deserts, low
prices and unspecified peril.

Reluctantly leaving Odin unattended, like a cowboy looking back nervously at his prized mount, I shot the indifferent-looking onlookers a beseeching glance and walked to the poorly ventilated old yellow brick building, joining the queue outside the door.

At the front of the line and through another door two men wearing olive-drab uniforms, military hats, and sunglasses sat behind a counter at ancient typewriters, stoically pecking away with two fingers, asking cryptic questions in flat, accented English, recording the responses on the forms.

After an hour I reached the desk and meekly presented my passport. The agent asked my name, age, address, and religion. Religion? Why would they want to know my religion? I knew Mexico was mostly Catholic, so I should say I'm Catholic. No, no, no, my thoughts raced. I'd heard something about anticlericalism in the government. OK, I'd say Protestant. No, that could be even worse. Protestants were missionaries, and they kicked them out of the country. I was on the verge of panic and held up my hands in confusion. The agent looked at me deeply, shook his head in despair, and wrote something down. Next he wanted to know my "method of transportation"? "Scooter," I said.

"Scooter?"

"¿Escuter?" The agent lit a cigarette and turned with an exasperated look to the man seated at the other typewriter. My heart sank. Would they reject my request for a visa just because they didn't know the word for what I was driving?

"Ah," one of them said, coming up with the proper Spanish word, "motoneta." I'd been rescued. That's one word I never forgot.

They asked to see proof how much money I was carrying. They had no use in Mexico for undesirables, beatnik types, loafers, hangers-on. Nervously I pulled out my billfold, clutching it all the while, and flashed my thin wad of bills, both pesos and dollars. A peso was worth eight cents, I knew—the price of a beer or two large Cokes. The agent hesitated, unimpressed, I'm sure, with the paltry sum, then nodded, grunted something Spanish, unsmilingly hammered my visa with a stamp, and signed it with a huge flourish. Years later I decided that was his artistic function, to decorate the lifeless forms with a robust

signature that couldn't be forged and would be easily recognizable to customs guards down the line. At the time I thought he
was just trying to make me more nervous.

The agent handed over my visa and looked past me to the
next supplicant. I left the building with a sense of euphoric
liberation, waving the document for all to see, my passport to
the mysterious land to the south. No one had molested Odin.
The same crowd watched with mildly curious stares as I kicked
the starter a few times. My self-consciousness increased until
Odin finally coughed to life. I climbed on, waved good-bye, and
chugged off, put-putting up the street.

Nogales, I would learn in later years, is Spanish for walnuts, and
it must have been named after the trees that used to line the arroyo draining the town. It was a fine setting for a ranch and not
bad for a town or small city, even with the congested traffic and
the houses built on hillsides so precipitous it seemed inevitable
they would jiggle loose and come crashing down into the creek.
It had 25,000 inhabitants, I read somewhere. All of them were
either watching me or driving cars that slowed me down. Bicycles
and small motorcycles clogged the streets, darting in and out of
traffic with a recklessness I both envied and resented.

Toward the southern edge of the city I obeyed a sign ordering
me to stop at what looked like an overgrown automobile repair
shop. A beaten sign over the building read "Car Permits." While
I was waiting in line, behind the same folks I had waited behind
back at the *aduana,* I glanced at my visa. According to it I was
born in Niw Yersei, was divorced, and lived in Pesciote, Arizona,
and to think I signed this document as being true and correct!
Suppose they should find out I was a 19-year-old bachelor from
Prescott? Would they throw me in jail for falsifying a document?
Should I drive back to the *aduana* and wait in the interminable
line again to inform the agent he had misread my passport? An
official rescued me from my anxiety, a nervous, busy little man in
an army cap wearing a faded gray shirt that bore a badge. He led
me to an office where another official filled in a form. Then the
little man affixed a decal to the windshield of my scooter and
waited around for a tip, holding the documents just beyond my
reach as a carrot. Reluctantly I gave him five pesos—forty cents.
He handed me the papers, and off I went. I stared at the papers.
Now I was divorced. I made up a name for my imaginary ex-wife.

Leaving behind the congested border city, Odin putted contentedly up over the pass at the south end of the valley, whizzed by the airport hidden in a forest of graceful sun-drenched oaks and tall grass, and began a gradual descent through the valley of the Río Magdalena, a fertile, green-and-silver band nestled among rolling hills where ancient Emory oaks stood guard over the abundant grass, fresh and just beginning to turn green after the spring moisture. From time to time I caught a glimpse of the sun reflecting off the stream that wound through the freshly budded cottonwoods, flowing past old adobe ranches and farmhouses. A distant mountain range to the west looked dark and cool. Dirt roads, sometimes only two ruts, led off from the narrow highway, teasing me with a sneak preview of freshly plastered and whitewashed farmhouses protected from livestock by fences of ocotillo and mesquite. I saw *sartas* of dark red chiles hanging from windows. Burros and horses grazed, and chickens scratched right up to the edge of the highway where speeding trucks and cars roared by. Every so often candles flickered from inside tiny shrines at the edge of the highway, some no larger than a dog house.

Red flashing lights and signs ordered me to stop: another inspection station where they would examine my papers with minute scrutiny. Once again my stomach tightened about nothing in particular. An olive-drab uniformed official studied my papers and frowned skeptically at Odin. "Wair aar jou goink?" he asked.

"Mazatlán," I said, remembering the destination indicated on my visa. He looked away, handed the documents back, waved me on, and resumed his unhurried demeanor. Now I could finally breathe a sigh of relaxation. From what veteran travelers had told me, this was the last checkpoint for a hundred miles. I was free, at least for the time being, of possible harassment by customs officials.

The highway followed the eastern edge of the valley, two narrow lanes frequently plugged by wide, flatulent diesel trucks, creeping along billowing black choking smoke that made me regret my choice of a motor scooter for transportation. The fields were bigger now—alfalfa, apple orchards, corn. Cows grazed everywhere, some foraging contentedly on the shoulder of the highway. How do they keep from getting killed? I wondered.

Not all of them did. The stench from a bloated carcass on the shoulder hit me, its legs protruding grotesquely like pipes from an inflated bagpipe. I held my breath till the corpse was far in the distance.

At Odin's top speed of forty-five miles per hour I chugged on past hamlets shaded by giant mesquites, cottonwoods just beginning to throw cotton, and eucalyptus. Mountain ranges blue and gray loomed on either side of the highway. Cowboys on horseback trotted by on the shoulder, seemingly oblivious to the traffic. I waved, and they waved back, staring for a moment at the diminutive vehicle I was driving. Abruptly, the highway climbed out of the valley, over a pass, down again, and through a shady grove of cottonwoods at a place called Agua Caliente. I knew enough Spanish to realize that meant "hot water." A few more hamlets and a brief hill, and I reached Imuris (stress is on the first syllable), a town bordered on the east by towering blue mountains. The village was named for Pima Indians who lived there, their village already ancient when the Spaniards arrived.

"Café," read a sign over a hut. *Tome Coca Cola* ("Drink Coke,") the brightly painted mural on the walls of the hut urged me. (In those days soft drink companies would paint people's houses in return for letting them use the walls for ads.) I sat at the tiny table and ordered *frijoles y tortillas.* The rear door to the café was open. Chickens scratched in the dirt just outside. Clothes hung on a clothesline, and a small pen held a goat.

The meal came quickly: good fried beans, great fresh flour tortillas and something else—two tortillas with fresh cheese melted between. It was delicious. I caught the waitress's eye and pointed at the last bite. *Quesadilla,* she explained and soon brought me another. They were invented right here in Imuris, inhabitants informed me years later.

I gobbled down the food, and the waitress presented me with the check. I paid the forty-four cents, said *grácias* and *adiós* and pulled Odin back onto the highway. I left the graceful valley and crossed some desert hills before descending to the Río Magdalena again. The brown, brushy hills merged into the verdant green of the valley. Off to the right was a tiny village nestled on a ridge above the river. I slowed and looked back to the right, seeing a distant white steeple. San Ignacio, the sign said. Someday I'd stop there.

Not far beyond lay Magdalena (renamed Magdalena de Kino in 1966), a bustling city almost hidden among the cottonwoods in the river valley. From a distance I caught sight of the steeple and dome of the large church. Father Kino's bones are now displayed in a weird crypt near the church, but in those days no one knew the whereabouts of the great Jesuit's remains.

All traffic—cattle trucks, semis, the massive crackling all-purpose Mexican trucks, buses, bicycles, horses—passed through the narrow streets of the city. The pavement was terrible, dusty, booby trapped with deep potholes, arroyos, even canyons, it seemed.

In the middle of Magdalena, Odin got caught behind a horse-drawn cart, ambling along at a leisurely pace, seats filled with a placid Mexican family. Children riding the rear eyed me curiously. Behind us loomed a very big truck bristling with impatience, its psychopathic driver not above squashing me and Odin flat in his rush to the south. Mercifully the cart turned off after only a couple of blocks, and I picked up speed again, left the bustling city behind, and continued through the tree-bordered fields of alfalfa, orchards of apple and persimmon, gardens of garlic.

That was how I met Sonora—on a motor scooter. Odin and I forged on south, through the big city of Hermosillo, across a drier desert to Guaymas and its serene bay on the Sea of Cortés. Then it was on southeast through thickening brush into vast Yaqui country and Ciudad Obregón, a new city built by the wealth extracted from the fabulous fertility of the fields of the Yaqui Valley and the high-tech innovations of the Green Revolution. We continued south to Navojoa on the semi-tropical Río Mayo and into the thorn forest with its wealth of exotic plants and animals, arriving at Alamos in the extreme southern part of the state late the following afternoon, almost four hundred miles south of where I had crossed at Nogales.

I've been back hundreds of times since then, the first only a few months later. I've gone by scooter, auto, boat, bus, plane, train, and even on foot. An indescribable attraction toward Sonora has become a dominant force in my life. Now I finally have a chance to begin to explain why.

ACKNOWLEDGMENTS

I could not have written this book without generous financial support from the Southwest Center of the University of Arizona under the leadership of Joe Wilder, who encouraged me and made it possible for me to travel to places I hadn't visited before and write about them. My wife, Lynn Fowler, was a terrific editor and showed superhuman tolerance for my meanderings through Sonora. Virgil Hancock came up with the idea of the book in the first place and spent many days driving through Sonora with me in the passenger seat of his truck. Merv Larson was a constant source of comments and his inn La Posada de Alamos a refuge on repeated occasions. Jesús García of Magdalena spent hours with me explaining Sonoran idioms and customs.

Numerous acquaintances knowingly and unknowingly made suggestions for the text. They include Tony Burgess, Barney Burns, Mark Dimmit, Bernard Fontana, Jim Griffith, Julian Hayden, Jim Hills, Fernando Ibarra, Gene Joseph, Cynthia Lindquist, Paul Martin, Jim Officer, Bill Risner, Tom Sheridan, Ray Turner, and Tom Van Devender. The late Howard Scott Gentry made several comments that sent me off to new and fascinating places. David Burkhalter spent a good deal of time with me in Sonora, making acute observations that may have wound up in the text.

Several individuals made editing suggestions, including Alberto Búrquez, Bernard Fontana, Greg McNamee, Carmen Villa Prezelski, Tom Riste, Tom Sheridan, Joe Wilder, and my patient editor at New Mexico, Durwood Ball.

Helpful and gracious Sonorans were many, among them, Joaquín Acosta, Eduardo Acosta, Memo Acosta, Armando Aguilar, Rubén Alvarez, Gustavo Aragón, Santiago Astorga, Alberto Búrquez, Cipriano Buitimea Romero, José Campoy, Carlos Galindo, María Garrobo García, Luis Guerrero, hijo, Dr. Jesús Armando Haro, the late Roberto Herrera, Ramon Hurtado, Don Johnson, Angel Lagarda, Braulio López, Rigoberto López

Estudillo, Angelina Martínez, Francisco Manzo Taylor, Cruz Matus, Dr. Samuel Ocaña García, Dr. Leobardo Quiroz, Alejandro Ramos, Ester Saucedo, Carmen Sinohui de Palafox, Vicente Tajia, Rita Terán de Valencia, Jesús Uribe García, Che Che Valencia de Terán, the late Carolina Valenzuela, Francisco Valenzuela Nolasco, and Lidia Zazueta. There were many more whose names I never got, including a nameless herd of *federales,* who helped a little or a lot in my efforts to put the book together.

SONORA: AN INTIMATE GEOGRAPHY

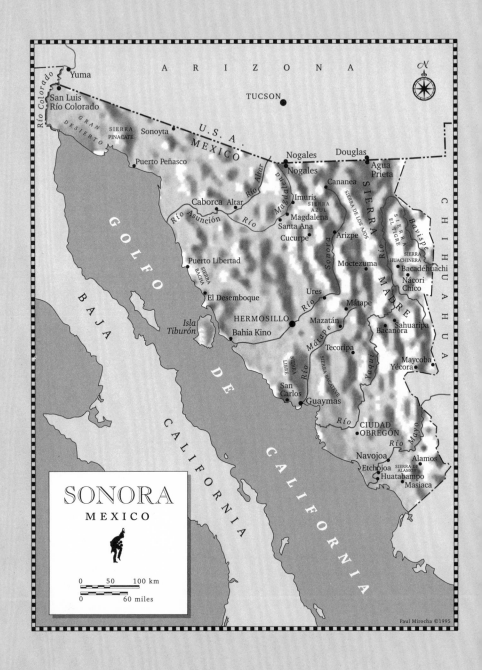

ARIZONA

Yuma

Río Colorado

San Luis
Río Colorado

TUCSON

SIERRA
PINACATE

GRAN
DESIERTO

Sonoyta

U. S. A.
MEXICO

Puerto Peñasco

Nogales

Nogales

Douglas

Agua
Prieta

Caborca   Altar

Río Asunción

Río

Río Altar

Río Magdalena

Río Concepción

Imuris

Magdalena

Santa Ana

Cucurpe

Cananea

SIERRA
AZUL

SIERRA DE LOS AJOS

SIERRA MADRE

SIERRA
EL TIGRE

CHIHUAHUA

Arizpe

Río Sonora

Moctezuma

Bavispe Río

SIERRA
HUACHINERA

Bacadéhuachi

Nácori
Chico

GOLFO

BAJA

Puerto Libertad

SIERRA
BACHA

El Desemboque

Isla
Tiburón

HERMOSILLO

Bahia Kino

DE

Ures

Río Sonora

Río Mátape

Mátape

Mazatán

Sahuaripa

Bacanora

CALIFORNIA

SIERRA
LIBRE

Tecoripa

SIERRA BACATETE

Río Mátape

Río Yaqui

Maycoba
Yécora

San
Carlos

Guaymas

CALIFORNIA

Río Yaqui

CIUDAD
OBREGÓN

Río Mayo

Navojoa

Etchojoa

Huatabampo

SIERRA DE
ALAMOS

Alamos

Masiaca

SONORA

MEXICO

0   50   100 km
0   60 miles

Paul Mirocha ©1995

PROLOGUE

Sonora—The Enigma

On successive trips to Sonora, I began to notice great and dark
mountain ranges to the east and vast desert plains to the west of
the highway. What lay out there? Where did the great rivers
come from, the ones that fill the dams and pour water into the
ditches that irrigate the endless fields around Hermosillo, Ciudad Obregón, and Navojoa? What were all these towns like,
whose names I saw on road signs and maps but hadn't seen in
person? Who were the people living there?

Through all my wanderings I have found common themes,
universal trends, unified complaints. As late as thirty years ago
parts of Sonora lived as though the rest of the world were a
mere story. Modern communications, especially television and
paved roads, have ended that timeless isolation. What happens
in remote villages like Bacadéhuachi is determined to a great
extent by market forces in Hermosillo.

My visits to the towns of the eastern half of the state reveal a
dying province—economically, socially and ecologically. The old
agricultural base is gone. Self-sufficiency is long forgotten. The
towns are drained of young men. Many of the ancient ranching
families have departed, replaced by a rapacious breed, the nou-
veaux riches of drug profits. In the east, only in isolated places
did I find optimism for the future. While some large-scale cattle
ranching is booming, it is at the expense of the small-time
rancher. Much, if not most, of the ranching prosperity is enjoyed by absentee landlords from the cities, not the country folk.

By contrast, the cities of the west are teeming, even prosper-
ing. Most of the growth, however, is a result of in-migration by
very poor people and of movement of water and commodities
from the east to the west. The west of Sonora has been enriched
at the expense of the east in a process that began a hundred
years ago. The countryside of the east is becoming impoverished
to maintain the wealth of the cities of the west.

Sonora's great beauty and incomparable natural resources have been compromised and are being seriously eroded. Its mountain forests are mostly gone, its tropical forests are in jeopardy, and its desert forests are falling rapidly to the blade of the machete and the bulldozer. Its surface waters are overallocated; its deep waters are approaching exhaustion. Its harbors are polluted, its ocean depleted, its beaches befouled. I've been unable to locate a single operating sewage treatment plant in the state.

The prosperity of a small minority in the cities has been at the expense of the other parts of the state. Sonora's indigenous population of Yaquis, Mayos, Guarijíos, Seris and Mountain Pimas is under intense cultural and economic pressure. The pastures of the Sierra Madre and the great plains of Sonora are continually being asked to yield a flood of riches to support the urban elite and a trickling for the urban poor. They have already reached the point where their yields cannot be increased.

All of the sad pictures I'm describing can be developed into scholarly publications. What I've found in my travels through lands I love and among people I've grown to respect deeply should be the subject matter for formal research. In the meantime the state's people and places speak for themselves.

One thing has not changed: the dramatic difference one sees when crossing the border. The language, culture, customs, even the countryside seem to change instantly. Nowhere else on our planet is a political boundary accompanied by such a vast social difference. Neither side knows the other well. The Mexican hand signal for "come here" is easily mistaken for American "good-bye." The Mexican workday is from nine to three with a long siesta for dinner. Then they work again (sometimes) in the evening. They eat at strange hours, don't use seat belts, toss trash with abandon, have huge families, stick together. They gather at shrines for reasons obscure to us. They party and pray at the same time. Huge rock paintings of Nuestra Señora de Guadalupe appear along superhighways and remote mountain passes. Pilgrims, rich and poor, light candles and make wishes. Their cities and towns end abruptly at the edge—there are no suburbs.

They like to be where everyone else is. They find our quest for solitude to be a perverse form of loneliness. There are no lone Mexican outdoorsmen—no John Muirs, no Henry David Thoreaus, no frontiersmen, no cries of "Elbow Room!" Few of them go camping, and when they do, they camp close together. Not only that, each (real) man is expected to build his own house.

They have a bewildering array of holidays, civil and religious. They lavish graves with decorations and have endless fiestas for rites of passage: births, anniversaries, confirmations, *quinceñeras,* baptisms, saints' days, wakes, weddings, Children's Day (in addition to the commercially important Mother's and Father's days), Easter, Christmas, Ash Wednesday, the Day of the Dead, and patron saints' fiestas. They vacation during Holy Week, when the cities empty in a rush for the coast, where they gather in happy hordes, each hoping the crowd will increase in size.

How, then, can I an American presume to write about a culture so different, so alien, so removed from my natural consciousness? My reply is simple: thirty years of digression, three decades of mesmerization with Sonora, hundreds of visits, many dozens of acquaintances, and several close friends. Sonora's differences attracted me; her perversity delighted me; her people's foreign presentation intoxicated me. My mind, my tongue, my wits are anglicized; my perceptions are shaped by Protestantism; my world view is Western. However, each time I return home from Sonora I find my own culture to be, in T. S. Eliot's words, "an alien people clutching their gods." I've stumbled into revelations, peeked into forbidden corners, pried into Sonoran consciousnesses, been robbed, duped, tricked, mocked, and ridiculed but my conversations with hundreds of Sonorans have shown me a breadth of humanity I'd never imagined. From a former governor to a dignified but destitute Indian, from a prestigious *diputado* to a desperate beggar, from a wealthy rancher to a hundred dirt-poor *campesinos,* I've learned about a different world. I write what I've seen as a *gabacho* (an outsider) who has roamed the inside of the state, where few Sonorans venture. I've pieced together a mosaic of what many have taught me in a hundred villages and a thousand pastures.

Back in 1961 I saw only a tiny portion of Sonora from the highway, the part most amenable to being crossed by a straight line. Even today only a brief sojourn from the main roads reveals Sonora to be still a land of ranches and small farms, of vast stretches of unspoiled countryside, of small towns, of tiny general stores and gossip, of Indians. Farther away from the trodden path lie mighty mountain peaks, deeply incised canyons, hidden villages, and unfamiliar peoples.

Sonora's population in 1990 was listed by the Mexican government as slightly over 1.8 million and growing fast. Demographers predict that Mexico's population problem will worsen dramatically in the next decade when its youthful population reaches reproductive age. One observer of Mexico has likened the republic to India in terms of the demographic, economic, social, and ecological problems it will face in the decades to come. However, the countryside often belies the crowding problems Mexico faces. Because rural unemployment is worse than urban joblessness, youths forsake the towns for the city, leaving rural Sonora a vision of the Old Mexico of Pancho Villa, of Alvaro Obregón, of *charros* and *señoritas*, of *vaqueros* and *barbacoas*, at least at a superficial glance. Sometimes only the ubiquitous red and gold Tecate beer cans and bits of plastic shopping bag that litter every possible road serve to remind us that we are in the dying moments of the twentieth century.

Sonora is a large state, 72,000 square miles, shaped vaguely like a right triangle standing on its apex. Wider than Arizona at the northern border with the United States, it narrows to scarcely fifty miles wide at its southern terminus with Sinaloa. Nearly five hundred miles separate San Luis, on the Colorado River, from Navojoa, the southernmost Sonoran city on Mexico Route 15.

The state is rugged. Gigantic escarpments tower over narrow valleys. Although the highest peak is under nine thousand feet, nearby river valleys are nearly always below two thousand feet. North-to-south flowing rivers separate parallel ranges that slice through the entire eastern half of the state, one range following another, each higher than the last as you travel east, each forming a barrier to east-west travel. No one has been able to tell me which is the highest peak in the state. Current aeronautical charts disagree. The most recent shows a peak in the Sierra de los Ajos as being 8,630 feet and another peak in the Sierra Huachinera ten feet taller. The official record will have to await an official expedition.

Only thirty years ago, without a high-clearance vehicle, a trip from Moctezuma to Hermosillo was an arduous journey. It was necessary to travel 120 miles by winding dirt road north to Agua

Prieta, west 110 miles to Imuris, then south 125 miles to Hermosillo, making it a nine-hour drive. I know: I've done the whole stretch—with my family. Now a paved road to the southwest of Moctezuma winds over the mountains and has shortened the journey to little more than a hundred miles and two hours.

The great river valleys—the Mayo, Yaqui, Sonora, Magdalena, Altar, and their tributaries—run generally north to south, paralleling the mountain ranges. Communication has historically run north to south as well. At the time I was first touring Mexico by motor scooter, no paved crossing from Sonora to adjoining Chihuahua existed. Even now, only two are completed—one at the extreme northeastern part of the state and another just finished in the central part. The northeastern route, completed in the early 1970s, has deteriorated so badly as to be slower than many roads of pure dirt. So rough are the ranges, so deep the canyons and valleys, so variable the flow of the rivers, so wide the Sierra Madre, that few highways have been built. In some places the border between the two states has not been surveyed. However, with the completion of Highway 16, *Chihuahuenses* can leave their capital and arrive at Kino Bay in little more than twelve hours, their first direct connection in history with the sea. The road, though paved and well engineered, is an unending series of curving ascents and descents, cliffs, forests, deserts and canyons that even power-steering can't make easy.

Nearly all roads leading east are still dead ends. The fifty-mile drive from Sahuaripa to Nátora, the last town going east in that part of the state, takes all day. North and east of Alamos, the Río Mayo Valley constricts until mile-deep rocky canyons and sheer cliffs preclude passage by any vehicle. So it is throughout the state. Eastbound roads wind up against the convoluted escarpments of the Sierra Madre. Only four-wheel-drive roads penetrate most of this vast mountain system, discouraging settlement and retarding communications to the east. To the south lie thorny forests growing from a muddy clay nearly impassable during the rainy season and rivers that routinely overflow their banks.

Geography served to isolate Sonora. Communications to the south and east were always difficult. To the north lay an alien English-speaking culture, an empire that gobbled up more than half of Mexico's original territory.

Lacking strong ties to the south, east or north, Sonorans were left to an isolation that developed a distinctly Sonoran ethos, a personality type. Sonorans are proud of their independence and always have been. They resent Mexico City's control, referring to residents of the capital with the disparaging term *chilango* (chile-eater). They find southerners to be uncouth and low-class, referring to them with the pejorative term *guacho* (something akin to "klutz"). They often express a closer affinity to the United States than to the distant capital in the south. Neither the strong United States economic presence in the border region nor the lure of the north shows any sign of abating. Despite invasions and interventions from the United States, Sonorans are attracted to this country. Several years ago rumors abounded that the United States would soon purchase Sonora from Mexico and make it the fifty-first state.

Still, Sonorans are Mexicans through and through and proud of it. Four presidents have been Sonorans, and Donaldo Colosio, the assassinated 1994 PRI nominee, was Sonoran. A deeply patriotic current runs through the people. Sonora was a strong base of support for the Mexican Revolution that restored the principle of constitutional government after it had been abrogated by Porfirio Díaz. Sonoran military forces were a key element in the overthrow of forces loyal to the aging dictator and his later supporters. In short, what Sonora has in common with the rest of the republic far outweighs any differences.

The origin of the name Sonora makes for heated discussion. Those who exalt Sonora's Indian past maintain the name is derived from a Pima word *sonot*, meaning corn leaf. Those wishing to link Sonora to Spain point to the name's proximity to the term for Mary, *Señora*, and view it as a corruption of the Spanish. The two sides will never agree. Nor do they need to. Sonora's personality, the character of her people, her physiognomy, her vegetation, make her distinguishable from all other Mexican states. I'll begin now where my trip on Odin ended, in Alamos.

PART ONE

Where it is Emerald-Green in Summertime

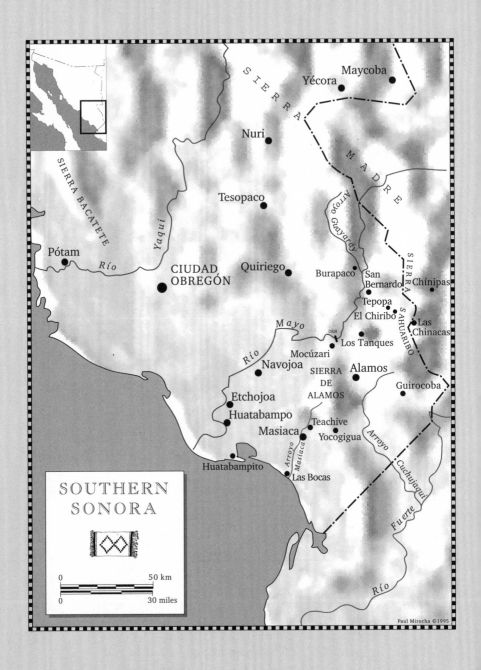

SIERRA

Maycoba

Yécora

Nuri

SIERRA BACATETE

Tesopaco

MADRE

Arroyo Guayardy

Pótam

Río   Yaqui

CIUDAD
OBREGÓN

Quiriego

Burapaco

San
Bernardo

Chínipas

SIERRA

Tepopa

Mayo

El Chiribo

SAHUARIBO

Las
Chinacas

Río

DAM

Los Tanques

Mocúzari

Navojoa

SIERRA
DE
ALAMOS

Alamos

Guirocoba

Etchojoa

Huatabampo

Teachive

Masiaca

Yocogigua

Arroyo Cuchujaqui

Huatabampito

Arroyo Masiaca

Las Bocas

Fuerte

Río

SOUTHERN
SONORA

0 ——————— 50 km
0 ——————— 30 miles

Paul Mirocha ©1995

CHAPTER 1

Alamos

"Go see Alamos, David. There's no goddamn place like it." He
was a grizzled, cigar-chewing, hardened veteran of travel in Mexico, a seller of insurance, real estate, funeral plots, used cars, and,
I suspect, snake oil. He had a paunch, a red nose and bags under
his eyes. His skin was a tough, leathery yellow from years of in-
gesting anti-malarial medicine. He was reputed to be an authority on Sonora. He sold me insurance for my motor scooter in
Nogales, Arizona. I knew nothing, absolutely nothing, about
Mexico. I was a young nineteen, obviously green. He told me
how to get to Alamos, and I went. I'd been working as a construction laborer in Prescott, Arizona. The lure of Mexico was
too great. I saved money, paid a hundred and fifty dollars for
Odin and headed south.

The road from Navojoa, thirty-four miles away, had been
paved just before my first visit. The highway rose gradually,
winding into ever-denser forests, skirting a steep range of mountains. The scooter put-putted around the curves. The forest rose
above the road, boxing it in. Odin topped a slight hill a few
miles from Alamos, and the steeple of the ancient church came
into view, soaring over ruined colonial mansions and the tropical
forest. I slowed down to a crawl when the pavement ended and
was replaced by cobbled streets, which suddenly narrowed and
jarred me like a jackhammer. I was enclosed on each side by continuous walls of white, with deep indentations for windows protected by stern bars of wrought iron. I let Odin idle along. Burros and horses parted to let me by, and pedestrians stopped and
stared. Odin's belch was amplified in the urban canyon into an
embarrassing sonic boom. I drove by a shaded square, onto another street too narrow for vehicles, with no sidewalk and no
curb. The alley suddenly emptied into a wide, sunny plaza surrounded by graceful old buildings protected by arched portals.
Half the buildings were in ruins. Others had deep, shaded

porches sustained by ancient beams and arches. There were purple, red, and orange flowers on the walls, wrought iron grates enclosing shuttered windows, and massive double wooden doors bleached by the ages. Horse dung abounded among the cobbles. The old church of hewn stone towered above, silent, brooding in the midday heat.

I chugged back to the shaded square—the *alameda*—and sat alone in cottonwood shade (*alamos* means cottonwoods) on a wrought-iron bench, feeling self-conscious. I was pale skinned in a sea of brown, light haired in a land of black. I watched patient taco and beverage vendors talking to each other across the street, listened to the rumble of hooves and cart wheels on the cobbled streets, and heard *ranchera* music blasting from a nearby saloon. As a kid I had dreamed of places like this, and now I was here. I ventured to a refreshment stand. With nerves of chilled steel and a quaking stomach I paid eight cents for a beer (in those days every refreshment stand sold it)—certainly the first beer I ever purchased and probably the first I had tasted. Not knowing just how to drink it, I tried to be cool, casual, feeling as though all the world was watching. The sudden chill and the alcohol rush made me sit down.

Children dressed in blue-and-white school uniforms crowded around me, their arms folded around school books. They admired my scooter and asked me innumerable questions I couldn't understand. Older youths stood back, watching. Cagier *viejitos* (old-timers) peered silently from park benches, pretending to take no interest in the gringo. These folk were curious but polite and unobtrusive.

The town market opened onto the alameda and overflowed with fruit. I walked past the stalls filled with produce, some of which was familiar, a lot unfamiliar. Merchants looked at me curiously, skeptically. I paid for a couple of ripe cantaloupes, sliced them with my pocketknife, and shared them with the kids. Four urchins competed to give my worn shoes a *bola* (shine). I couldn't speak with them because I didn't have enough Spanish. I had to be content with gestures. I also had to learn Spanish.

Even then I realized that Alamos is different from the rest of Sonora. Most Sonorans acknowledge that fact. It's only a part of Sonora today because the inhabitants pressured Mexico City to be split off from Sinaloa and included in Sonora when the states were divided after Independence in the early 1800s. They figured they would have more power as part of Sonora than as part of Sinaloa.

It was founded in 1682, after the discovery of silver in the nearby mountains and became the largest most important and most splendid city in Sonora. For a while it served as capital of the state. Within two blocks of the church (once a cathedral) and the plaza are around two dozen mansions, most restored. Early every morning the church bells summon everyone to mass with unambiguous tolling—the faithful and the less so.

Townspeople congregate on the alameda, two blocks away. They leave the more formal plaza for Sunday nights; the rest of the time it's used more by gringo residents and tourists. The alameda is as shaded as the plaza is sun-drenched. Food is never more than a few yards away, whether from the lunch counters in the market the mobile taco stands, a café, the three *cantinas,* an ice cream store, or the cornucopia of fresh food in the market itself. It—not the colonial plaza treasured by gringos—is the life and soul of Alamos, and Alamos has more life and more soul than any other town I know.

Sonora's wealthiest families came from Alamos. Their affluence was staggering; silver made them barons. In 1687 Father Kino reported forty-three silver mines in operation, each producing well, and many more sites where silver was believed to lie imbedded in rock. Legend has it that an Almada scion paved a path from his home to the church with silver bars for his daughter's wedding.

Silver poured from the earth by the ton. It was the richest silver-producing area in New Spain. Alamos became the seat of the king's coin mint. Fortunes came and went, and the fabulous city withered after the turn of the century, a whimpering ghost until the late 1940s when a few Americans trickled in, and restoration of the old places began.

On my early visits I'd sit on the portal of the Hotel Los Portales watching teenagers circling the plaza below us, the boys walking jauntily in a line in one direction, the girls, arm in arm, in another, making eyes at each other on every revolution. This custom has died out, people tell me, and now I see the young people running after each other just as they do in my own country. They hang out in pickup trucks with stereos blasting the international language of youth. Fabled Mexican modesty has vanished in young folks. The girls wear tiny, impossibly tight short skirts. The boys wear boots, Levis, and Wranglers, slouch on their pickups, drinking Tecate beer openly and notoriously. The cans are dangled with practiced nonchalance from their youthful hands. Young couples neck flagrantly.

A retired midwesterner with a heart problem told me over a beer that some 250 Americans now live in Alamos. Most have homes in the center part of town. They've taken over the colonial buildings: the sprawling, quiet, gracious mansions. Rebuilding the ruins is one of Alamos's principal industries, he told me. The presence of the wealthy North Americans is vital to the local economy. I sat tranquilly comfortable in a stuffed lawn chair with him and his wife, and chatted about New York while unripe mangoes drooped from a tree in the patio amid bougainvillea and jacaranda. Water trickled from a fountain. Parrots squawked from an aviary. A Mexican servant lurked in the background.

Resting his feet on an ottoman, the midwesterner explained that Mexicans live on the periphery. Their *barrios* were alive, crowded, and full of motion—too noisy for him, with lots of kids. He preferred a quieter existence in his retirement, and learning Spanish was too much work.

"For sale" signs—in English—are common. Gringos hide behind walls, some capped with broken glass set in concrete. Most have little interest in learning Spanish. "All us Americans support each other," one gringa told me confidently, adding disdainfully that she'd never tried to learn Spanish. She didn't need to, she said. That's precisely the problem, I thought. "They come and go," a Mexican citizen told me, "but they don't mix much with local folk." Their main contact with the community is through their hired help.

"Our roof leaks so much we hire a boy just to keep it intact," a jovial ex-Tucsonan bragged. His "boy" was in his thirties.

In 1964 I was chatting with a proud Alamosense on the porch when we were interrupted by the arrival of a Canadian car dealer who was staying at the hotel. He wore white shoes, gabardine slacks, and a white shirt. It was hard to confuse him with the locals. He'd made his fortune and was retiring to Alamos with his family, which included three teenage children (they'd be attending local schools). He'd bought an old place and had workers restoring it into the palace it had been. He loudly described its fountains and patios, fireplaces, and dining-room—how it would be festooned with boisterous displays of bougainvilleas. He extolled the tropical climate, the unhurried pace of Mexican village life, the hard-to-believe low prices; these were why he had pulled up Canadian stakes and moved to Alamos—at least for the winter months. Come summer, he'd pack up with his family and return to Canada, because summers in Alamos "are a god-dam inferno." He also complained that Mexico would be a hell of a lot better off if the people would work harder. Take the men working on his house, for example. They weren't reliable, they took forever to do the job, and they didn't do it right. I wonder just how much damage he did in the community. I wish I could remember his name.

Alamos folk live in their part of town, away from the restored mansions. In Alamos I've not seen the hustling personas of the big cities and tourist traps. A few years ago, thirty years after my first visit, I asked the operator of a soft drink stand where I could find the owner of a certain shop. He raised a hand and made a little gap between his thumb and forefinger, meaning, "Wait just a second." Then he left me in charge of his stand and ran across the street, asking three or four people who joined him in telling me where the fellow was.

The next evening I needed shoes fixed and found the *talabartería* (cobbler shop) closed. I managed to chase down the owner, a young man who couldn't have been more than twenty-five. I found him in his home holding his toddler son in his lap. Although it was already dark, he hopped on his bicycle and rode over to the shop. He let me in and repaired my shoes while I waited.

The cobbler's family owned a small ranch in the mountains, he told me as he worked over the shoe last with nimble fingers. They wanted to keep it beautiful, just as Alamos was beautiful. However, Alamos had problems. There were too many outsiders (he didn't use the ugly word *guachos*) from Chihuahua, Aguascalientes, even parts of Sonora coming to Alamos. Crime was up, people weren't as friendly any more. He apologized for a robbery that had happened to someone else. He'd been stunned when a relative, a well-known and liked mechanic, had been murdered on a lonely road. "It was better when there were just the people of Alamos and *Americanos*," he said. He was aware of the beneficial effect of North American construction projects on the Alamos economy.

His uncle, rancher Eduardo Acosta's home is nestled in a grove on a hillside next to a dusty street that doubles as an arroyo in the rainy season. When I visited, there was a truck parked next door, its engine was lying on the ground, and there were two men working on it who smiled good evening. A hen with a dozen chicks was teaching them to scratch in the grass near the doorway. Eduardo's wife Concha Nieblas met me at the door. "*Pásele, pásele*," she said, urging me inside. To the left of the arched doorway, hidden under great trees, was their house: living room, bathroom, and other rooms behind. Straight ahead was the living area—a palm-thatched ramada set on great pillars. The kitchen—stove, table, sink—was organized beneath in the open air, standing in perpetual shade. The thatch was lost in the great trees—figs, amapas, persimmons.

The floor was of cleanly swept, packed dirt. Dogs wagged their tails. A cat sat meowing in a windowsill. Neighbor children watched solemnly as we chatted. A young woman cradling a baby to her breast walked by and out of the door. She held out her hand and gently pressed mine, introducing herself as a neighbor. From both sides I heard competing *norteña* music. Concha offered me coffee, beans, and tortillas. I had just eaten. I would love to have stayed there.

Poorer folk, those who scratch a living from the soil or the forest, live on the outskirts of the town. On one edge live my friend Chapul and his family in a house of burnt adobe, which he built, as Mexican men are expected to. Immediately behind, Sierra de Alamos rises abruptly and appropriately. Chapul has spent much of his forty years gallivanting about the great mountain. He has often been my guide on the steep slopes, leading me through dark canyons, showing me unusual trees, and thoughtfully steering me away from vengefully guarded fields of poppy or hemp.

His given name is Jesús Sánchez. His nickname is Chapul, he says, because from boyhood he hopped and jumped wherever he went, just like a *chapulín*, the huge tropical grasshopper. His little sister, it seems, tried to call him a *chapulín* but couldn't mouth the final syllable, so he became "Chapul." He's an incessant smoker, thin as a rail, and tough as a frontiersman.

He scrounges a living any way he can, as a gardener and running a few cows on the mountain. One day I followed him up the slopes while he carried salt to the tiny herd that nibbled a frugal existence on public land on the forested mountainside. Half-way up the mountain he stopped and made a strange bawling sound. I looked at him as though he had been smoking funny cigarettes, but he bawled again. Before I could ask him just what the hell he was doing, a distant cow bawled a response, then another. We sat on the jungly hillside waiting, and presently four rangy cows appeared, hungry for salt. He left a pile of it for them, and we proceeded up the mountain. The mineral helps them gain weight, he explained and it makes them tame.

Early one morning he showed up where I was staying. He had promised to guide me up the mountain to a moist canyon where unusual trees were said to be found. "David," he said in his soft, anxious voice, "I just talked to a friend of mine. He says it isn't safe to go to Magnolia Canyon."

"Why?" I asked, curious that a tough outdoorsman like Chapul would be afraid of a canyon.

"Well," he said, lowering his eyes, "he says there are new fences there. I don't know if it's *mota* (marijuana) or *goma* (opium), but there are fences and irrigation tubing. He says we'll get shot if we go in there."

I could hardly argue the point, preferring not to be shot, so we stayed away. He told stories of drug raisers in the area, of killings, of mules coming home riderless, of whistling bullets. The people involved were not from Alamos, he said. He didn't know who they were, but he thought they were probably from Sinaloa—bad folk.

Chapul earned a small amount cutting down a variety of woods on the mountain and bringing down exotic plants to be sold to the inhabitants of Alamos. The work was very hard, for the mountain is steep and the few trails are tough going. Recently he was forced to stop collecting plants, for some of them were protected. I don't know what other source of income he can find except gardening and guiding gringos up the mountain.

Across the valley on the north side of town, Marcelino Valenzuela, a Mayo Indian, makes furniture in the ramada of his humble hut where he lives with his wife and four children. They get water from a single tap and use a privy. To get to his home one must walk across an eroded, trash-strewn ravine past several other shacks that house families. Mayos have lived in the Alamos area for hundreds of years but are increasingly marginalized. When Marcelino is not making his solid chairs, he and about thirty other men from Alamos spend their time in the *monte* (bush), cutting *vara blanca* (*Croton pseudonivieus*) poles, to be shipped to Baja California as supports for tomato vines.

Marcelino is a skilled chairmaker, the kind of craftsman whose numbers are fast dwindling. He harvests branches of *guásima* (*Guazuma ulmifolia*) during the full moon. If he harvested them at other times the wood would be too wet, and it would be soft and crack easily. With hand tools he saws and planes the branches into silky smooth chair legs, slats, and backs, then cuts mortises and tenons and fits the pieces together with a few nails and glue. The chairs, which he calls *sillas rústicas* (rustic chairs), last for years. For all his labor he gets about thirteen dollars.

Marcelino was out cutting *vara* one day when I walked up to his ramada. His wife explained that he was far out in the *monte* and wouldn't be back till the next day. I ordered a couple of chairs, suggesting that I pick them up the following afternoon. At the appointed time I returned, only to find that he had been called to a meeting of the *vara* cutters union. The government, his wife told me sadly, had announced a moratorium on cutting the stakes. Too many had been harvested, and the plant was in danger of extinction. No doubt the government was right, for millions upon millions of the two-inch-thick, eight-foot-long poles have been cut and shipped. This was going to be hard on the family, his wife said, because *vara* accounted for half of its income.

Well, I thought as I left, at least he can continue to make chairs, but later that night

I learned that the government had also announced its intention to declare a moratorium on the cutting of the *guásima*, from which he makes his chairs. Overharvesting of the tree had placed it in danger of extinction as well, it said. Ay, Marcelino, what will you do now?

Tourists who come to Alamos stay in hotels—mostly restored mansions. The Mexican hotel workers are helpful and reserved, but burst into smile when a North American addresses them in Spanish. I joked with a waiter in the shade of a mango tree. I asked him when the mangoes would be ripe. "August," he said. It was only March. I told him I couldn't wait.

He looked around to make sure no women were within listening distance and told me in a low voice. "Hey, mangoes are the best thing for, uh, well, if you can't get it up."

"Really, now," I said. This was useful information.

"O, sí," he answered happily. "Last year a guy from the United States stayed here. I heard he wasn't able to . . . ." He looked around again and raised his arm quickly, striking the biceps with his other palm so that his fist and forearm shot up obscenely straight.

"I told him to make a puree of two mangoes. He drank it and told me the next morning he did it all night!"

"Ah," I said, a hint of sarcasm perhaps tainting my tone.

"No, no," he protested. "It's true." Mangoes are now an important component of my pharmacopoeia.

For two hundred years prior to the rebuilding phase of the last fifty years, Alamos had its ups and downs. Even so it remained the wealthiest, most splendid city in Sonora, and one of the most prestigious in the Republic of Mexico. Its leading families were, and to an extent still are, the most prominent and powerful in the state. A long succession of Sonoran leaders trace their ancestry to the Salido or Almada families, clans whose numerous offspring and even greater land and commercial holdings extend throughout the state. From 1880 to 1910, during thirty years of the *porfiriato,* or rule of Porfirio Díaz as dictator of Mexico, Sonora was governed by the revolving triumvirate of Ramón Corral, Luis Torres, and Rafael Izábal. No important decision in the state was made without their concurrence, no political posts filled, no major enterprises undertaken. All three had their family roots in Alamos. An important leader of the Mexican Revolution, later president of the Republic, Alvaro Obregón Salido, was also derived from the powerful Alamos clan.

On my early visits, natural history appealed to me more than human history. Urged by an eccentric biology professor, I headed north of Alamos on the narrow dirt road out of the town, hoping to find my way into the Sierra Madre and locate reptiles. I only made it a few miles. The roadway was mostly a dry wash and the sand became too deep for my motor scooter. I flailed sideways, kept falling off, getting up, brushing off the sand and trying again. Finally, at the hamlet of La Higuera, I wobbled to the police station, a tiny whitewashed cement shack on a denuded lot in a little backwater town. Inside was a bare steel table with an antique typewriter, a metal chair, and a bench on an unpainted concrete floor. There was no phone. On the wall partially covered with flaking greenish paint was a faded picture of President Adolfo López Matéos trying vainly to look heroic. That was all. The police chief wore a long-sleeved brown uniform and a police cap. On his hip was a revolver. "You are looking for snakes?" He cast a confused look at his associate, then looked at me quizzically, surmising that I was a little daft. "Leave your *motoneta* here," he suggested amicably. "Take the bus to San Bernardo." He helped me pull the scooter inside the building. His lieutenant, who sat on the bench, jumped up at a command and trotted out to the narrow dirt road to watch for the bus. When the ancient *camión* rattled by, he flagged it down. I paid my sixteen cents and hopped aboard.

I quit ten miles down the road at Los Tanques, because it was too hot inside the bus, and a child vomited on the floor. The lady on the seat in front of me wasn't bothered by the commotion or the stench, or maybe she just didn't want to upset the rooster she held under her arm. I couldn't stay so calm. When the bus stopped, I got out.

I sat under a fig tree and sipped a Coca-Cola. By now I had learned some Spanish and chatted brokenly with some kids who were playing baseball barefoot in the road. The bus rumbled through on its return. I sheepishly climbed on, paid my fare, and rode back to the police station. The chief noted that I hadn't made it to the Sierra. "Bad road up there," he said gravely. "You're safer in Alamos." I came back with empty snake bags, feeling decidedly inept. In town I offered kids a peso for each green tree frog or snake they would bring me. While I was eating supper, one showed up and timidly handed me a paper sack. Inside were twenty-five pairs of eyes staring at me from iridescent green bodies. In my room that night they croaked, and croaked, and croaked.

Alamos is nestled among steep mountains in extreme southern Sonora, where the state tapers to an apex and the foothills of the Sierra Madre reach to within a few leagues of the Sea of Cortés. Between Navojoa near the coast and Alamos, the vegetation changes quickly in the space of a just few miles. Moisture and temperature make the difference: it doesn't freeze in Alamos, ever, and it rains almost twice as much as in Navojoa.

Scientists call the bush country around Alamos tropical deciduous forest. "Tropical" means the trees cannot tolerate frost. "Deciduous" means they drop their leaves, not in response to frost but to drought, which usually runs from October to June in this part of Sonora.

The mountains surrounding Alamos are covered with low thick forests, especially Alamos Peak in the Sierra de Alamos that rises to the south to nearly six thousand feet. I thought I'd check it out early one April morning, parking my scooter off the highway and striking bravely into the bush. After a hundred feet I quit. The forest and thorny trees were too dense and grabby. In a quarter of a mile, I'd be lost and scratched to a bloody mass. Everything was dry, the trees gray, the earth cracked. Flies and gnats buzzed me. Magpie Jays laughed at me, taunting me with their long tails of iridescent blue. It was late April and already dusty and miserably hot. I thought of the desolation of the coming summer and struggled back to my scooter.

May is a searing month; June is a burning hell. Temperatures routinely exceed one hundred degrees on the coastal plain. Those over 110 degrees are common. The sky is colored brown by smoke drifting high from the burning dead crops, the clouds of dust from the valley below, and forest fires. Evening brings relief, and the villagers move from their brick-oven-like houses of cement and adobe onto the streets to enjoy the cool. As the heat softens into warmth, the thoroughfares come alive, and the magic of Alamos is revealed. Myriad footsteps echo from the cobbles onto the long lines of walls. Chairs are dragged out from inside. Televisions materialize on the sidewalk, their umbilical cords extending deep into the entrails of the houses. The streets fill with music. Beer abounds. The chatter of children rises above the serenades. Huge families mingle with one another. Stereos compete. Stores stay open late. Young people flirt. Older people gossip. Lovers stroll back and forth, alert for shadowed nooks.

It's a small town. Everyone knows whose daughter is pregnant and by whom, which lads work hard and which are lazy (*flojos*), who is leaving town, who is buying what, who is mistreating whom. An old Chevy has been converted into a pickup, painted black, and called "Black Power." Another has a rag doll for a hood ornament. On the corners near the market unhurried traffic police have little to do except chit-chat with townsfolk and wave as they drive by. Even at the police headquarters, most of the force is seated outside in the open air, hobnobbing with other officers rather than frittering life away at a desk.

By day the Sonoran heat of late spring is relentless. Activity slows to a crawl. Siestas are long and inconclusive. The entire world is waiting. This is the time when cattle starve, and crops wither. (In the spring drought of 1994 over thirty thousand Sonoran cows died.) Finally in late June, masses of wet air stream northward from the tropics and crash into the Sierra Madre. The steep mountain slopes force the moist air masses upward. The mornings start out clear, but by noon great thunderheads boil up, and by early afternoon rain begins pelting the mountains. In a few days or weeks the showers spill out into the valleys. Sonorans watch the mountains and hope. Finally the flash of lightning and the crash of thunder herald an end to the dust and drought, and a deep existential happiness settles upon the town.

Alamos gets more relief than coastal cities. Navojoa on the coastal plain receives fifteen inches of rainfall a year, but will often go ten months or even more without a drop of rain. Alamos, thirty-four miles away and hardly a thousand feet higher, receives in excess of twenty-five inches, mostly because it's closer to the mountains. Points higher in the Sierra only a few miles away receive forty inches. The year revolves around rain rather than cold.

In 1990 I picked up a friend's copy of Howard Scott Gentry's 1942 classic, *Río Mayo Plants,* read a couple of pages and became a follower. Gentry wrote about a hundred or so kinds of tropical trees, densely packed on the hillsides and canyons until they give way—at about three thousand feet—to oaks and grassland and then pines. Local experts distinguish trees by their flowers, their bark, their leaves, and their shape. The amapa explodes with deep pinkish blooms in January, followed by its cousin, the amapa amarilla with flaming yellow flowers in February and March. In April and May it's the brilliant purple nesco and the fiery red chilicote. In July it's the delicate white of the cascalosú-chil. At other times of the year, depending upon rainfall, other species flower, including kapok, morning-glory trees, guamú-chiles, and a mishmash of acacias and mimosas. The most impressive tree of all, the great fig tree, provides an evergreen oasis along the watercourses.

Gentry came to the Río Mayo country in the 1930s to document its natural history. He spent several years wandering through magnificent wild country that had seldom seen a European. From time to time he would venture to the border, hand over crates of plant presses, fossils, preserved insects, butterflies, and lizards, then vanish once again into the wilds. He lived among the reclusive Guarijío Indians, plodded up massive peaks, and descended into jungled wild canyons, followed by a burro and, sometimes, a guide. He came to know the people of the Sierra, of San Bernardo, and of Alamos where he maintained a small home.

Gentry was a poet as well as a naturalist, infusing the wonders of the Alamos forest to his plant descriptions. Consider, for example, his description of the *amapa amarilla* (*Tabebuia chrysantha*):

> Tree, 7–15 m. in stature, usually unbranched for several meters, and with a rounded, spreading crown. It is in leaf from July to late fall. It flowers when leafless in February, and a colony or a single tree can be seen for miles, for it is like a great torch set burning with a clear yellow flame in the wilderness. Under the brilliant yellow canopy the sunlight is transfused to a new quality, and objects thereunder take on an ethereal yellow glow. [Gentry, *Río Mayo Plants*, p. 239.]

Gentry cast a penetrating, gently illuminating light over the Mayo.

I tried to identify the myriad forms of trees on the hills on my own and gave up; there were way too many of them. Over the years I've gotten ranchers to teach me. Even young cowboys distinguish at a glance between leafless trunks, rattling off names and morphological characteristics as though they were describing different automobiles. Men who cut wood for fuel and build fences, ramadas, huts, or furniture develop a keen sense of different woods. Joaquín, a cowboy lad of seventeen, taught me more about plants in an afternoon than I had learned in most classrooms in a semester. He showed me thirty or forty trees and as many bushes on the slopes of Sierra de Alamos, patiently repeating the ones I had forgotten, telling me in his quiet humble tone of authority of how each plant was used.

The forest abounds with creatures whose northern limit is the tropical deciduous forest. White-fronted Parrots and iridescent Military Macaws build nests. Macaws especially like the giant cypresses whose numbers have been decimated by timber cutters. A *viejita* from nearby El Tábelo has a pair that live in her house and leave to hunt and forage every day, returning in the evening. The Magpie Jays are sudden, rude, sensational brats, flaunting their foot-long purple-blue tails. Chicken-like *chachalacas* rather stupidly squawk their presence, attracting hunters. Russet-crowned Motmots stare sternly then flee silently.

Tropical cats pad their way through the forest. Seldom seen is the margay cat, a secretive feline smaller than a bobcat but with a luxurious spotted coat. Margays are tree dwellers said to have the uncanny ability to drop from a high branch, casually reach out a paw, grab a lower branch and swing upward with gibbon-like dexterity. Most natives have never seen one, although a rancher told me they're not rare. I never saw a trace of the margay, or the ocelote, or the retiring jagarundi, or the evasive *tigre* (jaguar)—the cats of the tropical forest. A rancher near Alamos reports losses of five or six calves a year to the *tigre*. He also confided that he loses cows to the *onza*, a different kind of cat. No scientist can produce one (although someone from a little town near Alamos is rumored to have a skin), but this rancher and others I've spoken with will swear on blood that the *onza* is a real animal, a cat smaller than a jaguar but bigger than a mountain lion—a cunning, ferocious cat with a spotted, pale brown coat. He told me, as mountain folk do with stern conviction, of the strength and cunning of the *onza*. The folks I've discussed the *onza* with haven't seen one. They all have a relative or cousin who has, however.

The reptiles that brought me to Alamos three decades ago are equally fascinating to Alamos natives. At any given time, three or four hotel residents are studying snakes and lizards, bringing specimens back to the hotel. The locals take it in stride, as they've learned to take gringos in stride, but even they show a hypnotic fascination with snakes such as boa constrictors, indigo snakes, poisonous Mexican moccasins and the blunt-headed tree snakes, found no farther north. Many live in mortal fear of a harmless gecko that crawls around walls by night gobbling insects, imbuing it with vast sexual powers and venom of frightful but fanciful potency. Beaded lizards, big cousins to the Gila Monster, scurry across the highway, often not making it. The two foot-long saurian—yellow, white, and black, while the Gila Monster is orange, white, and black—is every bit as poisonous as the northern relative but of a more mellow disposition.

Nowadays botanists, herpetologists, entomologists, and mammologists come and go all year. I hear the same lament from them all: "Another few hundred acres of forest gone. The bulldozers are at it again. Cows win out, as usual." It certainly was painful to see what had happened when I returned to Alamos in 1991 after nearly twenty-five years. In 1961 the forest extended nearly unbroken, from Navojoa, thirty-four miles to Alamos. Now most of the cover on the gentler slopes has been chopped down or bulldozed and replaced with pasture or dwellings. Thirty years ago only a few huts disturbed the forest between Navojoa and Alamos. Now there's an almost unbroken succession of chicken and pig ranches that give off a foul stench. Managers dump their offal into adjacent arroyos, making it somebody else's problem. Huge flocks of vultures hover near the coops, patiently awaiting each day's dumping of carcasses. Innumerable small dwellings have also popped up. Traffic has increased manyfold. The burgeoning population of Mexico must live somewhere, I guess.

Alamos is slowly growing, and its population is now in excess of six thousand. It's still a place of unfathomable serenity with an atmosphere of unreality, unmoved by the clutter, noise, and crime of the cities. Reality may be closer than they think, however, as the rest of Sonora will illustrate.

CHAPTER 2

The Bush

The white walls and charming patios begin to lose their charm quickly for me. Years ago I became more comfortable in the presence of Sonorans living on the edges than in the company of expatriate Americans basking in luxury. To get into the bush I drove my pickup north of Alamos toward the community of San Bernardo and the rugged and varied country of the upper Río Mayo and the Sierra Madre north and east of Alamos. From the plains rise steep, forest-covered slopes incised by sheer, deep canyons, softened by a heavy forest blanket, and unexplored by folk of European ancestry except for the venerable Gentry and a few mad ranchers and *gambusinos* (prospectors). As I first ascended the ever-steepening slopes, oaks appeared above, then pines. The temperature dropped by fifteen degrees from the oppressive tropical heat. From pine-forested Milpillas, unless I took the single winding road heading north, I could proceed only by airplane or on foot, horse, or burro into an area as inaccessible as any on the North American continent.

Ecologist Paul Martin, who has poked around the area for more than thirty years, describes the tropical deciduous forest as a cornucopia of nature constantly pumping new species to the North. Martin delves into what he calls "deep history," narratives left by communities of plants and animals over the millennia, even before people invaded from the North. Thousands of years ago the area that is now the Sonoran Desert had a cooler, moister climate. As the weather warmed and dried, living organisms—both plant and animal—crept northward, testing their ability to withstand drought and frost. The Sonoran Desert, the most interesting of all North American ecosystems, has its origins, its tropical roots, in the deciduous forest as seen around Alamos.

At the height of the rainy season, as Paul and I drove along a narrow road carved through the dense jungle, I remarked that the

26

forest seemed impenetrable. "You're right, David," he said. "It's so dense, so impassable, that no one has ever collected more than a few feet from the road. We have no idea what species and how many are to be found inside that unknown forest."

Paul and I ventured into the Sierra, far above the Río Mayo north of Alamos. On the rocky, sinuous road to Milpillas in Chihuahua, surrounded by the dense canopy of the forest, we came upon a tiny habitation called Agua Salada—Salt Water. It consists of one house, far from the nearest electrical lines: an ancient dwelling of crumbling walls and oft-patched, asphalt-impregnated corrugated cardboard roofing. The building sits astride a small ridge below a towering peak in the Sierra San Ignacio. The doorway opens to a view across the narrow saddle below to the lofty, pine-covered ridges of the Sierra Saguaribo, a few miles away. A family of seven somehow ekes out an existence here. One day I tramped up the little hill that leads to the front yard, watching my step to avoid assorted animal manure. A dog barked furiously but retreated when I glared at him. I called out a greeting, *buenas tardes.* There was no response. I called out twice more. Finally a tall, thin woman came to an open doorway, her face hidden by a dark scarf that she held in place. Remaining in the shadow of the dwelling, she asked briefly and in a muffled suspicious voice what I wanted. Maybe it was my gringo accent, but when I explained that my companion and I were studying plants, she became much more friendly, convinced that we weren't *federales* or drug dealers.

In the way that chicks appear from under the wings of a protective mother hen once she gives a reassuring cluck, three children—two boys and a girl—all less than ten years old, materialized behind the woman. After a few more words, two boys emerged, curious and confident.

The woman, Dolores Bracamonte, was the children's grandmother. One of the boys was an adopted Guarijío Indian, she said. Lowering the shawl, she told me with some pride that she and her husband had lived here for nearly forty years, raising a herd of goats, and growing vegetables in a small garden with a *milpa* (cornfield) far below the house on a saddle between two valleys and another far up the valley. Behind the hut were several citrus trees, a couple of papaya trees bearing green fruit, and a young mango tree. As we spoke she gradually became more talkative and described their life to me. She ground all their corn and made tortillas by hand, she said, clapping her hands to show me the motion she uses to form the cakes. Water is brought by bucket from a spring a hundred yards away. Her husband, who was not there (I dared not ask where he was) brings in some cash by making machetes and knives.

The boys, wearing only short pants, proudly gave me a guided tour of the open shed that is their grandfather's blacksmith shop. In it were a couple of foot-operated forges, an ancient but formidable anvil, and a huge foot-driven sharpening stone. From the ceiling hung several *bules* (hollow gourds used everywhere in rural Mexico for carrying water, until plastic jugs replaced them). The young fellows described to me how their grandfather Juan Cheno cuts the machetes from tractor discs he buys in Navojoa, sixty miles away. They proudly laid out his hammers of varying sizes, and indicated the woodpile for the forges and the stack of goat hides ready to be cut up into strips to make handles for the implements. From a hiding place in the ceiling, the older of the boys extracted several machetes and scythes lacking only the leather handles. Men came from all over the Sierra, they stated matter-of-factly, to buy their grandfather's machetes for thirty pesos, a little over nine dollars. They also showed me a couple of knives—rough hardy blades intended for tackling the bush of the Sierra Madre. These were not the pocketknives of gentlemen but working men's tools. Now, two years later, I still see Cheno's handiwork wherever I go in the Sierra, his distinctive design being easy to spot.

Once the boys had shown me their grandfather's workshop, they took me into their back yard and pointed out various trees, some unknown to me. Then they revealed a secret they guarded for special occasions. In a tall organ pipe cactus a swarm of stingless bees had made a perfectly round hole, perhaps a half inch in diameter, and lined it with dark clay. Inside was a hive of sorts. The tiny bees flew in and out of the exquisitely formed entrance, uninterested in our presence. The boy told me the insects produce a sweet honey that in turn sweetens the *pitahayas* (fruits) of the cactus. A few weeks after I visited, one of them captured the queen and moved the hive into a homemade *colmena* (beehive) where they can more easily collect the honey. The bees, or wasps as they call them, are harmless critters, smaller than

houseflies, and reassuringly gentle. Their honey is strong and
rich. The boys proudly showed me how the bees seal the entrance to the hive at night and open it in the morning. Not miss-
ing any opportunity, they also revealed to me a trail to the top
of the peak behind the house where they'd be glad to guide me.

I met Juan Cheno a few weeks later. He was hammering on a
machete while Dolores laboriously cranked a mechanical bellows
with both hands to keep the fire hot. He's a strong, tired-looking
man. His hand has been injured in an accident. His clothes are
worn, not recently washed. His life is hard, but he likes it here.
He's from somewhere down near San Bernardo but wants to stay
here where he has some land. He pointed to a distant hill with a
light-colored patch near the top. "That's my milpa," he said
proudly. It is an hour's walk away, at least. He invited me to
come back.

Juan Cheno's livelihood, as well as his blacksmith's skill,
depends entirely on the clearing of the forest. His way of life
would end if men for whom clearing the forest was a way of life
did not come to Agua Salada to buy his hand-fashioned blades.
Agua Salada would also cease to exist, and the family would in
all probability move to a city, probably Navojoa or, sooner or
later, a border city, to find work. I met fellows twenty miles away
clearing brush with implements made by Juan Cheno. If he were
gone I don't know where they'd get their machetes. When he's
there, the forest shrinks each day.

Roadways in the Sierra serve as the only practicable route for
driving herds of cattle in this land of large trees and thorny un-
derbrush. As I wound down the narrow road into a canyon below Juan Cheno's house, I caught sight of a herd coming down
the other side. Cows have the right of way on the narrow mountain road. When I reached the bottom I waited while the *hato* of
cattle descended.

I was fortunate; the canyon had a lively stream. Great fig trees
and huge *guamúchiles* lent luxuriant shade, while I watched the
cows mooing down the road. I spoke with one of the cowboys
who arrived first—on foot. He sat down wearily on a rock, a
week's growth of stubble on his face, his clothes the same ones
he'd been wearing when the drive began. They had set out from
Chínipas in Chihuahua, an impossibly isolated Jesuit mission
town one valley over in the *tierra caliente* at the bottom of a huge

mountain range. They were herding the cows another ten miles to Los Camotes, where they were to be pastured and fattened. It was a six-day trip, all on foot for him and four other cowboys. He figured they'd reach Los Camotes the following day, then turn around and walk back to Chínipas.

The wait for such a herd can be a long one. On Sierra Madre roads there are places with no turnouts for a couple of miles, and the cowboys aren't about to permit any mavericks to leave the herd. Vehicles must wait, no matter how impatient drivers may become. I thought of the romantic photos of horsemen lassoing cows on a cattle drive. These guys were too poor to afford horses. While the cows watered, I seized the opening to jump in the truck and return to Alamos.

Far up the eroded, rocky track the cows had passed over, above the thick, humid tropical forest, lies a cool land of oak and pine, of ranches, and small lumber mills. *Ejidos* (communally owned lands) and private plots dot the map. From them the *ejidatarios* and private landowners sell permission to cut down pines. Paul and I camped in a previously forested valley where piles of fresh sawdust and stumps oozing pitch showed that several large pines had been harvested that very day. A young fellow, also on foot, told us the rancher sold them because he wanted more open land for pasture. More pasture equals more cows, and a tree may bring in twenty desperately needed dollars. Long-term conservation goes out the window in the face of an empty stomach. The young man knew of no plans to plant more trees.

Paul and I ventured farther northeast on the rough plateau to the end of a tortuously slow road that ends at a place called El Chiribo. The tiny sawmill village is perched on a mesa whose towering cliffs drop off a few thousand feet to the Mayo Valley below. The mill, powered by a diesel generator, saws pine logs into thin wooden rods destined to become broom handles. The lathe that will round them into a smooth handle for wives to grasp is far away in Ciudad Obregón. Slash and sawdust mound up behind the great blade. When the pile becomes unmanageable, it is pushed off the side of the cliff.

As we idled through the little town, Paul noticed an especially attractive sotol—a yucca relative—growing in the fenced yard of a Chiriban family. While we inspected the plant, a man in his early forties with a three-day growth of gray beard came out of the wooden house.

"*Pasen, pasen,*" he said, holding his arm in the direction of the wooden porch of his home. Under his ample shake porch roof he pulled up the family's chairs for us and told us his house was ours. Angel Lagarda was his name. (The name Lagarda is common in this part of the country, a corruption of LeGrande, the name of a Frenchman who sowed his seed liberally among the impressionable maids of the Sierra fifty years ago.) Angel worked in the mill as well as in the fields of the *ejido.* He mentioned no other occupations.

He, as well as most other residents of the Sierra, keeps a decent supply of homemade *lechuguilla* (agave mescal). Angel insisted that Paul and I test his product. We submitted to his arm-twisting and steeled ourselves to the experiment. Angel produced a flask and handed it to me. He warned that it was stern stuff and that it should be tasted with caution. I took a mouthful—probably four times as much as I should have. I tried to swallow and couldn't. Powerful, lethal fumes wafted from my nose as I swilled the liquid in my mouth, managing to gulp it down only after my eyes had filled with tears. A burning sensation spread from my mouth to my throat to my stomach. I gasped a couple of times, reeled on my chair, and steadied myself on the wall behind me. Angel's wife and children who stood silently at a respectful distance, shook with soundless mirth at my improvident behavior. After thirty seconds or so, I regained my speech and asked them to their unimaginable delight what town this was and the time of day. I handed the now-shimmering flask to Paul, who had the maturity, wisdom and foresight merely to wet his lips with the elixir.

When my mind had cleared and Angel was able to wipe away the glee from his eyes, he asked us, out of the blue, "What took you so long to get here?" I was non-plussed, and not just because of the delirium induced by the *lechuguilla.* We hadn't reached the village the night before but instead had camped on a small meadow just over a kilometer from town. Paul had driven his four-wheel-drive Chevy truck away from the road. The ground was deceptive. On top it was grassy and firm, but a couple of inches below it was a sodden, squishy, slimy, clayey mass. The heavy truck had settled comfortably in the muck up to the axles a good seventy-five feet from the track. For a couple of hours the previous night and during most of that morning we dug, winched, jacked, and skidded the vehicle out of that oozing morass, sweating and fighting off biting gnats the whole time. It had rained all night, making the muck all the more gooey. "What do you mean?" I asked Angel, still confused.

"Well," he said, his eyes twinkling, "We knew you were on your way here. When you took so long, we began to worry. We were about to come looking for you!"

I looked at Paul, laughing. We had supposed that we were well hidden and that nobody knew we were in the area. Not a single vehicle had passed us in the last twenty-four hours. We hadn't encountered a soul on the road. We had been surrounded by forest. How the hell did they know? Maybe, I thought, they had seen Paul's blue truck cresting over the ridge above the village or spied it on the way down. I finally realized from that conversation that a news network runs throughout the Sierra Madre; our presence was as well known to the folk up there as an elephant's would be in a Kansas prairie town. Angel had lived in that part of the Sierra all of his life. He knows every hill, trail, footpath, and watercourse. He knows the sounds, the smells, the feel of the land. Any change is as noticeable to him as a siren is to those of us who live in the city.

El Chiribo was only five years old, Angel informed us, and in another two years the supply of pine trees would be gone, all cut down. I asked what he would do then. He shrugged stoically. "Find another business, I guess."

A year later we visited Angel again. I asked him if he could guide us to Tepopa, a place described by Gentry in 1942:

> Abandoned rancho on the northwest slope of Sierra Saguaribo. Founded about twelve years ago by two brothers, who terraced a steep canyon slope watered by cold springs, planting bananas, papayas, mangos, avocados, apricots, and peaches. The locality has a rich native flora. [Gentry, *Río Mayo Plants*, p. 26.]

That description lured us to Tepopa, and Angel had mentioned a year earlier that he could guide us there. I dispensed with politeness as we sat down and asked Angel bluntly if we could go the following day. He rolled his eyes. "I don't think so."

"Why?" I asked, confused. Paul looked despondent.

"Well, you see," he hesitated, looked around and leaned forward, lowering his voice. "There are soldiers here, now, stationed up by the school. We can't go anywhere without their permission." He stared at me briefly, laying out the challenge.

That explained his behavior. Soldiers had been dispatched to this part of the Sierra to convince the world that the Mexican government was controlling drug traffic. This area had the reputation of being a trade route. The *soldados* move from place to place, imposing themselves on the inhabitants, commandeering vehicles and demanding food and entertainment. Locals cynically suggest that the soldiers only want to get the dope for themselves. The soldiers instituted a military occupation. No one did anything without their permission. They were the law in El Chiribo.

I bolted from Angel's house and walked as fast as I could to the school yard, a quarter of a mile away. A couple of soldiers hardly out of their teens met me at the fence brandishing automatic rifles. They were from the South, they said. (Government policy keeps recruits away from their families.) They found El Chiribo boring. I asked them for permission to go to Tepopa with Angel as a guide. They said they couldn't give permission. Only their commanding officer could.

He sauntered up to the fence and looked down at me with disdain through his sunglasses. "What do you want?"

"Well," I said in Spanish, "We want to go to Tepopa."

"Where's that?" he demanded, staring off into the gathering clouds.

I explained. "And we'd like Angel Lagarda to guide us." Now he looked confused. Did we have guns? Were we really scientists? Of course, he said, without smiling, we could go. No guns. "*No eramos drogueros?*" (Were we drug runners?)

"Of course not," I told him. He nodded with authority and dismissed me with a flick of the wrist. I ran back to tell Angel the good news.

From our camping place half a mile away we heard music that night. The soldiers had requested that the townspeople sponsor a *baile* (a dance) for them. The villagers of course obliged.

The next morning we set off, itching from the bites of *baiburines* (chiggers) unimpressed by insect repellent. Angel and his young son who hiked barefoot led us through a cleft in the cliffs that tower over the Mayo Valley, below the pines and oaks down a switchbacking path. We hiked slowly as Angel told us the names of plants and bushes and trees and what they were good for. He wielded his machete effectively, hacking at protruding branches and cutting off samples for us to see. At the base of the huge rock face a mule had fallen off the cliff a few days before, and we had to detour around the stinking, fly-filled carcass. Vultures circled patiently as we hurried by, then resumed their grisly meal. Macaws screeched down at us from high in the sky. They like the cliff country where they're safe from marauders.

We reached the ancient *trincheras* (terraces) that had been painstakingly constructed sixty years before. A spring runs over them, feeding the heavy growth of vines and flowers that have nearly hidden the carefully placed rocks. The ruined house was still there, the orchard intact but untended. The bananas were not yet ripe, and the papaya trees had died of old age, but plump mangoes weighed down the branches of two majestic trees. We tore into the lascivious fruit, the juice running down our hands and face. We didn't bother washing until we had slurped all the delectable pulp we could. Angel watched with a tolerant smile.

We ate lunch at the ruined house. Looking out over the broad valley, greened by *las aguas*, we heard hoof beats. Three riders accompanied by a couple of panting dogs came into view from below. A young cowboy rode on one. He wore *teguas* (simple half-boots) and sheltered a child no more than two years old on the saddle in front of him. On another horse rode a shy young woman in a clean dress—his wife, we learned. On a third horse a somber boy of five or six sat alone, in complete control of his mount.

They stopped for a few minutes of polite conversation. Angel knew them. They were on their way to El Chiribo from a ranch a few kilometers below. The tiny store at the sawmill town was the closest for them. It was easier to take the impossibly steep and dangerous trail than to waste a whole day riding into San Bernardo. Besides, it was refreshingly cool above on the mesa and an oven in San Bernardo. They were impeccably polite, address-ing us Americans with "Sir." The cowboy smiled when we offered him and his family some lunch. He and his son wolfed down the food. The woman stuck hers in a saddlebag.

After a bit they begged our leave and rode away at a leisurely pace, the child-horseman leading up the switchback. I thought them the most handsome family I'd ever seen. I worried about the kid guiding that huge horse up the sinuous trail where a cou-ple of days ago a sure-footed mule had stumbled to his death.

A few months later I hiked to Tepopa from a ranch at the base of the escarpment, not far from San Bernardo. I then understood why the young couple found the ride attractive. For several miles the path leads through unbroken forest along a seasonal creek. As the pathway begins to climb, the views become scenic, and several small ranches with verdant orchards provide convenient rest points. I should be glad to be forced to take that trail often.

In 1993 Paul and I were joined by several scientists in an encampment near El Chiribo. We made friends with the townspeople who came frequently to visit and gawk at our tents and equipment. Angel and another resident—the incomparably knowledgeable Armando Aguilar—were our guides and informants. On a dark, rainy night we were awakened by two bandits armed with high-powered weapons who held us up at gunpoint. Issuing death threats, they tied our hands behind our backs. We waited and watched, standing helplessly in the rainswept blackness, while they looted our camp. For an hour they ransacked and vainly tried to steal a van, which they could not manage to start. Finally, laden down with booty they left, but not, as we soon learned, before a bandit had raped one of the women in our party.

The state police descended on the town. They arrested a suspect who was found with some stolen articles. He was sent to prison. A few months later, he escaped. The main perpetrator was not apprehended. He was well known to the authorities, they said. The weapons, captured by the police, were American arms provided by drug lords. The robbery had been planned well in advance, the police claimed. Before they would take action, they required that the raped woman submit to a physical examination to determine that she was telling the truth.

The people of Alamos were angry, as were the folk of San Bernardo. All shook their heads, first in disbelief then in despair, at the new wave of crime spreading over the great, wild Mayo country. Most felt it was a result of drug dealing. The police were loath to offer explanations. Drug lords, as we shall see, make *their* lives difficult as well.

A ranch on the other side of the mountain from El Chiribo is owned by the Alvarez family. It's no more than ten leagues from Alamos, a mere five hours for a high-clearance four-wheel-drive vehicle when the road isn't completely washed out. The headquarters sits in a splendid cool valley of oaks and pines, many of which have been cleared to make way for fields where corn and beans are raised. The valley and the ranch are big enough to support five brothers and two cousins and their families. Rubén Alvarez owns the first hut on the road. He pushes back his sombrero. His handshake is gentle, his smile shy, and his welcome sincere. On the slopes the brothers plant corn and beans together, he says. They eat the corn themselves. What they cannot consume they feed to cattle. Each year, Rubén explained to me, they save the biggest and best ears of corn for seed for the next year. He told me proudly that it's been done that way for generations, and the corn they produce is the best around. I can hardly argue, especially after sampling the fresh *tamales de elote* (green corn tamales) made by his wife, Ana María. The brothers also produce their own squash, fruit, and milk.

Biologist Phil Jenkins and I stopped by Rubén's house just in time for Ana María to offer us some fresh milk and cheese, along with delectable candied squash and some exotic corn cookies that she baked in our honor. They live simply, in an open-front house, built with their own hands, with thatched roofs and sleeping lofts. Chickens run free in the open fields; dogs guard against predators and foes. Rubén rides a horse into Alamos every couple of weeks. Other than that, the men's days are spent cultivating their fields, watching their herds, and (I noticed) frequently stopping to enjoy the profound beauty of their valley. Phil and I sat on a bench at the wooden table in the tiny open dining room, staring dreamily at the forested slopes, and the distant peaks of Chihuahua shimmering beyond the enclosing hills of the valley.

Ana María—a young, strong, cheerful mother with a radiant smile—came from a small town in the lowlands, she said, where her family had lived for generations. Did she miss it? Not for a minute. She smiled, holding two toddlers on her lap, her tidy kitchen behind her with its simple wood stove and its sparse but well-organized wooden shelves holding the few implements she needs to prepare the modest but tasty food that is the mainstay of her family's diet. She hummed a tune to the happy children.

Phil had come in search of new plants as part of the project he and Paul Martin have worked on for years to compile a list (or perhaps more accurately, a biography) of the plants of the Río Mayo area of southern Sonora, amplifying Gentry's classic.

Our destination was a canyon a few miles below the ranch, accessible only on foot. Rubén—a slim, handsome man in his thirties—graciously offered us his home to sleep in, but we were equipped with tents and sleeping bags, all that stuff we Americans take for granted.

He showed us to a flat place where we could pitch our tents, offered us supper and whatever other things he could provide us, then bade us good night. As he left, he turned and asked me, "Davíd, would you mind if I came along?"

"It would be an honor and a pleasure, Rubén," I assured him, elated over his request, for he knew far more about the country than Phil and I could hope to learn. A good guide in that country can easily double the knowledge gleaned. That night from our campsite I made out, far across the valley, the silvery beam from the Coleman lantern that is the source of night-time illumination for the Alvarez family.

Mid-morning found Phil and me staggering under the weight of our packs down a narrow trail in the canyon that drains the ranch. Rubén was patient, stopping with us frequently to point out plants and trees, most of which I'd never seen before. He could identify trees by leaf patterns alone. His sandaled feet moved with practiced grace through the bush, while Phil and I stomped with our boots.

As the canyon narrowed, the oaks and pines quickly gave way to trees and plants of the lower tropics. Rubén cited them and Phil followed with the scientific names in a bewildering flurry. "Lots of different trees and plants here," I remarked to Rubén.

"Just wait till you see what's in the side canyon below," he replied, smiling encouragingly.

He granted us a rest at a spring where lush, dense foliage and a plank cover nearly concealed a steady trickle of clear water from which he drank. Nearby was a distiller's cache from which someone brewed *mescal*. Later Rubén urged us to another halt in a cave with ancient rock paintings on its walls. The temperature rose as we descended; the biting bugs became more aggressive, the birds more raucous. Overhead a small flock of large, brilliant green parrots squawked. "*Guacamayas*," (macaws), Rubén reported. We paused for lunch. Phil and I munched on our American-style backpacking food. Rubén offered us fresh tortillas, bean burros, and cheese made on his ranch.

Down we plunged into the heat, past deep pools of clear

water. Cows stared at us, their curiosity mingling with suspicion. The canyon walls became steeper and the trees more exotic, taller, more exuberantly green. At one point Phil motioned for me to stop. "Listen to that bird, Dave," he whispered. "A Brown-backed Solitaire. Prettiest song in the world." I heard a complicated song, reminiscent of wind chimes and tinkling crystal. Rubén watched my expression and nodded with delight. "*Gilguero,*" he said. To this day, I have never heard a more enchanting sound.

We cached our packs, climbed the side of the canyon, then dropped into a deep forest of dense green, a place of the jungle-like flamboyance of rain forests a thousand miles to the south. Before we reached the bottom, completely obscured by the blinding green of the forest canopy, Rubén halted us. "Be careful David," he warned. "This plant is called *ortiguilla.*" He pointed to a broad-leaved short tree. "If you touch the leaves, they'll burn like fire." I was careful to heed his advice, for the canyon floor produced great groves of the nettle. We lingered in the bottom. "This is a place where you'll see trees never seen outside this area," Rubén reported proudly. "It's always green here. These trees never drop their leaves. See this tree? It's an *halla.*" I stood in the dark canyon bottom, a place smelling at once of freshness and decay, where the sun's rays never penetrate and where the trees have endured for thousands of years. I stared up at the canopy, trying to find the top of the thick-boled tree, unable to distinguish its leaves from those of the other leviathans, so inter-twined was the soaring mat far above us. "How tall do you reckon, Phil?" I asked him. We compared estimates and agreed it was at least a hundred feet tall. Rubén agreed with a height in excess of thirty meters. "This one is a *guasique,* that one's an *alar-rán.*" He pointed to one he called an *higuería* and another he named *chapote.* Some of them were familiar to Phil, some not, simply because they have never been found elsewhere in Sonora. Finally, Rubén himself admitted to being stumped. He pointed to a giant straight-trunked ancient with a rough bark. "I have to confess I don't know the name of this one," he said with a sly smile. "*No sé como se llama.*" It was the proud confession of a man of wide knowledge, one whose vast experience and sophistica-tion makes admission of ignorance a special event. Phil stared at the bark, craned his neck studying the leaf patterns far overhead, and shook his head. "It's new to me, too," he said.

Soon Rubén asked if it would be all right if he went home. His politeness overwhelmed me. He bade us good-bye and hiked out of the canyon by a different route, leaving Phil and me in awe at the marvel of nature and at Ruben's astonishing familiarity with the life forms on his ranch. He walked, moved, and lived with the humble pride of a people secure with their roots, bound to the land, yet liberated by its bounty.

In late 1993 Rubén reported that *narcotraficantes* were buying up ranches in the area and making life very difficult for his family.

CHAPTER 3

Mayos

In the very south of Sonora the tropical forest spills over into the basin of the Río Fuerte, which drains the great barrancas of southwest Chihuahua, including the famed Barranca del Cobre. The southern slopes of the Sierra de los Frailes, part of the Sierra de Alamos, drain into the coastal plain, the effective southern limit of Sonora. The land slopes down to the Fuerte, and Sinaloan and Chihuahuan mountain peaks are visible from many viewpoints.

It's Mayo Indian country. Small *rancherías* dot the forest-covered countryside. Mayos' living conditions are quite different from Yaquis', although the two languages are close. Whereas Yaquis tend to live in pueblos along the Río Yaqui, Mayos are spread out in small villages over the lower Mayo Valley and the western portion of the Río Fuerte drainage. The scattering appears to be voluntary, a *diaspora* after the theft of Mayo lands along the river by *yoris* (the Sonoran Indian term for Mexicans).

Mayos never possessed the military ferocity or messianism of the Yaquis and subsequently became more assimilated and were more handily dispersed by invaders. Hardly pacifists, they repeatedly joined in native rebellions. After the defeat of the Yaqui leader Cajeme in 1886, they were effectively neutralized and thereafter offered only scattered resistance to Mexican determination to steal their lands. Not as well organized to resist militarily as Yaquis were, Mayos were enslaved by farming and mining powers throughout the *porfiriato* and forced to work in mines or *haciendas*. In 1910 many men escaped from the *patrones* and joined the revolutionary forces supporting Francisco I. Madero. They attached themselves in large numbers to the army of General Alvaro Obregón, who espoused return of their ancestral lands to them and an end to enslavement and peonage. A museum curator in Huatabampo near Navojoa showed me a photograph of Obregón surrounded by Mayos bravely brandishing their bows and arrows. In 1915, after proving themselves valiant warriors, sometimes fighting alongside General Obregón in battles, they returned triumphant to their homelands, only to find their formerly communal lands divided up among non-Mayos, their homes destroyed, and their families separated. The revolution betrayed them. It was not until the 1930s that they were given *ejido* lands, and by that time the majority had been dispersed and their identity as a people severely compromised.

Some monolingual Mayo speakers remain today, and festivals featuring ancient dances still take place. Young people gravitate toward the more socially acceptable Spanish. In a small village I stood in the shade of a porch roof and talked with a family. Above my head dangled the pelt of a possum. "How do you say *tlacuache* in Mayo?" I asked a trio of young women holding an infant. They shook their heads.

"*No sabemos,*" (We don't know) one answered sadly.

Masiaca, which means "centipede hill" in Mayo, is the largest of several Mayo pueblos clustered only a few miles from Mexico 15. Masiaca itself is a village of a couple of hundred houses, some of them of Mayo construction, with woven cane walls, often daubed with mud. Several hamlets are found within about a kilometer or two. One of those tiny communities is called Teachive, "white ground" in Mayo, one of the last villages where heavy woolen Mayo rugs are woven. Thirty years ago the rugs were woven in *rancherías* south of Navojoa around Huatabampo. Now vast, manicured farms have gobbled up the *monte* where sheep once ran, and wool has become scarce. The blankets, or rugs, are ponderous and coarsely woven compared with Navajo rugs. Nonetheless, the Mayo are skilled weavers, and their rugs are serious works of art well known for their pleasant designs. The artists use wool of different sheep to produce varying effects.

The houses of Teachive stand well apart from each other, as Mayos seem to like it. The yards are swept thoroughly each morning, the homes neat. Teachive and other Mayo villages are the cleanest, most orderly I've seen in Mexico. Several women weave in their houses, including Lidia Zazueta, a thin serious women in her early fifties, who keeps a small loom strung and spins or weaves away as time permits. She was born in a house a hundred feet away, as was her mother María Gonzales who has passed eighty and still coaches her daughter and granddaughter in weaving techniques. María learned the art of weaving from her mother, who in turn learned it from her mother, and so on back through the mists of the ages to the time when Spaniards introduced sheep.

The weaving of *cobijas* brings with it a way of life. Lidia raises a small flock of sheep. She shears the *borregas* (ewes), washes, cards, and spins the wool, and gathers materials for the dyes. Years ago the flocks were large and varied enough in color that there was no need for dye. Now there are few black, brown, or gray sheep, so she must dye some of the white wool in a preparation made from mesquite gum to achieve the dark rich browns for her design, or buy the wool elsewhere. A blue shade has become more popular in her generation than before. Lidia tears off leaves from the *añil* bush (*Indigofera suffruticosa*) called *chiju* in Mayo, soaks them in water, then shreds and soaks them again. The resulting dye is a dark blue, almost black color that won't run (as long as it is soaked first in the urine of a little boy). After she has washed the wool in a soap made from agaves, a step necessary to remove the *"aroma,"* she says, laughing, she cards it, then spins it.

The weaving turns out to be the easiest part. The horizontal pieces of the loom are branches of *pitahaya* (organ pipe cactus), cut live, split, and stripped of bark. The vertical beams are made of tough *guayacán*. Lidia showed me how she forms the *tenido* (warp), carefully spacing the threads a quarter of an inch apart. Then she begins weaving the *trampa* (weft), altering the colors, depending on the pattern, her nimble figures flitting with practiced skill, pulling the shuttle, tamping the finished strands, all the while chatting with her family. One of her granddaughters, perhaps ten years old, looks on with a critical eye. She already knows how to weave and asserts she will one day take up the craft.

The weaving requires not only the skill of operating the loom, but intimate knowledge of raising sheep, gathering materials for the dyes, and selecting the proper woods for operating the loom. With the demise of blanket making, this knowledge will disappear, a sad loss for humanity. The demand for large rugs, called *matrimoniales*, has dwindled so that Lidia hasn't made one in some years (some of her neighbors have). It would be no problem, she says, if someone wished to order such a blanket. She would quickly construct a wide loom and begin the work.

For now the tapestries are a vital source of revenue. Employment for men is inconsistent and uncertain. A few from the village work as cowboys. A couple of fellows labored in a nearby sand and gravel operation during the construction of the new highway connecting Navojoa and Los Mochis, Sinaloa. Others find employment as field laborers in agricultural operations, but that work is on a day-by-day basis only. The jobs are back-breaking, and the pay is poor. A man stood by as I discussed weaving with Lidia. Soon he offered me his wares. He carves festival masks used by the *pascola* dancers—the old men of the fiesta—to sell to tourists. They are carefully sculpted and painted, with protruding tongues, fiendish horns, massive painted teeth, faces ringed with horsehair beards, and the grotesque images of spirits that protect the Mayos.

I worked for several days with Vicente Tajia, an older fellow, an expert in the Mayos' uses of plants. He guided me and my colleagues Tom Van Devender and Rigoberto López into the bush near Teachive. We tramped through nearby hills for many hours, while he recited a litany of plant names and uses. At the end of one session he asked me in private, "David, do you think my daughter (she was twenty) could find work in the United States?" I told him it would be difficult unless she could get a Green Card, and that could take years.

"Couldn't she just climb through a hole in the fence?" he asked, beseechingly.

"Yes," I told him, for hundreds of people do every day. "The difficult part would be for her to find permanent work on the other side. She could get hired as a nanny, but the pay would be poor, and she'd always have to be on guard for the *migra*, (the border patrol). They'd round her up and ship her on a bus to the border, just like that, maybe before she could collect her pay."

He asked me to bring books so that she could learn English. She was his one hope of getting out of the grinding poverty he lived in. In Mexico she hadn't a chance. I nodded, not wanting to discourage him. I'd bring her the books, all right, but her chances would be little better than those of the other millions of poor Mexicans yearning for a better life.

María Gonzales, Lidia's mother, watched the weaving operation and the plant discussions with an objective eye. She has put in her time weaving and working, and now she takes life more easily. She loves to tell stories of many years ago. She was waiting for me to ask her something as I sat in Lidia's veranda late one afternoon, enjoying the cool. I inquired about the Mexican moccasin, a venomous snake locally known as the *pichicuate*. Did they ever come into this village?

No, she said, but up in the nearby Sierra de Alamos they could be found. Once, years ago, two friends went deer hunting up in the hills. One of them was attacked and stung, yes *stung*, by a *pichicuate*. They're especially dangerous, María warned me, her eyes glistening with delight, her wrinkled face squinting from her smile, her ancient teeth long and protruding.

"You see, "she said, looking all around her, "the *pichicuate* has a stinger in its tail. Two of them. They don't bite with their mouth. They sting with their tail. That's why they're so, well, evil."

She had my attention and was loving every minute of it. The family gathered around. I noticed Lidia didn't let up in her weaving. She had heard this story before.

"Well, the man who had been stung died, just like that. And do you know that snake wouldn't let the other man get away? No. He kept circling around, watching the man. The fellow was terrified. The only reason he could go for help was that the snake finally went to sleep, and the man shot it. But by the time anybody came, the other man was dead, swollen up big, like this! But see! The snake got him with his tail, just like so." She showed me a fat figure with her arms.

So, the *pichicuate* has a venomous tail! I asked a Mayo cowboy in a village a few miles away what he know about the *pichicuate*. "They sting with their tail." He said. "That's why they're so dangerous." Other men around him nodded in agreement."But," he added, "they also bite with their mouth—a double menace." The reason for this belief (which, by the way, is not correct) may be the snake's habit of shaking and waving its tail when it's alarmed or surprised. *Pichicuates* are a nervous species, prone to strike at any movement, thrashing out with their tail.

I left Teachive reluctantly. The sun was getting low, leaving me little time to find a camping spot. The people of Teachive stood around happily, asking me to come back. "When you do, uh, what was your name?" Lidia asked. I told her. *"Pues, David,"* she said, "When you come back will you bring me a corn mill? You can get better ones than we can." I promised I would. Another woman, stout, smiling but shy, overheard me promise.

"Would you bring one for me, too?" She said quietly. I nodded.

"Por supuesto." (Of course.)

"Y, David, no quieres traer algo para matar cucurachas? Aquí hay tantas y son muy, muy grandes." She added that she wanted me to bring her something that would kill cockroaches. She said that they were great big ones, all over the place. I laughed and she joined in, and I promised to bring some RoachPruf. Now I had to go back. (I did.)

Action comes to Masiaca once a month or so on a Saturday afternoon, enough to raise the dust on the dirt streets. I happened upon the excitement purely by chance. I had stopped by a little general store, *tienda de abarrotes,* the kind that has a shuttered window and a counter from which you order. No one is allowed inside. I asked about local conditions and people, and bought a Coke out of consideration for the owner. While I was forcing down the syrupy liquid, I noticed truckloads of men heading north, followed by groups of men on horseback. Then two young men rode by on horses, leading a third horse covered by a white blanket. My curiosity got the best of me.

"¿Por que lleva la cobija el caballo?" (Why is the horse wearing the blanket?), I asked.

The store's owner was a fat man whose smile made me uneasy. "Va a haber carrera" (There's going to be a race), he answered. (Leave your bet with me!)

"Where?" I had to know.

"Oh, just north of town on the *pista.* You ought to see it; everybody goes. Just head north out of town. You can't miss it."

Indeed, I couldn't. A procession appeared to be heading north, ending at the local airstrip. At least thirty trucks of every sort and manufacture conceivable were parked on both sides, grills facing away from the *pista* that was soon to become a race track. It looked like about two hundred people were lined up along the track. I found a space, backed my truck into it, and joined a group of men, some on horses, some standing, who were taking advantage of the shade of a gigantic mesquite tree.

I chatted with them for a while. This was to be a real race, not a *chiruza* in which hacks or mongrel horses compete just for the heck of it. These were expensive horses, quarter horses, one man said. A lot of money would change hands that afternoon, a cowboy told me as he relaxed in his saddle, happily supporting a can of Tecate beer and the horse's reins in one hand, puffing on a cigarette he was holding in the other. After we had chatted for a while, and he had determined that I had not fought in the Gulf War and hadn't flown missions over Baghdad, his horse started to stretch. "Excuse me," he said in an unhurried fashion, "but you might want to step away from my horse just a little."

I lost no time and jumped about ten feet away, and the horse let loose with a waterfall of urine that splattered everything within six feet. I tipped my hat to the man, much to the mirth of the other cowboys around.

"Nice hat," he said. "Where did you get it."

"Nácori," I told him. He nodded.

"If you weren't such a *güero*, you might pass for one of us." He laughed and took a pull on his beer.

As we watched and waited, a second race horse was led onto the strip. Still truckloads of men, families, even children arrived on flatbeds, cattle trucks, pickups, sedans, horse-drawn carts, mule-drawn carts, and donkey-drawn carts. Men rode in on magnificent steeds, lowly burros, and nervous mules. Four or five men showed up on bicycles. A few, very few, walked. It was not as affluent a crowd as the one I'd seen at a race up north at Cucurpe.

I knew this was no random affair when a truck drove in, and a family set up a stand selling fresh *tacos de cabrito* (tacos of kid meat, green onions, and salsa). The father issued commands while the mother and children scurried around setting things up. He took the orders and money. The others did the work. From somewhere a man appeared pushing one of Mexico's ubiquitous ice-cream carts.

The two featured horses were paraded around by their jockeys, young men still in their teens. They were skinny. One was wearing no shirt, the other just a tank-type T-shirt. The kid with the T-shirt rode by near where I was standing. I asked my companions where he was from. They didn't know. Someone said they'd heard he was from up near Alamos.

A half-hour passed, an hour, and still the people and vehicles thronged to the airstrip. There had to be 750 people by now, and the crowd was getting happier by the minute, oblivious to the dust kicked up by hundreds of feet, hooves,and tires that now blanketed everything in sight. *Caguamas* (liter bottles of beer) were passed around and emptied only to be replaced by another and then another. "There's a beer truck over there," my cowboy friend informed me, pointing at a truck a hundred yards away. "They'll sell you all you can drink." I wasn't surprised.

I had difficulty believing there could be any more people within a twenty-mile radius. Men wandered out into the bush to pee. I pondered the problem faced by women in the same predicament. I had just decided to count the crowd, when a shout came from up the packed track, and the multitude parted. They cheered as the two horses came thundering by. Fast, very, very fast they came. The boy in the T-shirt won by a good length, but the horses galloped on past the end of the airstrip into the narrow road and vanished in the forest. A few minutes later they returned. The winner held his crop high in victory. The applause was faint and unconvincing. The local boy must have lost.

It was sundown when I left the race course and the happy gathering that by now was showing the effect of large volumes of beer. I drove a good ten kilometers to the north before I found an indistinct track leading off into the forest. I followed it a little way and found a clearing, where I pitched my tent, completely out of sight of the roadway.

I've never before camped in such an enchanted place. The moon cast shadows on the immense organ pipes and *etchos*, while the great trees of the forest maintained their air of mysterious and lofty indifference. Whip-poor-wills called, owls hooted. Far in the distance coyotes howled, and cows groaned. I meandered into the bush, scrupulously careful not to get lost, knowing in this flat forest every direction looks the same and no identifying landmarks are available, the distant mountains obscured by the canopy. Small animals scurried in the bushes all around. After an hour of listening and watching the cool of night in the deciduous forest, I climbed into my tent and fell asleep.

Thirty miles to the north of Masiaca lies an outpost of accessible civilization, the village of Güirocoba. An older Mayo explained that *güiro* in Mayo means *aura*, the turkey vulture, while *coba* means head. Thus, he informed me that Güirocoba means "vulture head." It's a good name choice, for a hill near the village looks just like one. It's a bumpy ride of an hour and a half from Alamos and is the end of the line, unless you have a four-wheel-drive vehicle and wish to continue to the smaller village of Choquincagui, another few miles up the rocky canyon. I wanted to go on but had been repeatedly warned that Choquincagui was heavy drug country with enough killings to keep all Sonoran morticians in business, so I reluctantly stayed away.

Güirocoba's Mayo huts are spread over a large area in a narrow valley surrounded by slopes covered with dense vegetation. At the north end of town lie the ruins of an abandoned *hacienda*. It had been owned and operated by an American, a few unfriendly men informed me as they relaxed under the shade of a huge *guamúchil* tree. However, the gringo was long gone, and they didn't know what he produced in the *hacienda* or at least were in no mood to tell me. They looked at me, answered my questions laconically, then turned away.

From the age of the sprawling crumbling walls, I gathered that the *hacienda* was the same vintage as the other ancient estates I've seen all over Sonora. It must have been abandoned some time after 1910, when gringos found they were no longer welcome to establish fiefdoms with Mexicans and Indians as their serfs. Closer to Masiaca at the village of Yocogigua a similar building lay in ruin. According to an older Mayo man, the Indians once produced *mescal*, a form of tequila from agaves. But the *dueño* (owner) had long since abandoned the scene.

A faded sign on the ancient wall reads *"Fabrica de Mescal. Se prohibe la entrada sin negocio."* (Mescal Factory. No admittance without business.) A few feet away a sign spray-painted in big red letters so faded as to be nearly unreadable set forth a political slogan of a leftist party.

As local residents tell it, the *patrón*—the boss, the *hacendado*—was General Carlos Yocupicio, a bigwig in the revolution of 1910 and former Governor of Sonora. He was born in Masiaca and took over the land at Yocogigua as one of the spoils of war. At least that is the story told me by several men seated under the *ramada* of a hut nearby the old building. It became the policy of the victorious revolutionary government to punish wealthy landowners who had supported Porfirio Díaz or his stand-in, Victoriano Huerto, by seizing their lands and turning them over to military leaders who had shown loyalty to the revolutionary cause. As governor of Sonora in the late 1930s, Yocupicio aligned himself—not surprisingly—with *latifundistas.* However he obtained the lands, Yocupicio built the *hacienda* and began producing *mescal.*

That's the local story. A Sonoran historian told me a different version: the *mescal* plant actually begun by a Yugoslav named Sugich in 1934 (the date fashioned in wrought iron over the central door). Natives refer to him as Súbichi. His family ran it until the 1970s when, the historian says, President Luis Echeverría expropriated so much land that the factory couldn't produce enough agaves. The town residents tried to maintain production until the 1970s, but the plant gradually failed, and the great building was completely abandoned in 1980. Maintenance of the structure must have been beyond the means of the local population. An older fellow told me that the residents felt that the *mescal* called Yocogigua was taking too heavy a toll on the men. They decided to cease production.

The crumbling factory is an eloquent testimonial to an era in Mexico when local warlords called *caciques* ran things pretty much as they pleased. Today cholla cactus and grass grow out of the roof tiles. Graffiti cover the inside of the building, which now serves as shade for livestock and a hide-away for lovers.

Fifty yards away from the hacienda is a Mayo hut. An Indian was seated alone at a tiny table in the yard formed by a fence of part living ocotillo, part dead mesquite poles. He jumped up as I approached and opened the makeshift gate. He swept his chair toward me, brushing it off in a gallant gesture of hospitality.

He was Tarahumara, he said, from the north, and he pointed to the endless series of mountains on the northern horizon. "And these guys are Mayos." (He indicated two slight youths who leaned on a fence post, taking in our conversation.)

He had been eating some bony portion of meat while an inestimably lovely girl with long, freshly brushed hair heated tortillas of corn on an inverted oil drum with a tiny fire built inside. "Can I offer you some *cabrito* (goat)?"

I had already eaten and couldn't bear to make inroads in his tiny supply of food, so I declined as tactfully as I could. He was there for the day only. He worked as a field laborer in one of the agribusiness megafields near Huatabampo. He felt lucky to have a job. Sunday was his day off, and he relished being with his family. Inside the adjoining hut were some people, probably too shy to come outside. I suppose he was in his late forties, although a man who works that hard ages early. Judging from the age of his daughter, he might have been younger. He was thin. His cheap cotton shirt was clean. Two younger girls passed behind me, giggling, bearing a bucket of water they carried between them on a yoke. The village well was two hundred yards away. When I left, he urged me to come back.

As part of a study of native uses of plants, research scientist Tom Van Devender and Sonoran plant researcher Rigoberto López joined me in Yocogigua. We asked an old Mayo, Santiago Valenzuela, to ride to a nearby hill and walk into the *monte* with us and tell us about the plants the Mayos used. We spent several days with him, listening carefully as he described in his gentle, unassuming voice the names and uses of forest plants. At the end of our session I paid Santiago, gave him a couple of shirts, and said good-bye.

On our return to Tucson, I discovered that Santiago had left his machete under the rear seat of the van we had ridden in. I was sick, knowing the importance of that implement to him. For the rural Mexican man, the machete is an extension of his being. He uses it for a knife, for protection, for lopping limbs, felling trees, cutting posts, digging, cutting, butchering, sawing, carving, and eating. Santiago would be almost crippled without his machete.

A month later I returned to Yocogigua. He saw me coming and came out to meet me. From a distance I saw his old face crinkle into a smile when he spied the machete. I handed it to him, laughing. "Ay, David," he said with a voice full of love and gratitude, "you can't imagine how much I missed this machete. I thought I'd never see it again. If you ever want me to cut something for you, you have only to speak and I'll cut it!"

CHAPTER 4

Guarijíos

North of Alamos in the drainage of the Upper Río Mayo live what are perhaps the most elusive *indígenas* of all Mexico, perhaps in all North America: the Guarijíos. Although they were visited by early missionaries, they were little known to outsiders until 1960 when Howard Scott Gentry published the field notes he had made on the Guarijíos in the 1930s. At that time they lived in the almost inaccessible fastness of the Sierra and retained much of their original culture. Even in Sonora, few authorities are familiar with them. Some evidence suggests that they are late arrivers in Sonora, appearing in the seventeenth century, a fact that may explain their peripheral involvement in the state's history.

In the early 1970s revolutionary guerrillas from Chihuahua filtered into the Guarijío country and seized a landowner from San Bernardo as hostage, releasing him only after a ransom of 1 million pesos was paid. Attempting to exterminate the trouble-makers, the Mexican government sent armed police and military personnel into the area. They claimed that Guarijíos were harboring and assisting the guerrillas. Guarijíos became victims of government oppression, including the capture and incarceration of one of their leaders. Reports still circulate of kidnapping, torture, and repression by government troops. The response of the Indians was to withdraw even farther into the mountains and to develop a heightened suspicion of outsiders. After a few months the guerrilla movement faded, but the hostility toward *blancos* (Mexicans) remained.

Most of the 1,800 Guarijíos still live in settlements or isolated ranches in the Río Mayo drainage, virtually inaccessible to vehicles. Mesa Colorada on the Mayo is accessible by tough dirt road. Some small villages have an airstrip, but most settlements require long trips on foot or by pack animal to visit. Guarijío tend to be secretive and uninclined to shower visitors with welcoming delegations. Attempts are in progress by the National Indigenous Institute to maintain *albergues* (boarding schools) in the remote centers. The town of San Bernardo, twenty-five miles north of Alamos, is now the site of Mexican government programs to assist the Guarijíos and provide them with social services.

Gentry was eighty-nine when I last spoke with him in Tucson in 1993. He was savoring an afternoon highball at his dining room table, a computerized aspirator next to him from which he inhaled various aerosols for his emphysema. I told him I was headed for Guarijío country. His old man's eyes lit up, and he told of his Guarijío guides in the 1930s, how they led him through isolated canyons and helped him collect and identify plants. He described the Arroyo Guajaráy, where I was headed.

"Oh, yes," he said, smiling, "you'll find deep pools half a mile long. Once I was swimming naked in one when I heard some women's voices coming down the trail to the pool. I ran up to where I'd left my clothes and dived into the bushes to hide until they left!"

Jesús Armando Haro, a Sonoran doctor and researcher familiar with the Guarijío, helped me obtain guides and pack animals. A tiny group of us set off on foot up the oxbows of the Arroyo Guajaráy, the heart of Guarijío country. We were the first gringos in the arroyo for a long time, a Guarijío said. Chalillo, one of the guides, was a quiet, brooding man in his early thirties, an *hechicero* (sorcerer) according to some. Seldom smiling, he uttered little more than grunts until I said to him: "Chalillo, you're as skinny as I am!"

He wore a black coat despite the heat of late spring and rode a horse unwillingly, leading the pack animals and the little troupe. Later, when he warmed up a bit, he confided that he'd much rather have walked. He walked everywhere he went, all over this part of the Sierra—walked for days, he said. By his own admission he was a *curandero* (healer). He volunteered herbal recipes, all of which we wrote down. Mix the bark of the algodoncillo with leaves of an amaranth and boil them. Then drink a glass of the tea each day for four days. It will get rid of colic or stomach pains, he announces. Dr. Haro says many of the local remedies target stomach pains, a sure sign of the prevalence of parasites.

We passed through Burapaco. Until 1990 the sleepy hamlet was but a clearing in a vast expanse of dry tropical forest. In the dry season most of the trees dropped their leaves so that only giant etcho cacti showed green on the landscape. When *las aguas* (the rains) came, the trees exploded into leaf, and the landscape became a glistening jungle almost overnight.

For many decades Guarijíos herded a few cows through the forest. Here and there they cleared small acreages for a *milpa* (cornfield), or cut an occasional tree for firewood, a fence, or a cross-post for a new hut. In their scattered villages they wove hats and baskets, raised pigs, and tended gardens.

Now the forest surrounding the town is gone. A host of hired woodcutters swarmed over the land, burning what they left behind. In their wake are a few thousand acres of scorched, devastated landscape. Here and there clumps of sowed buffelgrass spring up from the ground. Fifty or sixty kinds of tree, another fifty species of bush, and a hundred smaller plant varieties have been replaced by one foreign grass.

The cows come. At first a few, then many more, are trucked in to feast on the buffelgrass. Soon they too have trampled the pasture and reduced it to dust and the few tough, inedible plants that survived the fire. If the rains come, the cows will grow fat; if not, they will languish skinny and dull. Every day, drought or flood, more cows appear, and more land is cleared. The pasture expands. Buffelgrass takes over. The forest shrinks. The Indians retreat.

It's all part of the expanding drug culture of Mexico. The *desmonte* (clear-cutting) of the forest was ordered by a drug lord, local Indians say. He wants to run cows. Then his ledgers will show sales of beef and hides, many sales—far more sales than actually take place. It's a convenient way to launder money from drug sales. If the government wants to know where the drug lord's money comes from, he points to his cattle operation.

Everywhere in the mountains of northwestern Mexico, new clear-cuts, pickups, and cattle trucks are appearing, where only yesterday a small rural population eked out a life. Vast tracts of forest are cut down to provide a political cover for drug traffic. Across buffelgrass prairies waves of heat shimmer. Only months ago the forest cooled the earth, its fruits, branches, leaves, and roots home for a myriad of creatures. They are gone.

Beside a trail a few miles from the village a crude cross is stuck into the ground on top of a small grave. Buried below is an Indian who crossed up a drug lord and paid for it with his life. Indians walk by the grave silently. They have no comment on the marijuana industry. They say nothing and hope they will have no trouble. They walk in fear. They mistrust strangers.

Higher up in the mountains the old ranch families have left. The new dope cartels have taken over the land. They plant dope where they please, even on other people's land. They control the economy of the mountains. They pay a few *campesinos* generously to help till the crops and move the harvested *mota*. A few farmers prosper. A few protest and are killed. Others, frightened, pull up stakes, and move to the crowded cities. A rancher friend of mine, who loved his ranch and the forest, has moved into a town because he fears the new drug trade and the violence it has spawned.

Fear prevails everywhere. I was warned by low voices, "Stay away from there." "Don't go up there." When the topic of drugs come up, conversations end. Eyes wander or stare at the ground. The drug lords have established a reign of terror, and no one can counter them.

Marijuana has been a marginal part of mountain life for ages without any harmful effects, but the United States government threatens reprisals, cut-off of investment, and embargos. The Mexican government is puzzled as to why it should create huge, costly wars on a crop popular in the United States. Why should they interfere with produce in high demand across the border? However, the Mexican government does jump to the tune of the dollar. Officials create high drama with sporadic anti-drug campaigns. Soldiers, undercover cops, *federales, judiciales* abound. Sometimes, the people say, lawmen fight among themselves to control a share of the trade. They harass the people even further. The people don't know who to fear more: the representatives of law and order or the drug dealers.

Dr. Haro is the only physician in a thousand square miles. Indians wait quietly outside his rustic clinic. He knows the native people well and respects their quiet ways. He tells me that this terror—the creation of wasteland, the death of forest, towns, hamlets, and ranches—has been created by the policies of my country, the United States. Our punitive laws on marijuana have driven the cost of weed sky high, he argues. The profits from one successful shipment can provide a lifetime of easy living, but the drug lords must have absolute control over the harvest. To protect their life in the fast lane, they have a host of killers in their hire. Anyone who gets in the way must die. Sometimes it is necessary to make an example of an innocent victim. The doctor has seen too much of the violence.

"Why don't you consider, for once, how your country is destroying mine?" he asks with quiet bitterness and frustration. "Look at the billions you spend, the thousands of police, agents, helicopters, airplanes, you devote to keeping the price of marijuana high. What do the people of your country have to show for it? A siege mentality and a huge tax bill.

What do the doctor's patients have to show for it? A life of terror, a devastated countryside, a disrupted culture, and a legacy of violence and rural folk fearful of talking to anyone. He wonders aloud, "doesn't anyone in the United States understand the connection between deforestation and the drug trade? You've succeeded in nearly destroying the mountain way of life—the decent, congenial, hard-working folk of the Sierra. What have you done for your own people? Hired more police, deputies, border patrol, bigger DEA, FBI, CIA, Border Patrol, ATF.

"David," he asks, "why don't you get rid of laws against marijuana?" Overnight the price would collapse, and the drug lords would find their profits gone, he says. The payrolls of thugs and go-betweens would be eliminated. The barons would vanish from the highlands leaving the people there free from the reign of terror." I can't argue with him.

Miles away, across the valley, a field in an impossibly isolated canyon was planted with marijuana. A guide playfully pulled up a plant and offered it to us, injecting a note of panic in our midst. Along the trail in a different canyon lay snake-length sections of plastic water pipe, chopped up, a fellow reported, by government soldiers out to destroy the crop. The pipe had run from a spring down to a field where a marijuana crop was growing. It was part of a cleverly arranged irrigation system to nurse the crop through the searing dry season. Locals claim that the soldiers try to appropriate the pot for themselves. Our guide in that area said he seldom went to that canyon anymore, fearing he'd get in the middle of the drug trade. I think he meant he wanted to stay as far away as possible from the military.

The Guarijío guides led us stoically, keeping to themselves at night, politely answering our questions, warming up only after three days of leading us. Most of them make a living punching cows, one of them told me, but there's not even much of that work. He traveled to Ciudad Obregón once, looking for work, but he found nothing and came back to Mesa Colorada.

They also make a few bucks transporting marijuana along the steep trails of the Sierra, I learned elsewhere. The pay is good, and for people on the brink of starvation it's an excellent alternative.

Far up the river we went, finding out about plants, trees, and animals from our guides. They watched intently as we pressed plants, sorted specimens, and caught and released reptiles. They patiently answered our barrage of questions, shaking their heads when they didn't know, and asked us about what we were doing. On the way back we encountered a new fence cutting off the trail. Chalillo couldn't get his horse across the fence. He pointed to the path and indicated the direction. He would follow the fence line, he said, until he found a gate.

Chalillo was wrong. The directions he gave were bad. We wound up a mile above where we were supposed to be. I was curious to see his response when he showed up at the trail head. He was two hours late. He came on foot, fording the deep Mayo that reached his hips. He said nothing, plopped a bag of ours on the ground, accepted his payment, nodded, and plodded off into the Sierra. "He's not from around here," another guide added. "*No conoce muy bien el terreno.*" (He doesn't know the land very well.)

Back in Tucson I hastened to call Gentry to bring him up to date on the Guarijío he had dwelt with six decades ago. During my absence he had died. When I got the news, I sat on the curb and cried.

A year later I was back, this time guided by Cipriano Buitimea, a Guarijío who lives in an isolated rancho many kilometers from the Guajaráy but who knows the river intimately.

We plodded along the serpentine course of the river. I asked questions, and he patiently answered them. I asked him about the government oppression in the 1970s. "Yes, David, it was a hard time," he said. "We were afraid to go close to the towns. We didn't know when we would be attacked by the government, so we stayed hidden, but it was a time of drought, and we didn't have much food. We suffered a lot."

Cipriano makes sure that his children speak Guarijío at home. If they attend the *albergue* (boarding school) at Los Bajíos, a three-hour walk away, they'll be taught in Spanish. This was a deep man, I realized. Numerous Indians passed by on the trail going the other way. He stopped to speak with them all, speaking mostly in Spanish. He was in a bit of a hurry to get back to his *rancho*, for he had some cattle, three of them, I understood, to round up.

We sat on a rock and stared at the clear water of the stream. "What part of the year do you like the best, Cipriano?" I asked. He tossed a pebble into the water, thinking.

"I like it from the middle of May until *las aguas* (the rains) begin." I was rather surprised.

"Isn't it terribly hot then?"

"Oh, yes, David, it is very hot and dusty, but very early in the mornings it is cool and fresh. The doves begin to sing to each other, and then the other birds begin, each of them singing his own song. Then I hear the other animals talking to each other, and I can feel the soil calling to me and telling me it's time to dig in my *maguechi* (cornfield) and get it ready for planting so that when the rains fall the corn will grow up fine. That's the time of year I like best."

CHAPTER 5

Caminos of San Bernardo Revisited

A rocky, punishing dirt track leaves San Bernardo, crossing the Arroyo Taymuco to the north of the village. It forks a hundred yards beyond the concrete crossing, from which rusted sections of jagged reinforcing steel jut and deep potholes slow to a crawl the occasional trucks that cross. To the right the road curls off behind a mesa and ascends steeply to the new barrio that sits high over the north bank of the stream bed. To the left the roadway winds up a densely forested hillside and wanders northward into the convoluted, mountainous bush of the Guarijío country. About a kilometer from the arroyo, near a pass high above the valley, most of the town of San Bernardo comes into view. It's a place I'd hoped to bring Gentry. Fifty years ago he had written a brief article called "Caminos of San Bernardo," describing the roads and footpaths that tie the village together, how the *milpas* and their bounty are tied to the town. I had come back to San Bernardo to see what changes had manifested themselves. I'd hoped that from this new *camino* Gentry could describe the changes fifty years had wrought. It was not to be, for Gentry died before I could bring him back.

So I returned to San Bernardo alone. The town lies folded into an uneven valley surrounded by imposing mountain ranges, grayish brown (the color locals call *mojíno*) in the dry season, blinding emerald green after the summer rains. The dirt road from Alamos arrives rather suddenly into the populated area. On the outskirts lie the long warehouse-like, government-built offices of INI (the National Indigenous Institute), constructed to administer programs to the Guarijío Indians. From time to time groups of Indians can be seen, waiting somberly and stoically for a ride, south to Alamos or north into the Guarijío lands. Some have come to see a doctor or to spend their tiny savings on a few meager luxuries in the big city.

A hundred yards beyond, the visitor is suddenly in San

Bernardo. The town is more shaded than in Gentry's time, the dense braid of roads and paths lined with great figs—*nacapulis, chunas,* and *higueras*—strong, ancient mesquites, *palo chinus,* and eucalyptus, all now fifty years older. I plodded over every camino of San Bernardo I could find, hoping to speak with *viejitos* who recalled the great naturalist. I found only two: one in his nineties, another in his sixties. More common were folk who reminisced about Juan Argüelles—Gentry's assistant, his *mocito* Juanito. Argüelles eventually followed Gentry to California and worked on Gentry's farm where he is now retired. Today older men in the villages comment on Juan with the good-natured slanderous banter of men with time on their hands.

San Bernardo's character is shaped by its caminos perhaps even more than in Gentry's time. Pickups and cattle trucks penetrate everywhere a wheeled vehicle can possibly reach. Men in trucks the world over view landscapes as something to be ridden on, tested, defied, to be left alone only if nature or social indignation stand in the way. Trucks are, after all, quintessentially male, a fact accentuated in Mexico, where female pickup drivers are as uncommon as seatbelt users. Graves along the caminos have been replaced by defunct vehicles that died on the roadside and were too big to move. Gradually they sink into the sand and oblivion.

Footpaths remain, perhaps even more numerous than in Gentry's time, for there are more people now: between 1,300 and 1,400 (depending on how many are on the buses visiting Alamos or Navojoa)—at least a thousand more than the three or four hundred of 1940. Even so, the town has shrunk dramatically in a decade. The closing of the mine at San Rafael, fifteen kilometers to the southeast, caused an immediate plunge from a high of 3,500 souls in the early 1980s. The decline continues and paints a bleak portrait of the tearing apart of a community's soul by forces far beyond its control.

Gentry would hardly recognize the countryside around San Bernardo. Great acreages have been cleared of short tree forest and planted with African buffelgrass to improve pasture. Nevertheless, the town's physiognomy, its footprint, remains the same. The square is as barren as it was fifty years ago, its bleakness accentuated by a failed basketball court, now cracked and unplayable, backboards warped, rims bent. Most of the buildings of half a century ago are still in use. The old builders used *amapa* wood for posts, *palo colorado* for *vigas* and *horcones*, and *palo blanco* for bases. The porch roofs are still of dirt laid on top of *varas* of *vara blanca*. No porch could be better, no woods more resistant to the ravages of sun, water, and termites. With minimal maintenance those porches will last another fifty years, possibly longer than the town. The government has wisely issued decrees against further plundering of the forests for *amapa* and *palo colorado*. Future porches will not be bulwarks against time.

The *caminos* of today are strewn with trash, mostly cast-off plastic bags. Travelers pick their way gingerly. Polyethylene had not been invented in Gentry's time. Fifty years ago garbage consisted of the leavings of livestock, the detritus of human meals, a few paper wrappers, string, and an occasional tin can. Most of the garbage was quickly consumed by livestock. The cans rusted away. In San Bernardo the *camino* to the dump is the path to the nearest arroyo. There is no landfill, and residents have nowhere to dump their considerable trash. At the stores each purchase is plopped into a plastic bag which will wind up as garbage strewn along a *camino* of San Bernardo. Whoever introduced plastic bags to Mexico neglected to mention that they last forever.

Don José Borbón Borbón maintains a nearly permanent seat of vigilance on the plant-filled porch of his home just off the plaza. "He's a double Borbón," his son-in-law told me proudly. Don José gestured up the street to the house where Gentry lived. The white-bearded *viejo* is ninety. He remembered Gentry well, describing in his ancient voice how Howard brought pressed plants in great stacks from the *monte* into the town on a burro, scribbled voluminous notes, and entertained the locals by showing them his collections of plants, reptiles, and fossils. Before long Don José wearied of those memories and launched into vivid descriptions of life in San Bernardo during the two decades of unsettled political life that is now called the Mexican Revolution. His daughter Fermina stood by his side, helping her father describe the events.

The house of Doña Mercedes Rocha, across the small arroyo that splits the Mexican part of town in two, is well over a hundred years old. The roof over her kitchen/sitting room caved in a decade ago, and her children helped her replace it with practical uninteresting *lámina* (galvanized roofing). The porch is original. In her eighties, she is as gracious as a *viejita* can be. (The rural Mexican *viejita*, widowed and liberated, is possibly the most gracious soul on the planet.) She invited David Burckhalter, a photographer, and me in for coffee, heating the water on the *parilla* behind the house. She didn't remember Gentry, but she knew Juan Argüelles. "Ay, those days were so much better than the times we are living in now! Then everyone had a *milpa* for corn and beans and another field for squash and watermelon, plus a cash crop of *ajonjolí* (sesame seed). Now, nothing. Nothing."

She's right, of course, for the track of the pickup has obliterated what Gentry referred to as "the footprint of the brown man." (Gentry, 1942, p. 157) No *caminos* lead from San Bernardo to *milpas*, as his map indicated, for there are no *milpas* now. There are no fields, only a few gardens, most of them haphazard. The only products furnished to San Bernardo from the once-bountiful *monte* are occasional *panela* (farmer's cheese), *leña* (firewood), and *chiltepines* (fiery hot little chiles). Doña Mercedes grew up in Burapaco, up north in Guarijío country. "What a wonderful place it was," she says, but her face falls as she adds that now it has been taken over by *narcotraficantes*. I nodded in understanding.

A few more motor roads have been bulldozed: the northern roadway to Mesa Colorada and the Guarijío, the grinding fatiguing northeast route to Chihuahua, one leg burrowing into the great mountains and the mountain Guarijío settlement of Loreto, the other over a high sierra to the ancient valley village of Chínipas. These are not highways in any modern sense; Loreto lies sixty-five miles and fourteen hours away; Chínipas is forty miles and nine hours. Those who undertake journeys on those motorways will know weariness and hunger. A road to the now senescent mine of San Rafael extends ten slow miles to the southeast. Alamos is but an hour and a half and thirty miles away by a dirt road Gentry would have pronounced agreeable.

Some of the foot *caminos* remain. Corohui is four hours by horse to the east, a steep climb from which mules have been known to fall, Don José warned me. Once while I was hiking to Corohui from the Sierra Saguaribo above, I was passed by an unfriendly fellow on horseback on his way down to San Bernardo in the valley below. We chatted for a bit as he readjusted the insecticide sprayer he was carrying. "Four hours to San Bernardo," he said nervously and hurried on. Some crops require careful attention.

The great trail through the deep Arroyo de Los Mezcales is still passable, a rancher told me. It was the original supply route to Chínipas, Chihuahua, which even today depends on Sonoran roads as its supply routes. Another well-used trail near the mouth of Arroyo Mezcales connects San Bernardo with Chorijoa, a Mayo village eight miles to the north on the Río Mayo. An old man leading a burro with a *carga* of brasil wood (the best for firewood, most say) plodded by me on his way to San Bernardo where he will get a little over three dollars for the load.

Another *camino de pie* passes through the Arroyo Gochico to the east. Isauro Ramos, in his late sixties, still owns the Rancho Gochico, a four-hour ride by horse from San Bernardo. His daughter lives in a nice house in town with a satellite dish, and he visits her often. There is little traffic in the arroyo now, he says. Often he'll see no outsider for many days. There is not much need for the trail, except for cows. There is nothing to bring in. He'd heard Gentry was interested in plants and offered to show me some rare and unusual specimens high up in the *cajón* (box canyon).

To the southeast the trail into the lush terrace of Tepopa, one of Gentry's favorite plant collecting locations, is still well used. Tepopa sits at the base of a huge escarpment, and from there the trail leads into the "pleasant land of the oaks" (Gentry, *Río Mayo Plants*, p. 266) and the pine forested mesas of the Sierra Saguaribo. Travelers on foot, horse, mule, and burro still arrive in San Bernardo on this path from the cool country, eager to learn the latest gossip and attend the *tianguis* (merchant's market) on the square once a week when truckloads of merchandise, spread in the shade of a portal on a corner of the plaza, become San Bernardo's main source of general merchandise.

In Gentry's day a couple of houses in San Bernardo doubled as cafés. Now there are no public eating places. Two saloons compete for the bar trade and two *depósitos* dispense beer by the six-pack or case, one selling Tecate, the other Modelo. The Tecate distributor hangs out in the pool hall across the street, glancing only occasionally in hope of spying customers. He complained that business was terrible. "Nobody has money to buy beer anymore," he lamented.

All the village *caminos* lead eventually to and from the arroyo, called San Bernardo by Gentry, now called the Taymuco. For most of the year it has a respectable flow, but it usually dries up in the searing drought of late spring. It is where the villagers gathered for eons to celebrate San Juan's Day, June 24. Don José's daughter Fermina recalls the jubilation they had, underscoring Gentry's remarks: "We'd celebrate by putting on red bathing suits or red skirts—anything red—and run down to the river and bathe. It was the only time we'd do it, running around and swimming like crazy. Then we'd come home and stuff ourselves with watermelon. They'd be good and ripe then. Oh, what a time we'd have.

"Nobody does it any more," she added, sadly. "In those days every now and then someone would slaughter a pig and have a party; somebody else would bring a few hens, then we'd all turn out, eat, and dance all night. Now nobody has parties. The town is full of strangers. There are robberies, murders. You can't even have a big wedding party here for fear of violence. It's a terrible disgrace! There's a new *barrio* up there." (She pointed to the northeast.) "I don't know anything about the people there."

Gentry mentioned that the sandy arroyo on the southwest side served the mischievous function of letting people bypass the more public roads for whatever reason. Ramón, our Guarijío guide, used it as did some young Indian-looking folks leading pack animals that I passed on the path. It serves the Barrio El Coyotero, a poorer, more Indian part of town. From my *casita* at the southeastern end of the pueblo, from which most of the town slopes down, I watched a steady trickle of folk emerging from the arroyo via a trail so ancient the rock had been worn down a good foot. Men on horses, men leading burros, men carrying bags, women carrying bundles, and children bearing groceries appeared and disappeared into that anonymous track of sand. Good-sized trees and shrubs along the arroyo limit the view of the *camino* ahead to a few meters. It's perhaps the town's best hope for privacy, the closest it can come to anonymity and the human activities that demand privacy.

Cipriano, my Guarijío friend, lives on a tiny *ranchito* far away in a remote mountain village. It was a fifteen-hour walk to San Bernardo, he said. Sometimes when he walks to town, he goes by the main *camino*. Other times, though, he wants to be alone. On those occasions he takes his own, private pathway through the forest and hills, so that he won't have to stop and talk to someone along the way. He uses the arroyo in San Bernardo as well.

The *barrio* called El Frijol in Gentry's day is gone. An old timer verified that it used to be where the *barrio* known simply as San Bernardo is today. Two others now complete the town's social fabric: El Coyotero, at the lowest part of town, and Los Jacales, built on the bluff across the Taymuco to the north, where the inhabitants are all Guarijíos. San Bernardo is still a biracial town.

Gentry's map shows but one building on the present site of Los Jacales. Now it could easily be a separate village, except that there are only tiny, closet-sized shops. For groceries and supplies the inhabitants must descend the steep path from the bluff, cross the Taymuco—impossible or difficult during *las aguas*—(the rainy season)—and ascend the mesa that supports most of the town and its five shops, only one of which carries more than food. The *barrio* is tightly knit, the houses rigidly separated by carefully built fences of ocotillo or vara. About thirty homes (it's often hard to determine what constitutes a discrete home unit, since many huts are connected and may contain more than one family) make up the *barrio*. The city government has constructed a water line leading to a couple of central spigots, which is a vast improvement. It is frequently out of order, however, as it was when I spoke with the inhabitants. When such breakdowns occur, *barrio* residents are forced to descend by *el camino al río* and fill clay *ollas* of about five gallons apiece. These they carry, one on each end of a *polanca* (yoke), staggering up the steep incline to the mesa. In times of drought, when the arroyo is dry, they dig *pocitos* and scoop water into the *ollas* from deep pits.

Los Jacales is united by Guarijío culture and language. Spanish is the second language, although all except small children seem to speak it well. I visited a belt weaver and potter named Chémali, whose yard was protected from unauthorized entry by a maze of vara fencing. Guarijíos still observe their customs, he told me, relaxing in his clean-swept yard in the shade of a spreading guamúchil tree. He told of a young man from the *barrio* who is being trained to dance the *pascola* and of a couple of musicians who accompany him. Their fiestas are in December, not in Holy Week as is the case with Mayos and Yaquis. This may reflect the growing influence of Protestants among them, for the converts frown on Catholic traditions, including Easter pageantry, which smacks, they say, of idolatry. Others say the Protestant converts are ostracized by non-converted Guarijíos.

My skillful and knowledgeable guide in the *monte* (bush), Ramón Hurtado, is a zealous Protestant, a member of the Apostolic Church. Although he still sings Guarijío songs (one fellow declared that Ramón has been known to sing for twenty-four hours without repeating a song), he prefers to speak Spanish and had forgotten Guarijío terminology for plants. He assured me that all around us were signs of the end of the world. He gently denounced the drinking, smoking, and gambling vices of the folk around him and quoted scriptures liberally. "Twelve years ago I began reading the Bible," he said, "and at the same time I gave up my old vices." An indefatigable worker, he carves Guarijío masks, and builds harps, drums, and *angarillas* (clam-shaped baskets made for carrying supplies on burros). He works alone under a small *ramada* in his backyard. He lives at the opposite end of town from the other Guarijío, but is in close contact with them. "I'm not a preacher," he confessed, "but I can still spread the word of God." Ramon's comparative prosperity is the result of his dogged work and thrift. He spends no money on alcohol and cigarettes, and he doesn't gamble. He owns no television and no large portable radio. He owns no motor vehicle and has no aspirations to own one. No roadway reaches within a hundred yards of his house, located on the south side of the dry arroyo, the only dwelling there. Ramón has isolated himself, spiritually and physically, from the rest of San Bernardo. He does not participate in politics or protests. He had no comment to make on the recent Indian uprising in Chiapas.

The *caminos* of San Bernardo are still used more by horses and burros than by trucks, and even more so by foot traffic. People come and go incessantly to the shops on the plaza, even as they did in Gentry's day. Affluent men wear boots; the less affluent wear shoes; the poor wear *guaraches* (handmade sandals of varying styles but always with a sole of tire). The very poor go barefoot. The footpaths are covered with foot-shaped tire tread marks. Most women still wear long skirts or dresses, a sign of the deep conservatism of the community, but others, especially younger women or wives of more affluent men, wear pants and short skirts.

A tall, thin, cowboy-looking fellow wearing *guaraches* stopped to chat with David and me as we sat on a plaza wall next to a store. I told him what we were doing in San Bernardo. He put his shopping bag on the ground, and we talked at length while his two young sons romped around the dusty, desolate plaza. Angel Ramos Maldonado was around forty years of age. There was a hole in his shirt; his brown trousers were mended along the crotch with white thread. His face was tired, his outlook grim. That is what his dossier would say. Angel moved into San Bernardo a decade ago from a *rancho* near Chorijoa, to the north, so that he could be near his children, while they are going to school.

Angel has seven children, all except one in school. I asked him how he makes a living. He lit a cigarette and stared off into the plaza. He told me that he herds cows and breaks saddle-broncos—whatever it takes. "There's not much work here," he said softly and sadly. A rumor was going around that the government would soon create a new *ejido* (communally owned land) to the north. We gazed at the hills to the north at the area supposedly to be purchased. It was covered with heavy tropical deciduous forest. I asked if once it became an *ejido*, it would be *desmontado* (cleared of forest and seeded with alien grass). "Yes," he nodded. "I'm sure it will."

"Doesn't that make the land ugly and hot?" I asked. He shrugged.

"Sure, but at least it will give us work, cutting down all the trees. Hell, we've got to have work. Nobody has any work here. My children will have to leave. My oldest son already has, and the government does nothing. Nothing."

His sentiments were echoed by another former rancher. I saw him sitting on the edge of the old basketball court on the plaza and sat down to chat. He shook my hand vigorously. "Santiago Cázares Miranda at your service," he said, and launched into a description of what San Bernardo was. He had owned a ranch on nearby Arroyo Los Mezcales, a beautiful place with plenty of grass and good water.

"Why did you sell it?" I asked. He thought for a moment.

"The drug trade was making it too difficult to be a rancher there." He didn't elaborate, and I didn't ask. It's a touchy topic. Santiago has a decent pickup truck painted a rich brown he calls *chocolata*, and a nice old house off the plaza. He proudly showed me his ancient home with its posts, *vigas* and *horcones* of ancient hardwoods. He also owns farmland in the Yaqui delta near Ciudad Obregón, which he bought with the proceeds from the sale of his ranch.

"I don't know why I stay here," he mused. "I suppose it's because I know everybody, but now it's not safe. There are killings, robberies, assaults. None of the fields is planted. Why, I used to raise corn, beans, squash, sesame seeds. Now there's nothing. We have to buy everything. There's no work. The graphite mine down on the Mayo employs ten or twelve men at the most. We can't survive on that."

I asked him why he didn't still raise sesame seeds. He responded that the market price had dropped. He couldn't make any money. It wasn't worth the cost of shipping them to the market. He couldn't compete with the big farmers in the valleys. He decided to join them instead.

Santiago knows most of the bootleggers in the region, known locally as *mescaleros*. He produced a bottle of local *mescal* and insisted that David and I take a sip. Not far away three tipsy cowboys were nursing their own *mescal* inside the fenced yard of an apparently abandoned house. Their mule was enjoying the shade of the stepped porch. They called to David and me and begged us to join their revelry, reacting with disappointment when we passed on to find better conversation.

So the picture developed. San Bernardo is dying a painful death. Young men between the ages of eighteen and thirty-five are almost non-existent. They have no hope of employment and have left town. A group of boys in their early teens race through town in new pickups, almost certainly purchased with drug money. They party in the shade of a great *palo chinu* tree near the stream, guzzling Tecate beer with practiced style and ease. Several older folk lament the way the boys throw away their money on beer that costs five dollars a six-pack—nearly a day's wage for most. I asked several times where they got the money for the expensive pickup trucks. There was no reply.

Across from the town's only general store, playground equipment, once state-of-the-art, sits rusting. The merry-go-round has been torn from the ground, and the slide is bent near the bottom, making it a dangerous game for the few children who try to use it. The swings are gone, a rusted chain all that remains.

What dark forces brought on this decline, this wasting disease that could so drive down a village full of life and excitement fifty years ago?

It is easy—too easy—to point to the numerous satellite dishes and television antennas and denounce television for bringing to an end the old practices of conversation, story telling, family conversation, evenings in the streets with neighbors, hours of delicious gossip, and informal psychologizing. No doubt, *la tele* has spread its venom of urban uniformity on San Bernardo, but it alone is not responsible for the town's decline.

The closing of the mine at San Rafael also dealt a powerful blow to the community. The elimination, nearly overnight, of 150 well-paying jobs had a ripple effect. One hundred and fifty families no longer spent money in shops, no longer needed *guaraches*, no longer ate, no longer had school children, no longer rented or built houses. Around a thousand San Bernardans were directly affected by the mine's closing. Within a year or so another thousand were indirectly affected.

Nevertheless, San Bernardo was a strong community before the mine. Mining towns are always subject to boom and bust. After all, most ghost towns were mining towns, dead as soon as the mineral deposits no longer proved worth extracting. San Bernardo had a land-based economy and should have been able to endure the closing of the mine.

Over San Bernardo lies the shadow of the Green Revolution. Ironically, the birthplace of Norman Borlaug's innovations— varieties of grains highly responsive to agricultural inputs such as water, fertilizer, and herbicides—is in Ciudad Obregón, barely sixty air miles away. Borlaug's hybrid wheat, corn, and rice increase yields manyfold, but they require careful nurturing that only those with large acreages can afford. The enormous fields of the Yaqui and Mayo valleys are tended mostly by machines— tractors, combines, reapers, and cotton-pickers—mechanical giants no peasant can dream of affording. The crops need ongoing and massive infusions of fertilizer, regular irrigation, and the assistance of herbicides to control weeds. They are often especially susceptible to insect depredations, thus requiring the application of heavy doses of insecticides, typically by airplane. *Milpas* and the peasants who work them do not fit into the agricultural model of the Green Revolution.

The Green Revolution was successful in vastly increasing production of basic grains. In doing so, it drove down the prices. A hundred San Bernardo farmers (and thousands more like them in Sonora) raised corn, beans, and squash on their *milpas*, consuming a part, and selling or bartering the rest. These small producers, always marginal, were driven out of the market, especially those not in a position to benefit from government credit, government-built dams, government-sponsored irrigation districts, government-sponsored scientific advisors, government-constructed highways, and government-subsidized diesel fuels. It made little sense for anyone in San Bernardo to raise corn for sale when townspeople could purchase corn raised in the valleys for half the price. The same was true of beans and squash and sesame. The Mexican government provided enormous subsidies for *latifundistas* (owners of vast tracts of land) to increase production. Such subsidies were not available to *campesinos* (peasants), who were mostly rural and poor. Subsidies to rich farmers put poor farmers out of business. They could not afford to plant their *milpas.* The new world order hates small farmers.

Thus, the *milpas* of San Bernardo vanished quite simply because they made no economic sense. While rural Sonoran farmers still raise corn on *temporadas* (dryland fields) to feed livestock, even those make sense only in areas where rainfall is reliable (around Yécora in the Sierra Madre, for instance). Rainfall around San Bernardo, while often abundant in summer and winter, fails often enough to make *milpa* farming too risky.

A similar revolution affected cattle raising. In Gentry's day many families kept a milk cow and a calf or two for beef. Beginning in the 1950s, however, the Mexican government undertook a program of "modernization" of the cattle industry, namely, organizing the industry along modern capitalist lines. Each segment of beef production was compartmentalized, from breeding and the raising of calves to the butchering and marketing of beef. To the small ranchers, those who lived in remote areas such as San Bernardo, the market assigned the task of raising calves, easily the most risky portion of the vertically organized industry. Today buyers come to San Bernardo to buy yearling calves. What they will pay is determined by the international market and is generally far less than what they will sell them for at the urban markets. Ranchers living far from San Bernardo, especially those without trucks, must drive the calves to the village. The calves lose weight from thirst and lack of feed along the way. The peasant ranchers must sell at the price the buyers offer, losing the revenue that the lost weight would have brought them. The buyers deliver the calves to a feed lot, usually near Ciudad Obregón or Hermosillo, where they are fed and watered, immediately regaining the weight lost in the journey from the ranch to San Bernardo.

This "rationalizing" of the cattle industry also removed from rural families the staples of milk and cheese, which formerly were an important part of the rural diet. Milk is now fed to calves to increase their weight, rather than consumed by the family. Heavier calves bring in more money. The family must then *buy* what they used to make, the first sign of the end of a subsistence economy. Families are hooked into a cash economy. Whereas in Gentry's time a vigorous system of trade linked town and country, today nearly every item purchased by the people of San Bernardo is produced in the great cities. The complex relations between the village and surrounding farms and ranches have become simplified or nullified; the trade that linked the village and the hinterland has dried up as both have become impoverished.

Finally, in the absence of a strong land-based economy, San Bernardans resorted, in varying degrees, to the only income source they could identify: drug trafficking. It is nearly impossible to determine the percentage of the town's income related to the drug trade, but I suggest that without the movement of drugs and the immense profits involved, the payments for shipment, and the commerce created by the flow of currency, San Bernardo would have collapsed even more quickly than its current schedule of demise. The economy of marijuana and (to a lesser and hard to determine extent) opium poppies rumbles in the background of every local conversation about the economy. New trucks—and there are many—are invariably viewed as a sign of participation in the lucrative trade. Equally hard to determine is the amount paid to local men to assist in planting, growing, harvesting, guarding, and shipping *mota* by burro, horse, truck, or airplane, but it is substantial.

The darker side of the drug traffic is the destruction of the moral and social fabric of the community. One older woman lamented the fact that one of her daughters had become so involved that she and her husband moved to Navojoa (it's a shipping point, she said) where they are highly successful participants in the distribution network. With high money stakes, human passions run even higher. Murders are routine. Competitors weed out their rivals. Suspicions that someone may be a government informant lead to an atmosphere of paranoia. Ramón, our Guarijío guide, expressed great dismay at the death of a young man, a friend of his children, in a drug-related murder only a few days before. "He was just sitting in his house when they came up to the door and shot him!" he exclaimed, outraged. Ramón expressed great fear of being in the *monte*. He accompanied David and me to a nearby canyon to show us medicinal plants. When we returned to the village he was most relieved. "They rob and kill anybody. They'd even rob me, even though I have nothing." Dependence on drug revenues breeds a dependency worse than that induced by any drug. Crops or shipments are frequently disrupted by the Mexican army that regularly patrols the area, especially in the mountains, with varied and often cynical results. On other occasions *judiciales* (state judicial police) appear to be involved in drug busts; sometimes *federales* (federal judicial police) take part. Some locals believe the military and the police appropriate drug shipments for themselves. With each interruption in the flow of *hierba*, as a local woman called marijuana, local incomes are shut off, creating a desperation for money that leads to assaults and robberies.

San Bernardo's demise is the inevitable result of the internationalization of commodities, whether they be grains, beef, minerals, or illicit drugs. Ironically, the agrarian policies in the United States, generally tied to the interest of the immense transnational agribusiness firms, have led to the end of *milpa* farming in San Bernardo. Mexican President Salinas conceded that the North American Free Trade Agreement will hasten the decline of small Mexican farms. At the same time draconinan United States drug policies have elevated marijuana prices, vastly inflating potential profits and corresponding risks. In so doing they have created the drug production culture that has destroyed the fabric of life in hundreds of rural towns in Latin America. San Bernardo has been viciously affected.

Ramón hitched a ride with David and me back to Alamos. He

needed to purchase paint and sandpaper for producing his carved Guarijío *pascola* masks. Packed and ready to leave, David and I waited for him at our *casita* which offered us a splendid view of the *camino* below. People came and went on the foot *camino* from the arroyo, their movements languid, unhurried. When Ramón appeared, we watched him walk the final hundred meters, hurrying along, toting his humble travel bag. He had worked until the last minute, he said apologetically, trying to finish a harp for a customer. Now he was anxious to get to Alamos and take the return bus home to San Bernardo to resume his work.

Gentry remarked of the differences between Indian and Mexican in San Bernardo that "not until the last pure Indians of Mexico have gone will the differential undercurrent cease to flow and make a ripple here and there." Fifty years later the Indian *caminos* are still distinct; the other, more modern roads are ambiguous and shifting.

We stopped briefly a few kilometers south of town. The scar of a newly bladed road to the north appeared as a diagonal line on a hillside. Gentry never saw that mark, but he would have understood it as part of "an ever-present, yet labyrinthine and ambiguous source book." The *caminos* of San Bernardo have become a living portrait of savage forces that rip apart the vanishing old. At the point of starvation or a gun in the face, the imperative new beckons.

CHAPTER 6

Navojoa: The Market Town

For Alamos, San Bernardo, and Teachive, Navojoa is the urban center. It is the main city of bustling farming region at the head of the vast and fabulously fertile delta of the Río Mayo whose seemingly unending farmlands, reeking of pesticides, were made lush by the construction of Lake Mocúzari on the Mayo, twenty miles upstream. The Mayo, only half as large as the Río Yaqui to the north and west, drains an area only one-third that of the Yaqui. Its length is proportionally small, and its flows are more subject to fluctuation.

Navojoa was a sleepy Mayo town until the 1880s, when the railroad made shipping easy and awoke enterprising individuals to the possibilities of milking the rich soils along the Río Mayo, the southern part of Mexico's Mesopotamia (the Yaqui is the northern) for export-oriented agriculture. The families who first irrigated large acreages were powerful groups originating in Alamos. Uprooting and chasing away the native Mayos was no problem. Ironically, as the big families turned their attentions to farming in the lower Río Mayo, they began to forget Alamos, which underwent a financial decline that has continued until today.

I first knew Navojoa as a flourishing small city of 30,000 inhabitants back in 1961. I met Carlos, an old Mayo, in a *barrio* that he had converted to Protestantism. He spoke some English and knew the Mayo Valley well. He told me about Mayo customs, but railed at the idolatry of their ceremonies. He lambasted liquor, dancing, and women cutting their hair. He and his congregation were building a tiny church. Catholics were sabotaging it, he complained. He pleaded for help from me.

"David, the United States is Protestant. The Catholics won't let us worship. Can't you help?" I shied away from involvement, knowing Mexico was sensitive about foreigners' religions. The constitution forbids missionary work, prohibits clerics from wearing habits in public, and says churches can't own land or operate schools. With that sort of touchiness I wanted nothing to do with anything that smacked of religion. Finally a policeman came and assured Carlos he would be protected. Oddly enough, the vandalism ceased.

Mexico is still overwhelmingly Catholic. While evangelical Protestant sects are growing, Protestants are still associated with the United States, so much so that some Sonorans refer to North Americans as *aleluyas* (hallelujahs). A Sonoran friend related a conversation with a Mexican customs agent while he was trying to clear a group of old folks through customs in advance. "How many *aleluyas* are you bringing?" he asked. "Fifty? No problem."

It was hot in late April when I met Carlos. I asked how hot it got in the real summer. "David, it's so hot you want to die," was his reply. I stopped by once in August. He was right. I sat through an interminable evening church service. The temperature inside the concrete-and-brick building must have been over a hundred degrees. I can't recall what I needed to find out from Carlos that would have led me to sit through that bit of hell.

Thirty years later Navojoa is a small metropolis of 175,000 inhabitants and growing. Buildings are going up fast, subdivisions are invading fields greened by the best in modern fertilizers, and new trucks are zipping up and down the highways, many of them loaded with produce, grain, or agricultural supplies. A huge department store has just been built. A red-light district looking like a movie set has been built east of the city. Navojoa was a Mayo town many years ago, but the Mayos found most of their lands taken by non-Indians. Progress has left them behind. They now constitute only a tiny percentage of the population. Affluent residents speak of Mayos affectionately as quaint decorations from an irrelevant past.

I asked a clothing merchant about life in Navojoa. "It's dusty. I have to keep all my merchandise covered with plastic, or it gets filthy. Then I have to watch the customers' children. Middle-class Mexicans never discipline their children. They tear things off the racks, try things on, and throw them on the floor. It's not that way with people from the mountains. They're polite. Their kids are well-behaved." She knows everyone, it seems. She calls at passers-by and waves at autos. She describes a small town grown out of its clothes.

She calls me *Davicito,* as she introduces me to the other shop-keepers. She phones when she and her husband visit Tucson. She sells only clothing imported from the United States. "Here they think Mexican clothing is *corriente* (junky)."

"It's crazy," her husband told me. We go to the United States to buy clothing imported from Taiwan, Singapore, and the Filipinos. It doesn't matter. As long as the label is in English and it's imported from the United States, the people here will buy it."

The long main street of Navojoa is packed with fruit stands, restaurants, saloons, video movie rental stores, boutiques, and parts stores. The central market is much cleaner, quieter, and far less interesting than it was thirty years ago. No longer is it a repository of the fascinating handcrafted items I used to find when I wandered among the numerous kiosks and booths. I once bought a pair of *guaraches.* They were the universal footwear of men and boys of the working class—comfortable and cool—that wore like iron. Now they're seldom seen. A professional from Hermosillo told me, "Sonorans view *guaraches* and *teguas* as a mark of poverty and won't wear them."

Other market booths would specialize in locally manufactured belts, hats, and tiny stoves made from flattened beer cans (they ceased to make those when the steel beer can went the way of glass milk bottle). There were hand-woven shopping bags, hand-made knives and machetes, stools, and tables made from tough branches of the *guásima* and *chopo* (*Mimosa palmeri*) trees with a top of tightly stretched still hairy cowhide. There were heavy and colorful Mayo blankets and even fine *serapes* from Saltillo, plus a myriad of other indigenous products. The stools are still there, covered with cured cowhide, but the other things are mostly gone, replaced by plastic items or assembly-line manufactures of dubious interest and questionable life span. It's as hard to find items of regional or local manufacture in Navojoa or in any Sonoran city as it is to find them in any United States shopping mall. To find the native crafts, hand-carved wooden trays and spoons, chairs and tables, one must visit tiny villages where isolated individuals still ply their trades.

Twenty-five years ago a friend and I limped into Navojoa in his Jeep, which had broken down a hundred miles away in the foothills of the Sierra Madre. He showed me a place where for a peso (eight cents) a glass we bought all the beer we'd ever wanted from a congenial bartender who asked about work in the United

States. That place is now closed. Beer is available exclusively in bottles manufactured in the best modern way. It is now a dollar a glass and has the uniform taste of United States beer.

Navojoa is infected with the same transforming curse that has stolen the souls of Phoenix, Los Angeles, and most other cities. None of its residents seems to recognize the developing blight, except for the rural folk who descend on the city in desperation. "I'll probably have to move to Navojoa or Ciudad Obregón," a cowboy told me stoically. His future in the cities is as dim as the future of the cities themselves.

PART TWO

Cows and Cowtowns

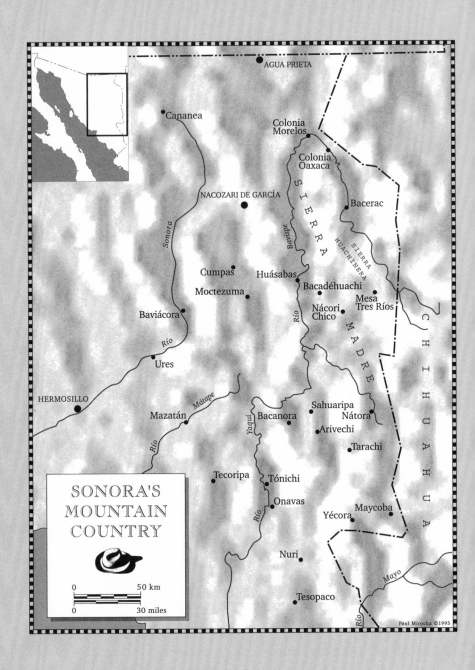

AGUA PRIETA

Cananea

Colonia
Morelos

Colonia
Oaxaca

NACOZARI DE GARCÍA

Bacerac

Sonora

Bavispe

S I E R R A

H U A C H I N E R A

SIERRA
HUACHINERA

Cumpas

Huásabas

Moctezuma

Bacadéhuachi

Mesa
Tres Ríos

Baviácora

Río

Nácori
Chico

M
A
D
R
E

Ures

Río

C
H
I
H
U
A
H
U
A

HERMOSILLO

Mátape

Mazatán

Yaquí

Bacanora

Sahuaripa

Nátora

Arivechi

Río

Tarachi

Tecoripa

Tónichi

Onavas

Maycoba

Río

Yécora

SONORA'S
MOUNTAIN
COUNTRY

Nuri

0   50 km

0   30 miles

Tesopaco

Mayo

Río

Paul Mirocha ©1995

CHAPTER 7

Bacadéhuachi

In 1980 a Tucson friend who knew I was enamored of Sonora
suggested I visit some of his relatives in Bacadéhuachi. I was still
a county supervisor with many duties to perform as a public servant, but the pain of a divorce made the wilds of eastern Sonora
more attractive than ever. I took a week off and headed south of
Douglas, Arizona. My friend's teenage son joined me in my
Volkswagen bus which had grown accustomed, through years of
life in the Chiricahua Mountains, to tough unmaintained dirt
roads. From Agua Prieta we drove south through oak-studded
grasslands, past the new copper smelter at Nacozari, down a verdant valley to Moctezuma. Then we headed eastward up a steep
mountain range, descended into Huásabas in the Bavispe Valley,
forded the great river (it was the dry season and the ferry wasn't
needed), and began the arduous drive to Bacadéhuachi.

I could have chosen a more easterly route. I could have taken a
pounding dirt road to the Bavispe River and the old Mormon
settlement at Colonia Morelos, then gone east around the great
bend in the river, past the rugged and deep Púlpito Canyon that
drains the pine-covered southern Sierra San Luis, and past the
nearly hidden fertile fields of Colonia Oaxaca. Then I would
have headed southward up the Bavispe Valley, between the high
ranges of the Sierra El Tigre on the west and the Sierra
Huachinera on the east. However, that scenic route would have
involved crossing the deep river twice. The last time I crossed,
the four-wheel-drive vehicle I was riding in was nearly washed
away by the powerful current at each crossing, so even though
the roadway traverses some of the fairest oak and juniper mesas
and mountains in all of Sonora, I took the easier route, which
isn't easy at all.

Bacadéhuachi is nestled in a soft valley that narrows quickly
into a gorge descending southward into the Bavispe. Father Juan
Nentvig, a Jesuit curate who was stationed in quiet Huásabas in

the mid-eighteenth century, described the last few miles of the trek to Bacadéhuachi:

> Once at Huásabas it is necessary to remain a few days to rest, recuperate, and brace ourselves for the eight-league trek to Bacadéhuachi during which a fellow missionary feels obliged to commend himself to Saint Ignatius while climbing and descending such mountain passes replete with declivities and precipices the likes of which he had never encountered in one stretch, not even in the Tarahumara.
>
> [Nentvig, p. 87]

Bacadéhuachi has been remote for centuries. Getting there from the west still requires an ascent of the impossibly steep *Cruz del Diablo* (Devil's Cross), an almost sheer cliff bisected by a narrow, deep crack of a canyon that gives the appearance of a cross. The escarpment, the same described by Fr. Nentvig, kept the pueblo effectively isolated from major traffic for centuries, until an improved but rough road was blasted through in 1947. It was paved for about ten miles east of Huásabas in the early 1980s, and work had begun on the next section when the construction abruptly and inexplicably ceased just where *El Pirinola* (The Top)—named because of its uncanny symmetry that resembles a spinning top—comes into view. I asked a Bacadéhuachi rancher, a man of power and influence, when it would be finished. He shrugged and changed the subject. I've since learned that Mexico's ruling political party provides and withholds roads as political favors and punishments. Somebody up there in Bacadéhuachi must have sinned.

Bacadéhuachi was an Opata Indian town when first visited by Jesuits in the early seventeenth century. The church they began (with Opata labor) at Bacadéhuachi and completed in 1659 glows like a swan in the sunlight. The earthquake of 1887 toppled one of the bell towers, and it was not replaced for fifty years, but the church is mostly unchanged. Its serene presence defines the personality of the town, a luminescent bulwark in a compact neat village.

I remember that first visit clearly, walking disconsolately into the plaza in the fading daylight, still stunned and weakened by my inability to maintain the most important relationship in my life. The church stood shining and silent in the east. At sundown I sat on a bench in the small plaza. My skeptical will was irresistibly pulled towards the altar by the slight concavity of the gentle facade. I realized that the church's architects must have had that subtle optical phenomenon in mind as a tool for gathering the faithful and faithless into the fold. I could hear a quiet conversation taking place on the steps of the church from a block away. The mayor walked by and interrupted my spiritual reverie. We talked for a while. He made it clear that this was the finest church in Sonora. Nothing in the big cities could compare. He was right.

I tiptoed inside. No priest was about (he came only a few times a month), but several devout residents were praying in the sanctuary, their humble clothing and fidgeting bodies contrasting sharply with the timeless dignity of the images and the stunningly beautiful altar of gold and black. I was torn between being captivated by the altar, which I wanted to see more closely, and my fear of being disrespectful to the worshippers, so I went half-way and stopped. I couldn't kneel, genuflect, or say a rosary, even though I had once memorized the ritual. I wasn't a Catholic, and my soul was too secularized, but I heartily sympathized with those who did. For reasons I can't explain, that church remains my favorite in Sonora, and Bacadéhuachi remains my favorite small town.

A great tragedy struck the community in September of 1990. A local priest, a native of Bacadéhuachi, with whom I'd played a pick-up game of basketball on another visit, had come home to the village along with two colleagues in preparation for a national holiday festival. Before the fiesta, the three clerics ventured into the mountains to the east to spend an evening camping and meditating in the pines. A storm came up, and they took refuge in a cabin, lit a gas lantern for light and warmth, and fell asleep. They never awakened. Two days later their bodies were discovered by a young man from Bacadéhuachi who had gone to look for them, worried when they did not return on time. Apparently they had succumbed to carbon monoxide asphyxiation. It was a staggering blow to the village and to the church. Priests are scarce; priests from the hometown, are almost unknown.

The church today is maintained in excellent condition by the local inhabitants under the generous leadership of Doña Rita Terán de Valencia. Mrs. Terán, a gracious and devout Catholic, is a fourth-generation Bacadéhuachian who works tirelessly for civic betterment and, above all, to see to it that the church's beauty remains pristine and its itinerant priest adequately fed and clothed. She is married to José "Cheché" Valencia, a prominent rancher, also born in the village. They live in a gracious but modest colonial home on a narrow cobbled street only a block away from the plaza. Most of their children have moved away.

Chess, my mongrel terrier, and I visited them a couple of times when he was growing old. He grew accustomed to lying in their doorway, content to view the constant parade of people, vehicles, cows, horses, and burros that paraded by. Doña Rita fussed over him and brought him bones, much to his delight. When she'd come around, he'd wag his tail so furiously his body would double back and forth like a hinge.

Around their dining room table, after a *serrano* breakfast of eggs, refried beans, tortillas, and coffee, the two of them would relate stories about their youth. Bacadéhuachi had no road until 1947, no electricity until 1974, and still has no phone service, although the town does have a parabolic antenna that brings televised soap operas into the homes.

Cheché's eyes filled with nostalgia as he recalled a cattle drive when he was a young man. He leaned on the table sipping a cup of coffee, his face tanned brown, his forehead a lighter color. "Ay, David, you would have loved our cattle drives." He and a brother rode to Tarachi, deep in the mountains southeast of Sahuaripa, to buy cattle for their annual drive. It was a ride of four days, he said, and having seen the terrain, I was amazed he could make it in that time. They began buying cows and amassed a herd, driving the bunch north over rugged mountains from Sahuaripa to Bacadéhuachi. From there thirty cowboys pushed a herd of between five hundred and a thousand cows over the crags and high ridges of the Sierra Madre to the railroad in Chihuahua, a twenty-day trip. Three cooks rode ahead and set up camp. They had food and camping places ready by the time the herd arrived. Once the cows were sold and shipped, the cowboys returned to Bacadéhuachi in only five days.

Even today Don Cheché owns a ranch—La Ventana (The Window), accessible only on horseback. It takes an hour and a half by truck to get from Bacadéhuachi to Granados, a large town near Huásabas. Don Cheché says with a look of amusement that they used to make it on horseback via the ranch in three hours. Doña Rita, her warm eyes laughing, would also relate tales of horseback traveling. She, as many other Sierra women, had to be an expert rider as well, able to ride side-saddle for the several hours it would take to reach a road or highway, capable of handling a pack mule or burro to bring supplies from the distant market to their home. Her eyes would glisten with pleasure and her serene, ageless face would radiate love as she related the fun she had as a young woman in the isolated but renowned village.

The clop-clop-clop of horseshoes on cobbles is more common than the rumble of motors in Bacadéhuachi. The village's plaza is fenced with white-painted wrought iron, and the gates are closed to protect the flowers and grass from wandering burros, horses and cows. One morning a decade ago, as I sat reading on a plaza bench, a burro wandered over to the fence, casually craned his long neck over, and scarfed some flowers. I noticed more recently that no flowers are planted anywhere near the fence. Some towns have installed turnstiles at the corners of the plaza to allow people in and keep livestock out.

Horses in the street are no more noticed than people. I was visiting some years ago with Don Cheché and Doña Rita when his younger brother Pancho stopped by. "David," he said with a swashbuckling voice, "I've got to round up some cows down the arroyo. Would you like to go?" Although I knew my legs would hurt the next day, I said I would love to go. He was back shortly. He tethered the horses at the front door.

We spent the day herding cattle in the canyon bottom. It was there I came to appreciate the virtues of *chaparreras* as leg protectors. Cows don't mind crashing through the thorniest of brush to avoid being driven to where they don't want to go. Horses are trained to follow right along through the brush. Without the heavy leather protecting my legs, my Levi's would have been tattered, to say nothing of the skin on my legs. Pancho punched those miserable "beeves" through the brambles while sucking on a can of Budweiser. I struggled to hang on.

That night Doña Rita insisted I eat more food. "We've got to fatten you up a little, David," she said. "You're feeling better, aren't you," she added after dinner. "I can see it in your face." Who wouldn't be better in Bacadéhuachi?

For a cowboy, his hat, boots, or *teguas*, and belt are terribly important, but they are insignificant compared with his horse.

Anyone can wear cowboy clothes, but only a real cowboy has a horse. Less affluent individuals and young men and boys often can only afford a burro.

I swapped stories with a couple of fellows who trotted by on burroback as I sat reading in the shade of a mesquite tree near the village. Burros were good mounts, they agreed, informing me that they are more intelligent and durable than horses, stronger and much less expensive to buy and keep. A good burro could be had for thirty dollars or so, while a horse was seldom available for less than ten times that amount. They conceded that burros are a stubborn lot, but argued that they can easily be trained, can live on a godawful variety of plants most of which a horse would sneer at, and don't need as much water. I hopped on one of them gingerly and took a stroll. The burro complied with only minimal encouragement from me, although I detected a look of extreme skepticism behind his sleepy-looking eyes. The ride was surprisingly comfortable.

Thus, there's a lot to be said for burros, but they can't rival horses for speed and grace, and most cowboys would no more be caught riding a burro than ordering quiche in a saloon or wearing an earring. Somehow the image of a gallant cowboy rescuing a town from robbers, waving goodbye, and jumping on his burro to ride off into the sunset doesn't mesh with the lofty traditions of the Old West. Sonorans reveal their lack of high respect for burros by referring to groups of them as *licenciados* (graduates) or *diputados* (legislators). A horse, on the other hand, is a worthy status symbol.

In earlier times, Don Cheché says, especially before the road was built, the people of Bacadéhuachi provided most of their own needs. They raised beans, potatoes, corn, wheat, and vegetables for their own use. Everybody had chickens, and a few people had dairy cattle and made their own cheese. However, the development of subsidized modern irrigated agriculture on the coast west of Hermosillo eliminated the market for homegrown products. Now folks buy much of what they eat, and their fields are used almost exclusively for raising alfalfa and feed for the calves they sell. The last time I visited Bacadéhuachi I saw teenage girls carrying cartons of milk from a grocery store and, perish the thought, packaged tortillas.

Still, most families grind their own corn for meal. Doña Rita

makes tasty hand-shaped *tortillas de maís* every day, and other
women pat out paper-thin *tortillas de harina*. *Machaca* (sautéed jerky
with spices) is the meat mainstay, but the most interesting food
of all is strictly native. A cowboy showed me some prime habitat
for *chiltepines* (*Capsicum baccatum*), red round chile peppers the size
of a pea with a powerful flavor and a fiery hot disposition. They
grow all along the arroyo near town. I picked a pint of them and
took them home.

Most tables in the town offer a salsa made from these prized
chiles, although it must be eaten with utmost caution and in
homeopathic doses to avoid setting the mouth on fire. People
come to Bacadéhuachi from all over to gather the tiny flaming
red fruits from plants that flourish in the river canyons. In the
Sierra Madre, a cowboy breakfast consists of *machaca* (when beef
is available), *blanquillos* (eggs), *frijolitos* (mashed and fried pinto
beans), tortillas, and coffee, with a little homemade cheese on
the side and *salsa de chiltepín* to add flavor. Doña Rita always keeps
a jar on the table. There's no other flavor like it in this world.

Bacadéhuachi is growing, a school teacher told me. The *ayun-
tamiento* (municipal government) has bladed off an area on a mesa
above the town for new home sites. Even so, the population of
the entire *municipio* (county) is under 1,500. Ironically, eligible
young men are scarce in the village. To the dismay of the town's
young unmarried women, young men of marriageable age have
left for the big city or for the United States, a few to complete
high school (Bacadéhuachi like many smaller towns has schools
only through grade nine, roughly equivalent to a sophomore year
in high school), the others to look for work. A young woman
told me that in her family are five grown sons and three grown
daughters. Four of the sons live and work in California, while
the daughters remain in Bacadéhuachi. Ranching provides many
jobs but cannot absorb the numbers of young men being produced by large Mexican families. If a father divides a ranch
among several sons, the acreage will be too small to support any
of them.

Ranching is far more expensive than it was a generation ago.
Everywhere I go in the Sierra I see huge, costly cattle trucks, necessary because fences and higher costs have put an end to cattle
drives. Modern ranching includes breeds less hardy than the old
criollo cattle. They are more susceptible to diseases, so the rancher

must be a veterinarian, watch the herd closely, and buy expensive medicines. Furthermore, ranchers universally believe the climate has dried out, so fewer cattle can chew away a living in the pastures. A custom has evolved that one son works the ranch, while the others look for work elsewhere.

The girls are stuck in the village, far outnumbering the boys. It's socially quite acceptable in the United States for single women from rural areas to move to the city, but not in Mexico where a young woman on her own is considered a slut. An even graver problem exists for an unfortunate young widow in Bacadéhuachi. I talked with her in some friends' living room (they diplomatically left us alone). Her husband had died of cancer two years earlier, leaving her a childless widow in her early thirties. She was still *de luto* (in mourning) decked out in an amorphous black dress. I toyed with asking her but dared not how long she would continue to announce to the world that her husband was dead. She loved Bacadéhuachi dearly and intended to live out her life there. Her chances of finding a husband are discouragingly slim in a culture that cherishes virginity in brides and in a town where the young men are gone. Her face showed resignation that she was destined to live single for the rest of her life.

On one of my earlier return trips to Tucson I gave a ride to a cowboy who still lived in the village. He talked for hours about his family's life and about work as a cowboy. Suddenly, out of the blue, he said, "David, I've got this problem. I wonder if you could help me."

"I can try," I answered, baffled.

"Well, you see, it's that, well, I don't seem to be able to satisfy my wife. I'm terribly ashamed." This was delicate ground. One false move and he might be forever offended. I told him I understood, and that many men felt that way sometimes.

"No, David, it's all the time. I'm afraid she'll stop loving me because I'm no good." Why me, I thought, but upon reconsideration, I recognized that his asking me was an expression of trust. I wondered if his problem was premature ejaculation.

"Yes. That's it. It makes me feel terrible."

I smiled at him. "Well, I can assure you that it's not a serious problem." That was easy for me to say. My mind raced for what to tell him, especially since my fluency in Spanish did not extend to clinical descriptions of sexual activity. Finally the answer came.

"Manuel, do you have someone you can level with, someone who knows English?"

He nodded, "my brother." Like so many other Mexicans, his brother had worked for several years in the United States as an undocumented alien in the United States and had learned passable English.

"Good." I said. "I have a book for you. I'll mark the place. You have him read it to you and translate it. I can almost guarantee results."

He was at once greatly relieved. When we reached Tucson, we drove by my house before I dropped him at his relatives' home. I rummaged through my bookcase and found my copy of *The Joy of Sex*. I scanned the index. There it was: the section on "Hair Trigger." I marked it, wrapped the book in a plain paper bag, and gave it to him. "Here," I said, in my most professional, counselling voice, "this section should help."

I never got to find out, but I saw him a few years later and he gave me a shy confident smile. His wife served us breakfast and kissed him on the neck as she passed.

CHAPTER 8

Nácori Hats

The mountainous dirt road winds across another mountain range and through a four-thousand-foot pass to the east of Bacadéhuachi—about an hour's drive—to Nácori Chico, a cow town if there ever was one. In spite of its isolation, Nácori is a bustling place of about two thousand souls. Its streets are dusty from cattle trucks, and the picturesque valley is checkered with irrigated fields of alfalfa and cattle grain.

At the entrance to the town a uniformed soldier stood in the road. He couldn't have been more than seventeen and handled his automatic rifle uncertainly, much to my discomfort. He peered cursorily through my belongings, glancing at me hesitatingly every few seconds, and asked me casually if I was carrying any drugs. His interest perked when I said I was heading for the mountains to the east. We both knew it was drug country. Immediately my passage was blocked by several more soldiers from their camp adjacent to the road. No vehicle could pass without their assent.

Presently they were joined by their commander, who sauntered down the from the camp above the road and eyed me suspiciously through sunglasses. He leafed through my papers, tapped with his hand on my pickup, and in tortured English demanded to know where I was going. I told him, in Spanish. He walked twice around the truck, banged on it with his palm, then motioned me on.

A fellow in town told me the *soldados* had been there for several months and were prepared to stay several more. "Lots of drugs up in the mountains," he said solemnly. From what others told me, everyone in the town (including the soldiers) benefits economically from the drug trade.

Nácori Chico is nationally famous for its sombreros, which are actually made in Buena Vista, four miles of verdant alfalfa fields to the south. Irrigation of the fields is guaranteed by a dam built during the administration of Governor Samuel Ocaña. Buena Vista is hardly an affluent town, a rude gathering of fifteen or so houses on a bluff above the arroyo. I drove into what appeared to be the closest thing to the village square and parked. Faces peered out at me from doorways. They were not friendly and not unfriendly, curious, perhaps, or maybe there was a hint of Sonoran suspicion.

A man was carefully siphoning gas from a small barrel into his late model pickup, trying to avoid splashing gasoline on his polyester trousers. His affluence suggested either a big ranch or drug profits. He looked at me quizzically. "Where can I find a hat for sale?" I asked him.

He pointed at a house fifty yards away. "María Gorrobo García makes good ones," he said with an air of expertise. I thanked him, noted that his hat was probably of North American origin, and drove over to the house he pointed out. Three middle-aged women in simple cotton dresses, one wearing a shawl, were standing inside, peering out at me. No men were in sight. "Good morning," I said. "*Busco un sombrero de palma. ¿Aquí hay?*" (I'm looking for palm hats. Do you have any?) They returned my smile.

The door opened. "*Pase, pase,*" they all said, simultaneously ushering me inside. I ducked under an impossibly low door jamb and squeezed through a tiny but tidy kitchen into an inner room. The women pointed to a fourth. "That is María," they said and sat down on a twin bed that nearly filled the room, their hands in their laps. María said not a word, but with a shy, faint smile produced from a bag three hats, perfectly woven, soft-textured, high-peaked. I tried one on and told her I'd buy all of them if she'd tell me a little bit about herself and show me her *huuqui* (weaving cave). (I've come to the policy of never haggling about prices when dealing with native artisans.) Her smile broadened. The other women nodded with enthusiasm. One of them asked me where I was from. Hearing Arizona mentioned, she smiled broadly and asked me if I knew her son, Juan, who works in Phoenix. She was disappointed when I couldn't place him.

The hats and the baskets the women produce are woven of palm gathered from nearby canyons. Some of the women gather it themselves. María does. It's hard work. She has to find someone to take her to the foothills to find good trees. Then she has to find branches low enough that she can harvest them, hack them off, cut away the part she can't use, and pack the material to her home. That's why some women purchase the palm from men who collect it. María cuts the fronds into tiny strips no more than an eighth of an inch wide, then soaks them before tearing them into the even finer strips used to weave.

Only when all this work is done does the unique weaving begin. Palm fibers tend to dry out and crack in the desert climate. They must be kept moist at all times while being woven. Each woman constructs a *huuqui* (a subterranean hut dug four feet or so into the earth and lined with stone, with a roof of thatch built over). The moisture from the earth keeps the palm strips pliable and soft. In prolonged dry spells, the woman splashes the floor of the cave with water to maintain high humidity. María has to squeeze into her *huuqui* and sits cross-legged on a mat on the dirt floor. She sits and weaves for hours, her fingers flying nimbly along the unfinished edge of the hat.

María is a large, slightly heavy woman of *mestizo* appearance. She was taught to weave by her mother when she was eleven years old, she said, weaving rapidly all the while. Weaving was taught to daughters by their mothers as far back as anybody can remember. Most of the women of Buena Vista weave. She doesn't know where her ancestors learned weaving and isn't sure if any of them was Indian. Some probably were.

In other parts of Sonora, Lower Pima Indians fashion baskets called *guaris* from palm fibers. In the tiny Jova village of Pónida, in the municipio of Arivechi, residents still weave palm into baskets, mats, and hats. They too construct special huts they call *huuquis*, similar to the caves in Buena Vista. Small villages on the Río Moctezuma, now flooded out of existence by Lake Novillo, were also known for palm weaving. It's just possible this marvelous craft has its origins in a pre-Columbian group who transmitted their knowledge to a purely Mexican village. María says her great-grandmother came from somewhere down near Sahuaripa. My guess is she came from Pónida.

Whatever their origin, demand for the hats of Buena Vista (or Nácori, as they are invariably labeled) always exceeds supply, so I felt fortunate to have found three. Eleven years earlier I found only one hat in the whole village. Everywhere I go in Sonora, people comment on my hat. One older fellow from Moctezuma was especially enthusiastic. "It's the best hat you can buy, David. It's double, so it keeps your head cool in hot weather and warm in the cold." A retired lumberer from Mesa Tres Ríos told me the same, as did a housewife from Huásabas.

"You must like Sonora," she commented to me as I sat on the curb in front of her colonial-style house watching Virgil Hancock photograph an ornate, crumbling adobe across the street. "You have a hat from Nácori. They make the best hats in Mexico there." A Mayo Indian from Yocogigua recognized it as well, as did a cowboy from Sahuaribo, high in the Sierra Madre.

María's hats are two layers thick, marvelously pliable and strong. The women of Buena Vista weave two different types of hat: the regular—a work of art in its own right—and the exquisite showpiece—which is woven from *palma pelada,* (peeled palm). To weave the latter the women use a fingernail to split the palm strips in half, then use the point of a needle to split the soft interior fibers into strips hardly wider than thread. A hat woven from this fiber is a wonder to behold, as soft as any Panama hat and of double thickness. Not many *sombreros de palma pelada* are made. It takes about six weeks to make one, and the price (upwards of fifty dollars) is more than most people want to pay for a hat. They're worth the investment. They breathe enough to keep the head cool and are flexible enough to be soft and marvelously comfortable. They are also strong enough to withstand wind and rain. María confided in me, however, that the regular type, which I bought, will wear longer. "The *palma pelada* type," she assured me in a low voice, out of earshot of the other women, "is just for people who want a little luxury. Wealthy people like to wear them."

What of the future? María doesn't say. The work of gathering palm fronds is difficult and time-consuming. The twelve dollars or so a woman gets for a regular palm hat leaves her with precious little money for her efforts. A machine-produced hat sells for about the same and most (but not all) cowboys prefer the Texas-style hat. I don't. I bought a palm hat in Buena Vista in 1980 and wore it regularly for ten years.

If the women of Buena Vista find the work is too long and hard for the money they make, their families will be forced to move to the big city in search of work. Another native craft will be lost to the incessant march of machines, another culture killed by a thousand tiny surgical cuts into the fabric of indigenous life.

CHAPTER 9

The Halls of Moctezuma

Bacadéhuachi's supply center is Moctezuma, located on a tributary of the Río Yaqui. The 350-year-old town is sedate, proud, elitist, and fading. Some of Sonora's wealthiest families are from here. It remains conservative and strongly Catholic and competes with poorer Cumpas, a few leagues to the north, which is liberal and anticlerical. Moctezuma's massive and magnificent church with a unique wooden dome in a side chapel dates from the early seventeenth century when the town was still called Oposura. At the time of their expulsion from the New World in 1767, the Jesuit blackrobes planned to establish a *collegium* (a college for prospective priests).

On one of my first visits the plaza was deathly quiet in the early spring mid-afternoon, especially for a town of nearly three thousand inhabitants. I sat alone on a bench. No young men hung around; there were no groups of chattering young women walking back and forth—only one despondent vendor and one man on a horse. Muffled music trickled fitfully from a saloon: No one went in or came out. The great church gleamed tranquilly. It was spooky. This was hardly a bustling commercial center.

Moctezuma flourished during the *porfiriato*. When mining was at its highest point, toward the end of the nineteenth century, a small group of Mexicans prospered, collaborating with the Yanquis, acting as their local lieutenants, working closely with United States interests to exploit the mines and keep profits high. These folk were instrumental in suppressing strikes and arranging with government officials to keep taxes on mining operations to a minimum. During those years of their prosperity, they retained architects, masons, and carpenters to build mansions of unmatched splendor, living in opulence like the great Spanish families of old. Today the house of Don Pepe Terán, a well-known official of that day, is a magnificent ruin, a crumbling masterpiece of portals, arches, and barrel vaults, with deep basements and ornate designs of carved stone and terra cotta.

An older Moctezuman showed me the ruined house, along with others, on a walking tour of the pueblo. "*Arnoldo Santa Cruz, para servirle,*" he said, introducing himself (Arnold, at your service). A large man, sporting bushy brown hair, dressed a little on the seedy side but speaking impeccable Spanish, he was born and raised in this old town. I was seated on a bench inside the *talabartería* (leather shop), while the owner made me a belt. Arnold shuffled into the shop, his large frame a dominant force, and asked the cobbler how things were going, how much work there was. When he spied me, he inquired who I was, not in an unfriendly manner but as though the shop had just gotten a new rug or sewing machine. When he found I was a Spanish-speaking gringo he began to wax eloquent on the history of Moctezuma. Had I seen the old house with carved monkey faces on the lintels? Well, we had just better trot right over there because I was going to be impressed.

We paused frequently as Arnold greeted people, old and young, on the street, made appointments, asked about the health of relatives, and inquired whether there would be fresh beef in the store today.

"*De aquí viene mucho dinero, David.*" (A lot of money comes from here, David), he informed me solemnly. "Important families. Conservative. Powerful." Seeing the fading mansions and imagining their magnificence during the *porfiriato*, I readily believed him. "I could buy Don Pepe's crumbling palace for a couple of thousand bucks," he said in a low voice, "from some lawyer in Agua Prieta. But to fix it up? Ooooh, a lot—fifteen, twenty million pesos." He wanted to know if I was interested in mines. Most gringos who come to Moctezuma are, he confided. He had figured me for a prospector or mining speculator. He himself had an opal mine in Jalisco but was experiencing difficulty in working it because of drug dealers and other brigands who kept stealing from him. Terrible thing, those *narcotraficantes* were.

He asked me to go and see his house and shuffled by the plaza and up a silent street. His home shared walls with dwellings on either side. The inside was nearly devoid of furniture, dusty, and dark. It had high ceilings and an odor of despondency. There was a faded print of French countryside on the walls, a cracked, ancient photo of a small family, and a rusting, disheveled cot. He lived alone. "This is my house, David. Not pretty, I know, but I've been here all these years. Here, let me show you an opal from my mine in Jalisco."

I didn't stay long. The place was like a tomb. Our voices echoed in the emptiness. Before I left, though, I bought the opal from him and promised to keep in touch. He wanted more than it was worth but quickly accepted half of his first price. "*No quiero chingarte, David. Ese ópalo es una verdadera joya.*" (I don't want to screw you, David. That opal's a real jewel.) He's symbolic of the city, once a center of influence and power, now a somnolent cow town, recalling its days of glory and despairing of its dwindling future. Young people leave, as they leave most Sonoran towns, looking for better work, more excitement, and a more promising future—any future at all.

CHAPTER 10

Of Cowboys and the Cattle Business

I knew I was seeing a clash of eras when I saw a cowboy punching a herd past a newly installed satellite dish. Worldwide communications are coming to Sahuaripa. They tell me that fax machines will soon be available. Still, old eastern Sonora refuses to yield to the new west. Of course, some things have changed, such as the recent dedication of farmland to raising a little or a lot of marijuana as a cash crop. Other modern touches intrude, like the ubiquitous pickup trucks treated to a daily pummeling by the bumpy roads. Unlike Dodge City, electric wiring, TV antennas, and satellite dishes have joined the scenery in most of the towns. These features do alter the old west image, but most of the mystique is intact. Horses still outnumber trucks. It's not unusual to see a horse tethered outside a store, while its owner is inside buying something or visiting inside a house. Cowboys on horses carry plastic bags of groceries in one hand and hold the reins in the other. Hell, I've seen a cowboy on horseback drinking a can of Tecate with a grocery bag clutched under an arm. He'd have a rough time lighting a cigarette, but maybe he'll figure out how to con the horse into holding the groceries. It wouldn't surprise me to see a cowboy talking into a cellular telephone, while he drives a herd down the highway.

Sahuaripa and a hundred towns like it are still part of the old east. Cows roam the streets in every town in eastern Sonora as well, and burros still have the right of way. Fenced yards in these towns serve to keep livestock out, not burglars or prowlers. More prosperous towns have fences protecting the flowers in the plaza. Most of the men wear cowboy boots or *teguas*, and *all* men wear cowboy hats, usually even inside their homes. A man without a hat is like a day without beer.

What are *teguas*? They're a sort of half-boot, with two side flaps of leather that lace together to cover the instep in the front. The slightly pointed toe and the smooth sole let them slide

easily in and out of the stirrup, while the heel (a half-inch of tire) limits the movement in the stirrup and gives support on the ground. They're easy to get on and off, surprisingly comfortable, nice-looking, and inexpensive, and they wear like iron. They're the ideal footwear for the working cowboy who must walk on the ground from time to time as well as ride a horse. Cowboys hate to get off their horses for *anything*, resenting having to get off even to take a leak or open a gate. I once spoke with a mounted cowboy who was waiting for a companion in the shade of a cottonwood along the Río Moctezuma. The friend was late, but this fellow remained in the saddle. After a wait of fifteen or twenty minutes, he climbed down, walked into the bushes to pee, came back, and hopped onto the saddle and waited another fifteen minutes. I swear he almost nodded off to sleep up there.

However, work is work, and cowboys of the Sierra Madre have to do multiple jobs, most of them on the ground. They plow, plant, cultivate, harvest, tie, brand, castrate, build fence, feed, water, doctor, pull calves, chop wood, clear brush, repair buildings, buy groceries, lay adobe, and even, perish the thought, cook. For all these tasks they need a multi-purpose shoe. On the ground *teguas* feel more like moccasins, so when a *vaquero* has also to work in the fields or string a fence, he'll be equally comfortable on foot.

I've never seen *teguas* worn anywhere other than in the Sierra Madre and its foothills. They're made in Moctezuma, Bacadéhuachi, Yécora, Sahuaripa, Tarachi, Valle de Tacupeto, Nácori

Chico, and Baviácora on the Río Sonora and in almost any *ser-rano* (mountain) town. I've been told by numerous sources that in Sahuaripa, Beto Pacheco will measure your feet and in a day or so fit you into some of the most comfortable footwear you'll ever know. Luis Guerrero of Yécora, although he's well advanced in years, can do the same, as can the *talabartería* in Moctezuma. You'll have to tell the cobbler whether you want them *cosidos* (sewn) or *clavados* (nailed). The former wear longer but the latter are cheaper. Even for the best you won't pay more than about twenty-five dollars (United States currency).

I sat for an hour or two in the *talabartería* (leather shop) in Moctezuma waiting for my pair. Customers came and went, some of them more than a little curious about the gringo sitting in the corner. Each person had some information to impart, some to pick up. One rancher from fifty miles away in the Sierra Madre came in to order a new belt and saddle for his son. He talked about rain (ranchers and farmers always talk about the weather), about the road, about the price of beef and everything else, and about acquaintances—men's gossip. When he realized I was a North American, he asked me about the war in the Persian Gulf and asked if I had fought there against Saddam Hussein.

Cowboys wear *teguas* until they separate in front and start yawning, the foot appearing in the gap like a dusty tongue. Some tough old *vaqueros* seldom take their *teguas* off. Just as North American cowboys are rumored to do with their Levis, they wear them till they fall off, then hop to the nearest shop and order new ones.

Teguas aren't in demand the way they used to be. It's odd that more men don't wear them. One rancher told me he doesn't because he has forty acres of field to plow, and the dirt gets between the flaps and works its way into the shoes. That's reasonable, but the real reason is that they're a symbol of the old-fashioned, self-reliant way of life. Boots, snap-on cowboy shirts, and straw hats from Texas are more in keeping with the cowboy image of television and billboards. I don't see boys and young men wearing them, only men in their mid-thirties and up. The younger guys (and better-off older men) wear more fashionable boots made in the factories of Mexico City, or, if they're even more affluent, in the United States: Tony Lamas or Justins. The high heels make a man stick out his butt and his chest, which a cowboy shirt then accentuates—real macho image. Some younger men even sport Reeboks or Nikes. *Teguas* are definitely not high-fashion footwear in spite of their practicality and comfort. They're worn by traditional men who harbor no aspirations to the affluent life or the macho image. *Teguas* anchor a *serrano* to the land, for better or worse.

Teguas are a microcosm of the Sierra Madre. Virtually every town has its *tegua* craftsman, much as every northern European town before the Industrial Revolution had its cobbler. *Teguas* are designed for the cowboy and made of pure leather, except for the heel fashioned from recycled tires. (Sometimes the sole is made of tire as well.)

Cattle is king in eastern Sonora—ungrammatical but true. Sonorans are obsessed with eating beef. For most Sonorans no meal without beef is a *real* meal. Anyone who refrains from eating beef is suspect, weird, wimpy. Beef is a symbol of the good life, a goal of the poor, a status symbol of the well off. It's not that the dietary hazards of a high-meat diet are unknown, for I was given an informal lecture on the dangers of high blood cholesterol by a rancher and his wife in the kitchen of their home in an isolated Sierra Madre village. They have cut way back on their meat consumption to lower their serum cholesterol. They are an anomaly, however. Dietary knowledge makes little difference to the meat eaters of Sonora.

Cows are sacred in Sonora. All of Mexico seems to be obsessed with eating beef, but nowhere more than in Sonora. Cattlemen's associations are as powerful here as they were thirty years ago in my home state of Arizona. Every town, no matter how small, sports a building housing the local cattlemen's association. Herds of cattle have the right of way on rural roads. Round-ups are real and ritualistic. Cow dung is as common as rock. Cows abound everywhere, everywhere. Only in a few microsites where cows are prohibited—fenced out—and in some areas inaccessible to the hardiest breeds are cows absent.

Sonorans consider beef to be a basic food. "Ay, David," said a Sonoran environmentalist friend to me, "*esta noche vamos a comer carrrrne,*" (Tonight we'll eat beef), he said, burring the "*r*" with pleasure at the prospect. Not that beef is accessible to everybody; its high price puts it out of the range of the majority. In 1987, for example, the price of a kilogram of beef was 125 percent of the daily minimum wage. Nevertheless, beef is the dietary element that defines good eating. The fantasy of most Sonorans is to eat beef at practically every meal, but at least once a day is a goal. Eating beef is a sign of virility, social standing, patriotism. In Sonora beef is not merely real food for real people, for many Sonorans it's the *only* food of stature. However, the reality is that beef is a rare treat for most, virtually unknown for many.

The ubiquity of cows is part of a government plan. Until the early 1970s, no paved road penetrated the Sierra Madre or any part of eastern Sonora. During the 1970s a vigorous campaign of road construction into the mountains was undertaken, including a highway through the valley of the Río Sonora. The paving was done to make it easier for cattle growers to get their meat to market, to connect large ranches with the urban centers of Hermosillo and Ciudad Obregón. Dams on minor Madrean rivers were constructed primarily to impound water for irrigating alfalfa and feed grains for cattle. The cattle industry became the basis for eastern Sonora's economy. If cattle production were eliminated in the Sierra Madre, economic and social catastrophe would follow. The livelihood of all the towns in the Sierra Madre, and many others as well, is derived mostly from raising livestock and marijuana.

In many towns livestock is the only industry. Even farming exists primarily to provide supplemental feed for cattle and only secondarily to provide food for people. The whole social and economic life of the area is determined by livestock grazing. Take away the cattle industry, and there will be no cowboys. Without cowboys there will be no need for *teguas* and no need for the leather workers, who make saddles, belts, laces, chaps, saddles, *reatas,* and every other leather item. Another industry will be dead, another craft vanished, another talent lost. I cannot think of anything that could replace it. The Sierra would be depopulated, while the already overcrowded cities would swell even more. Towns like Sahuaripa, Bacadéhuachi, Guisamopa, Tecoripa, and Soyopa would become instant ghost towns.

Ironically, beef is also a preservable food for many who can afford little else. Most ranches are small and have only a few cows. The small producers slaughter a cow but once or twice a year. One Sunday morning, while I was seeking directions on

a back road in the mountains, I came upon a butchering. It was a
joyous household, the whole clan at work in the shade of a giant
palo chinu, preparing for a rare feast. "Looks like a party," I called
from my pickup to a man busy hacking away at a carcass sus-
pended from a wooden rack. "Am I invited?"

He looked up from his work and saw my smile. Though I was
a total stranger, he nodded enthusiastically. "*Seguro que sí. Bájate de
tu camión y prepárate a cenar,*" (Of course you're invited), he answered, smiling magnanimously. (Get out of your truck, and get
ready to eat.)

I made up some lying excuse, thanked him, and wished the
family luck. From the looks of their place, they could use it.
There was an ancient adobe house, a broken-down tractor rusting in the sun, and an ancient pickup with a doubtful future.
When they have eaten all they can, wolfing down mounds of
fresh roast with tortillas, beans, and *salsa,* they'll carve the rest of
the meat into thin slices and hang it out to dry in the intense
sun. The head will be boiled up for a Sonoran delicacy *tacos de
cabeza,* the stomach and intestines stewed into *menudo,* the heart,
liver, and kidneys eaten fresh, and the milk ducts barbecued.
The hide will be saved and either cured on the ranch or sold to a
buyer. I don't know what they'll do with the hoofs and the
skeleton.

Because beef jerks well, the dried product can be stored without refrigeration. The jerked beef (*machaca*) will constitute the
family's only red meat source for months. They will eat it in
small portions and infrequently, savoring it on special occasions
when they combine it with the inevitable tortillas and beans or
potatoes that make up their diet. In rural Mexico, few families
have access to a refrigerator. They must eat all of their food
before it spoils, so *machaca* is hardly a luxury. Although a treat, it
is also a dietary staple, a supplement to the ubiquitous tortillas.
Beans are so expensive that some families cannot afford them.
Machaca fills the void.

The biggest, noisiest celebration in Hermosillo is not the
national day of independence or a religious fiesta, it's the annual
Cattlemen's Festival. I was serenely reading in a hotel room one
night when from the distance came a cacophony of truck horns.
I ran out into the front porch to see a huge parade clogging the
streets, slowing traffic to gridlock. Hundreds of flatbed trucks

were carrying thousands of young people decked out in country western fashions. They jammed the downtown area, swarming over each truck like brightly colored ants with cowboy hats. Trucks, tractors, and pickups were festooned with banners representing every town in Sonora. Red Tecate cans reflected a thousand points of light. Cows, cowboys, and cowgirls were the themes. For three hours no other vehicle could move. The honking of a thousand horns made conversation impractical.

The night clerk at the desk was mildly apologetic when I inquired when I might expect to sleep. "It's a noisy celebration," he offered lamely, looking up from a comic book. "They're going to crown the Queen of the Fiesta." He went back to his comic book, and I seethed off to my room, a concrete baffle with ringing tile floors that echoed and buzzed with the clamor. The noise went on most of the night. Cows had the right of way.

I spoke with a former high official in the Sonoran government. He tells me that since the late 1960s times have become more difficult for the small rancher. Years ago each family kept a cow for milk and cheese, providing its own dairy products. If family members were fortunate, they also had a small *milpa,* where they raised corn, beans, squash, and a few other vegetables. As the market for beef soared, cattle feeders began to appear. They needed calves to fill their feed lots, and the government pressured small ranchers to produce the calves as their part of a modern marketing system. Before the calves were a year old, they would be sold to larger producers who would fatten them in irrigated pastures or feed lots before selling them for slaughter, either in Sonora or north of the border. It is no coincidence that raising calves is the riskiest and least profitable part of the beef industry.

In the space of a few years, the official says, hundreds of small producers began raising calves. The *becerros* (that's what calves are called) need their mothers' milk and additional pasture to gain enough weight so that buyers will accept them. During this period, beginning in the 1960s and continuing to the present, many small ranchers stopped producing cheese and milk for their families. The calves needed the nutrition instead. In turn, they hoped to buy the dairy products with the cash they received from the sale of the calf.

Cheese is still made in most Madrean towns. Somebody has

stuck to the old ways or has found a local market for her product. It's available in Mazatán and Doña Rita Terán de Valencia makes some tasty stuff in Bacadéhuachi, but vendors in most of the towns now sell cheese from far away—Hermosillo, Chihuahua, or even Mexico City. The art of cheese making is fading all too fast, its demise hastened by the conversion of milk into food for calves rather than for people.

At the same time Madrean families were turning their cows' milk into food for a calf, they converted their fields to growing alfalfa or field corn for the livestock. The food they used to produce for themselves now had to come from the nearest store. In the space of a few years, hundreds and hundreds of families went from a subsistence economy—one in which they raised most of their own food—to a cash economy—one in which they must purchase their food. I have found no economists willing to state that the small rancher is better off for the transformation. Most seem to agree, however, that a small number of big producers has done extremely well. As is so often the case in the modern economy, efficient local production is undercut, eliminated, and supplanted by the cold inevitabilities of the international market.

New cattle breeds, especially Charolais, but also Cebu, Hereford, and Angus, have been encouraged by the government because they gain weight more rapidly than the rangy old *criollos*, the longhorned, ornery cows that crashed through the thorny brush a generation ago. The government's line has been that production will increase with better breeding stock, but nothing is free, including weight gain on beef cows. For the new breeds to gain weight fast they need gentle pastures where water is handy and the grass convenient. The southern third of the state has little grass, only dense uncompromising forests ranging from scrubby to towering. The solution has been for the ranchers, mostly the rich ones, to scrape off the forest and plant grass.

I sat with a young rancher who was working his family spread, a huge place not far from Alamos. Carlos had hired a host of peasants to cut down all the forest and plant buffelgrass on the flats and on the steep hills. That year the drought was a grinding, cruel force, and almost all the grass was gone, even though it was only mid-April. As we sat under the shade of a great *guamúchil* tree, I looked up and saw in a pasture far above the ranch house a Charolais pulling tentatively at grass on a hillside that only a couple of years ago had been covered with a nearly closed canopy of tropical trees.

Charolais do not like to climb hills at all. They do not even like to climb knolls. They prefer flat pastures or those that only slope downward—in all directions. I asked Carlos how he managed to get that lazy beast up the slope. He thought for a moment and shook his head. "It wasn't easy. That *pinche* bastard fought me all the way up, and now he'll hardly eat."

At least he had the cows. Most of the small-scale ranchers were selling off their stock. The ones best off were those few who still kept the old criollos or *ganado meco*—the surly old critters that for centuries have roamed the Sierras. They can live on just about anything and will range for miles away from water, while the "improved" breeds need water close by. Most of the peasant ranchers have been too poor to buy the new breeds, but this particular year they were fortunate not to be stuck with the lazy new herds pushed by city slickers and the government.

Small producers in the Sierras have stubbornly kept the old breeds. I hiked one day for nearly five miles with a Guarijío Indian who was driving a yearling calf to Mesa Colorada, where, if fortunate, he would find a truck to carry it to San Bernardo and the buyers who venture there. This *criollo* calf, just weaned, was ideally suited for the trip, my companion told me flat out. He could go a long time without water and nibbled on various shrubs and trees each time we paused for a rest. A Charolais would not have lasted a mile. Nevertheless, the Indian would take a loss on the shipment, for the cow would lose weight due to dehydration and lack of food, and the buyer pays by the pound, not by the cow. At the feed lot the calf will gain the weight back in a couple of days, much to the delight of the new owner.

Criollos or *mecos* do not bring high prices on the market. Their beef is tasty but tough as shoe leather. It's not the tender, marbled stuff increasingly popular in Sonoran supermarkets. It is a cowboy's beef, meant for a man who has time to chew and chew for the gratification of the incomparable flavor of *serrano* beef.

Overgrazing in Sonora is staggering, and with the government push for more production, it gets worse each year. By May, with two months of drought left until *las aguas* (the summer rains) every blade of grass, almost everything edible, is gone. Cows resort to cactus, yucca, and agaves, and even the bark of trees. When those are gone many starve unless they are given supplemental feed. When rains fail, cows congregate around watering spots, trampelling into oblivion every plant not big enough to avoid a cow's hoof. There is a certain late-spring smell in Sonora. It is the aroma from a mixture of windmill-area dust, the sweat from listless cows crowded into the shade of a mesquite or cottonwood, and cowshit- and urine-drenched soils that have been pulverized into flour-like consistency. I have smelled it in a thousand pastures for thirty-some years. It is a desperate smell, and when summer rains hit that mess, it erodes like ice cream under hot chocolate sauce.

I sat at a desk in Hermosillo across from Don Johnson, a United States–born government agricultural official and an expert on cattle and grasses. Sonora has about 2 million cows, about the same number as people, he says. While big ranchers prosper, the small producer is not faring well. "How about overgrazing?" I ask him. He's a big man, wearing cowboy boots and shirt, equally at home on the range or in a government office. He looks at the ceiling.

"Overgrazing is a serious problem," he acknowledges. "We don't seem to be able to get ranchers voluntarily to limit the numbers. Most of our range is in pretty bad shape. Now the cows are eating things they've never eaten before, we're seeing a decrease in overall biomass."

He stops and thinks about the problem. "Production is down. Each year it seems to be less. Forage is disappearing. Maybe in years of good rainfall, it'll go up a little, but cow production doesn't respond quickly, you know, you have to build up herds over the years. A lot of small ranchers have more horses and burros than they need. They keep 'em like pets, although they eat a hell of a lot. The small ranchers don't improve their breeding stock. They'll keep around some old bull who's genetically not very good, but the family loves him. It's hard, hard.

"The *ejidos* aren't doing well. *Ejidatarios* don't even get a hundred acres. That's not enough to raise a herd. They run too many cows. The food's all eaten up. Then . . ." His voice trails off sadly. He has worked for years to improve rangeland and has introduced better forage grasses and better management techniques. Sheer numbers are overwhelming, and the inexorable fact is that small ranchers now dependent on cash sales *must* sell as many calves as possible in order to survive, even if it means destruction of the range in the long run.

He didn't discuss the absentee landlords whose only concern is the bottom line, but another range expert did. "They'll seed the range with a new grass, and production will go up, so they'll double the number of cows and in a couple of years it's back to where it was or worse. They want a fast return on their investment. We never quite catch up."

The omnipresence of cattle and the concomitant overgrazing is not surprising in light of the popularity of beef. The trampled, denuded pastures blanketing the state make a bleak statement about Sonora. About thirty years ago the economy of grazing in the state was changed forever when a new forage grass was introduced, largely through the work of Don Johnson. Its significance was driven home to me when, from the top of a hill near Navojoa, I saw huge swathes stripped of forest and filled with yellow grass, all the way up to Alamos Mountain, sharp lines delineated by fences. The thorn forest and tropical forest once covered thousands of square miles of mountains, valleys, and flatlands. Hundreds of thousands of acres have been cut down, some for crops but mostly to make way for cattle pasture sown with a South African import, buffelgrass (*Pennisetum ciliare*).

First introduced into Texas in 1946, the grass found its way to Monterrey Technical Institute in the Mexican state of Nuevo Leon in 1954 and from there into pastures throughout the Republic of Mexico. Proponents point to the grass's potential of raising forage production dramatically under proper management. One ranch in central Sonora saw an improvement of a thousand percent. The Sonoran government claims that 400,000 hectares (1 million acres) have been planted with the grass. The actual figure is probably more than twice that and growing fast.

For the grass to be successfully introduced, the pasture must be stripped of existing vegetation and the seed planted, a machine-intensive operation usually involving bulldozers, which rent for an hourly rate in excess of the monthly income of most peasant ranchers. Cattle gain weight quickly from the high protein in the green leaves and blossoms. The grass flourishes in the hot desert climate, but for best results the range must be burned every few years to eliminate invasive plants like mesquite and the ubiquitous semi-tropical thorny scrub, called *chírahui* (*Acacia cochliacantha*).

All over Sonora vast pastures of buffelgrass have appeared, huge sweeps of monotonous yellow in the dry season, bright green in more moist seasons, from north of Hermosillo to the Sinaloan border, from Guaymas Bay to the foothills of the Sierra Madre. Across the plains of Sonora, kilometer-square tracts of thorn scrub, and in the south, the tropical deciduous forest, are being cleared of every plant except for a few columnar cacti, morning-glory trees, and token legumes like *palo verde* and ironwood, which stand out like abandoned, doomed sentinels. After a couple of years, all are dead. Following the clearing, the area is seeded. If the rains are good, the new grass grows rapidly and soon fills the pasture with thick forage of a rich green.

Trouble is not far behind. I sought out Coahuilan range management scientist Fernando Ibarra, who has worked for a decade with buffelgrass. He told me that ranchers tend to react to the new grass by increasing their herds well beyond the long-term carrying capacity of the land. Then pest plants, such as mesquite and *chírahui*, reappear and become an even greater nuisance than before. Ibarra lights a cigarette. "Buffel pulls nutrients from the soils," he laments. "Desert soils are rich in nitrogen and the grass sucks it out." He showed me pictures of the grass, shriveled and ugly, after an invasion of spittlebug, an insect predator that can devastate large areas. The bug not only eats the leaves, it injects a venom into the plant that accumulates until the plant is killed. In some years, huge acreages are destroyed by this pest, which seems to thrive in years of good rainfall.

Buffelgrass is very, very popular. Pickups park along the highways where cows are fenced out. Collectors run huge gathering sieves through the grass on the median and the shoulders, collecting the seed for their own pastures or for sale. Unemployed, landless peasants reap grass and seed and sell to buyers. Mayo friends of mine have travelled across the state gathering buffel seed and making relatively good money at it, as much as fifteen dollars a day.

Ibarra showed me photographs of a well-run ranch owned by a bigwig from Hermosillo, a gentleman rancher, a *latifundista*. This guy does things right, he says. Most others do not. "Sure, buffel can increase cattle production significantly if the rancher plants in coordination with a careful management of the *system* of which grass is a part. Unfortunately, most ranchers are more interested in rapid profit than the long-term well-being of the soil. They load the range with more cows than it can support, and in five or six years they've wiped out what would last indefinitely with good management." He crushed his cigarette, his handsome, moustached face a study of frustration.

Small ranchers, only marginally surviving, have an incentive to extract every possible ounce of forage from that pasture and hope that the next year will bring good rain and proper growing-season temperatures. Good management for them is an ivory tower consideration applicable only to *latifundistas.* If they can plant buffelgrass and raise another calf, it means more food in lean times and a hedge against inflation. "The danger with this picture," Ibarra adds grimly, "is that the soil and the people and ultimately the planet are the losers. When any resource is managed for maximum current yield instead of maximum long-run yield, whether it be rangeland, forest, or cropland, those who live closest to the land suffer the most." Replacing a diverse ecosystem with a single grass is an anathema to nature.

In early 1994 the Sonoran government announced that it would pay one-third the cost of converting pastures into buffelgrass.

CHAPTER 11

Sahuaripa

If any area typifies a Sonoran ranch town, it is Sahuaripa, and if
any valley exemplifies ranching, it is the Sahuaripa Valley. The
Arroyo Sahuaripa originates in high mountain ranges near
Yécora and flows northward through a broad, green, tree-filled
valley, between two steep, parallel mountain ranges, finally emp-
tying into the Yaqui fifteen miles north of Sahuaripa. Normally
the river runs all year, its flows regulated by a dam and reservoir
just south of the village of Cajón de Onapa, one constructed
during the administration of Dr. Samuel Ocaña. A cowboy
named Manuel from Santo Tomás, a village of five hundred a
few miles south of Sahuaripa, told me the uniform flow helps
him raise more predictable crops: alfalfa and grain sorghums,
both to feed cows, and garlic, for a cash crop. In the drought of
the early 1970s, he said that the reservoir dried up and there was
no flow. He had no crops for nearly two years. It was a hard
time. He had to sell off part of his herd but somehow survived.
Others didn't. Some have gone to Hermosillo, some to Mexico
City.

We sat talking on a bank above an irrigation ditch brimming
with clear cold water, watching his cows of mixed breeds—
Zebus, Charolais, Brangus, and even a few Herefords—grazing
placidly in the field beyond. It was February, and the bugs were
dormant, the temperature balmy, the hills a light green from
substantial *equipatas* (the Sonoran term for winter rains). Life
seemed very good to this cowboy. His hat and *teguas* were new.
His young son sat beside him, tossing pebbles into the ditch,
fascinated by the plop they made when they struck the water.
Manuel was born and raised in Santo Tomás. Unlike many men
his age, he has never worked in the United States. "I've always
worked here," he said simply. All his life he has ranched and
farmed in the Sahuaripa Valley. He likes the peace and tranquil-
ity in the valley. He confessed that the summers are long and hot

and full of bugs, but he wouldn't ever want to move away. I hesitated to ask him how many cows he had. An Arizona rancher once complained that it was rude for people to ask ranchers how many cows they had. "I don't ask them how much money they have in the bank!" he said testily. Since hearing that story, I've stifled my desire to know. Manuel would probably have told me, but my rancher friend was right. It's none of my business. Manuel is certainly not rich, or he would not have been riding a horse along the bumpy, dusty road I had been driving on. Nonetheless he is healthy and pleased with his fields and his son. It occurred to me that his roots that would serve him well psychologically in times of need, giving him a sense of place and relatives and friends willing to assist him if necessary. I envied him the roots and the peace but not the summer heat and the unending isolation or the inevitable squeezing he'll encounter by international forces he'll never hear about.

Sahuaripa, 130 miles east of Hermosillo, is a busy, noisy town, not unpleasantly so, but robust enough to show signs of restless activity often absent from other Sierra Madre towns. The difference may be the economic stability brought on by the more or less reliable waters released by the dam. The central part of town is a good kilometer long, though only a few blocks wide. Common-wall homes, each painted a different color, stretch on both sides of the street in one continuous wall on a terrace above the Arroyo Sahuaripa. As I looked down the main street that curved slightly in the distance, it was like looking into a narrow, multi-colored canyon. On one side of a prominent building a broad sign was painted artistically directly over the bricks. "Mr. Peasant," it read, "don't let your crops include drugs. Help protect our young people." Such signs are often seen in the rural towns as the Mexican government carries out an anti-drug program. Sahuaripa is rumored to be a drug distribution center. I've been there many times, and no one has mentioned it to me. However, a student from Hermosillo gave me a hint—"Look for new pickup trucks. Wherever you see a lot of them, you can bet there are *narcos* around"—and Sahuaripa has a lot of trucks, *a lot.*

Sahuaripa once basked in affluence and influence. A major mining center as well as a commercial hub, in the early part of the nineteenth century it boasted a population close to ten thousand. Wealthy families lived in mansions. Miners, especially from the nearby mine at La Trinidad, spent their earnings in Sahuaripa, spawning a robust merchant population and a flourishing service economy as well. The city wielded political clout throughout the state. In the 1880s financiers and industrialists, mostly from the United States, the source of most railroad capital, made the decision not to extend a railroad to Sahuaripa. The town's fortunes began to decline. A new and powerful merchant class from Hermosillo gradually came to dominate the state, siphoning political power away from eastern towns like Sahuaripa and its *hacendado* class. Near the turn of the century, mines in the area fell victim to labor unrest and failing production, the economic vitality of the area dwindled, and it lapsed into relative obscurity.

Today, Sahuaripa, as other once-prominent eastern towns, Moctezuma, Huásabas, Arizpe to name three, has seen the economic power of the state shift permanently to the west. The revolution of the second decade of this century broke up large landholdings, brought down great fortunes, and demolished empires. The newly emerging landed class lives in the new cities, not in the old towns. Reminders are everywhere. Crumbling adobes were once stately mansions with walls of adobe or stone, often sheltering portals with ornate columns, and majestic old doors of cracking weathered cedar or thick pine. It's as if these grandiose old structures are irrelevant to the current towns. They lie waiting for an improbable renaissance, fragments of an age long forgotten.

Sahuaripa offers two hotels, both of the type known in Mexico as *de viajero* (for travelers). Neither would be recommended by the AAA, but for a historian or a sociologist they're ideal subjects for study. Tourists are almost unknown in this part of the country, so anyone staying at a hotel is involved in some business or other. I had to roust the manager from the TV set, even though it was early evening. Ten United States dollars was the price. The only competition had inexplicably closed, perhaps because termites had devastated the portals, so when I came to Sahuaripa I stayed at Hotel Pie de la Sierra (the Foot of the Sierra Hotel). It was austere, to say the least: a hard crooked bed, a toilet that worked only partially (no toilet seat), cold water for a shower, towels so worn I could count the threads, windows that might have closed had I known the magic formula, cockroaches the size of mice, and mice the size of rats, but at least it had a roof and walls.

I chatted with three pleasant chaps from Hermosillo who were staying in the room next to where I was stowed away. They worked for the Federal Commission on Electrification and wore khaki-colored uniforms with great pride. One offered me a cigarette and asked if I had fought in the Gulf War. Their work takes them to numerous small villages, which reminded me that these men are a valuable source of information about road conditions, descriptions of the landscape, and the latest gossip about what's going on in the boondocks. They're as up-to-date in rural gossip as a traveling salesman should be.

The traveling salesmen also plod from *rancho* to hamlet to village to farm in big box-like trucks, often with a plastic-covered couch or stuffed chair or two lashed to the top. They take orders from rural customers or sell them goods on the spot. They are to rural Sonora what Sears and Roebuck was to the rural United States two generations ago. Their arrival in a town is a major social event. Most citizens leave behind what they're doing and gather around the truck to see what's for sale. Even grown men watch attentively from a distance. Once, on an impossibly narrow road in a high pass between Huásabas and Bacadéhuachi, I met one of these trucks. Neither of us was in a hurry, so we leaned on our face-to-face trucks and talked about their business. The driver and two companions were returning from a buying/selling trip to Nácori Chico and were heading for Ciudad Obregón. They carried clothing, shoes, candy, paper goods, electric fans, blankets, sheets, pots and pans, dishes, tables, chairs, beds, mattresses, and dozens of other items. They had visited everywhere they could get to, offering their wares to anyone, even suggesting credit terms. They've got creditors in every village and town in eastern Sonora. They gave me accurate and invaluable information on road conditions and asked me to deliver greetings to a hatmaker in a tiny town far in the distance. Sixty years ago the same could have happened in my country.

Saturday night at the Hotel Pie de la Sierra was lively. Rooms were rented out by the hour as well as the night. It was far too noisy for sleep. Beer and *bacanora* flowed freely, *ranchera* or *norteña* music throbbed loud and inescapable, and emotions ran high.

I watched the plaza from a high curb. Trucks clogged the square, the bulk of them bearing license plates from the United States, although all were driven by Sahuaripans. Single cowboys paraded around the square. The more affluent leaned on their pickups, their shirts freshly laundered and ironed, their faces clean-shaven except for the inevitable moustache, their boots brushed and polished as much as possible. Most had just come into town, harboring flickering hopes of finding love—temporary or permanent—or at least a little action. All drank beer: red-labeled cans of Tecate.

To my dismay I found that Sahuaripa isn't a town of active restaurant-goers. A couple of cafés offer meals from time to time. Sometimes only *machaca* is available, sometimes chicken, sometimes pork, rarely cheese enchiladas. Sometimes it's impossible to get a meal, period. On one visit I could not find anywhere at all that would serve a meal until I tracked down Teresita López in a little store just off the plaza, who rustled up a nice Mexican plate for not much *lana* (slang for money). It was generous of her, for her extended family was also enjoying a fiesta in the café, and she served me along with them, just another plate on the table of Sahuaripa.

I missed by only a day a small caravan of gypsies who provide travelling cinema in tiny towns without theatres or electricity. Their strange-looking vans, gypsy-looking trucks that appear in even the most remote villages, contain chairs, a projector, a generator, and an admission booth. They often drive in caravans along main highways then splinter off into obscure pueblos. Their days are numbered, however, for solar-powered satellite dishes are springing up everywhere, and their quaint movies are no longer in much demand. Video rental stores in isolated villages are putting the gypsies out of work. Gypsies, of course, are a resilient bunch, accustomed to harassment, economic adversity, and changing societies. I hope someone will follow them closely and report on what they turn to now that international media conglomerates are putting them out of business.

CHAPTER 12

Bacanora *from Bacanora*

The upper Yaqui Valley is almost as famous for its moonshine as it is for anything else. The fiery distillate known as *bacanora* is revered and enshrined in songs and tales throughout the Republic of Mexico. The practice of producing moonshine *bacanora* in adroitly concealed stills shows no signs of abating. It's also an important source of income for many hundreds of *mescaleros*, or *jimeros*, as distillers are called locally.

Twenty-five miles to the west of Sahuaripa in a narrow valley constricted between two steep mountain ranges, nestles the town of Bacanora. The first *bacanora* I bought came from this quaint town of the same name of a thousand or so, located in an isolated valley watered by a tributary of the Río Yaqui. On the outskirts of Bacanora a sign reads "Founded in 1627, elevation 420 meters."

From the mountain range that rises sharply east of the pueblo, the road to Sahuaripa overlooks the clear stream and green fields of alfalfa and sorghum that border Bacanora in one of the most unforgettable views in all of Sonora. The church with its graceful bell tower and the dark red town hall immediately adjacent to it dominate Bacanora, contrasting quaintly with the various pastels of the homes and stores clustered on a bank above the watercourse.

I found Bacanora to be a tranquil, unhurried backwater town, quieter than Sahuaripa, caught between the onslaught of a new and advancing paved highway and its ancient isolated existence. Once a bustling mining town, it is now a self-sufficient cattle village dreaming of a past when flourishing mines brought a fleeting prosperity. I'd described it so to Virgil Hancock and he came to photograph. Eyes stared at us through open windows as we bumped our way through the narrow streets. Virgil parked the Toyota on the plaza, his photographer's vision darting among the colorful buildings, seeing numerous settings. I wandered in the direction of a group of men seated on a shaded curb in front of a *tienda de abarrotes* and enjoying the quiet Saturday afternoon by chewing the fat. I approached them without hesitation, having learned through years of travel in Sonora that people in this part of México, though proud, independent, and somewhat aloof, are always polite and willing to discuss things with strangers. One of the men looked especially friendly. "*Buenas tardes,*" (Good afternoon), I said

"Buenas tardes," they repeated in unison. I would have no problem here. These men were happy and friendly. Their cans of Tecate rested on the curb beside them.

"*Pues, es que dicen que uno se puede comprar por aquí un poco de bacanora. ¿Es así?*" (Well, I understand that it's possible to buy a little bacanora around here. Is that right?) It was important for me to be somewhat oblique in my request because making bacanora is strictly illegal. From time to time, I'm told, the state judicial police conduct raids throughout the Sierra Madre, wiping out stills and seizing the contents for their personal use. At least, that's the allegation.

The man I spoke to looked slightly amused and turned to the others. There was silence for a few moments, while he sized me up. I needn't have worried. I could no more pass for a Mexican undercover policeman than I could for a defensive football line-man. "Well," he told me, "a lot of fellows make it." I could find it in various houses. By the way, he wanted to know, where was I from. I told him. He wanted to know if there was any work there. I told I didn't think so. Lots of Mexicans came looking for work, and I didn't think many of them found anything good.

I brought the subject back to *bacanora*. Could he be a little more specific? I had heard a man in a house up near the highway sold some. Was there anybody nearer?

The man shifted his *teguas*, took a drag on his cigarette and motioned up the street with his head. He told me a name and pointed to a house a block away. "Go ask him. He sells a lot." I asked if anybody in town had a reputation for making the best hooch. He told me that everybody made good stuff. It was stupid of me to have asked.

Knowing that twenty or so pairs of eyes were on me, I saun-tered up the street, trying to look nonchalant. I knocked lightly on the steel door. It echoed inside. There was silence. I rapped again, this time a little harder. The door swung open, and I was confronted by a young woman in her teens. I explained that I had been told I could buy bacanora here. Was it true?

Inside, a television set with terrible reception was blaring some old United States–produced melodrama, probably a rerun of *The Untouchables* busting bootleggers. Several people in the room ignored me, their eyes riveted to the TV screen. The young woman studied me, then, apparently deciding I was harmless, said she'd get her father. I was prepared to go through a rigamarole of leaving a ten-thousand-peso note on the sidewalk, walking away, and coming back in a half-hour to find a jug of hooch, but such clandestine behavior was unnecessary. I only waited a few seconds in the street before the young woman invited me into the house. I was offered a chair and had barely sat down when a thin man in his late thirties invited me through the television room into a run-down patio. How much did I want, the man asked. "Just a little," I said. A liter? No, perhaps less than half a liter.

He couldn't find a smaller bottle. Finally, he chose a seven-ounce beer bottle, rinsed it at a faucet in the patio, and pulled a glass gallon jug from a cupboard. Carefully, he poured the beer bottle full and corked it with a carved wooden plug. An older man with a cane approached and offered me a narrow glass with an inch of liquid in it. "Try this," he said. "See what we make here." I took the tiniest, most hesitant sip I could. The old man watched my every move. It was pure, smooth fire and warmed my gullet as it spread into my stomach. I am not one who drinks hard liquor, but I knew now where I would start if I ever were to take up the habit. There was no aftertaste, no sensation of impurities or warnings of impending hangover, just a powerful, slightly sweet burning liquid. I nodded.

"*Muy fuerte, muy bien hecho.*" (Strong stuff, well made.) The old man nodded in agreement.

"Be careful," he warned. "Don't drink it too fast. It goes to your head *rapido, rapido.*" He swung his head wildly to underscore his point. I accepted the bottle, paid the younger man, and indicated I'd be back some day to buy more. I kept my word, returning a month later to buy two bottles. They made great gifts for sophisticated friends.

Bacanora-making is a complicated ritual. For the *jimeros* it's an important source of revenue. For many people it's the only affordable alcoholic beverage. Mexico's excellent beers are far too expensive for them. A beer costs about a dollar. For a third of that you can get enough *bacanora* to make the world spin, even if you won't have the experience of holding the red Tecate can in your hand. Drinking *bacanora* is an indigenous vice, not one introduced by marketing experts from a beer conglomerate.

According to a *jimero* from Bacanora, *bacanora* is made as follows. The process begins with the harvesting of agaves that grow in the surrounding hillsides (*Agave angustifolia* and *Agave palmeri*), known locally as *lechuguillas* or *magueyes*. The *jimero* locates as many of these as possible when they are about to produce a shoot. He cuts off the shoots and leaves the plant in the ground for a few more months, perhaps as much as a year. This time period, I'm told, encourages the plant to increase its sugar content. It also requires the *jimero* to retain a remarkable geographical inventory of agave sites.

When the appropriate time has passed, the *jimero* pries the agave from the ground and lops off the leaves with a machete, leaving only the core or *cabeza* (head), as it is called. He transports these by burro to his still, which is in a hidden location to prevent seizure by the police. In a pit he builds a fire and roasts the heads carefully for a day or so. Then he cuts them up with an axe, soaks the pieces to soften them, and places them in water in a large vat. After a day or so, he shreds them once again with an axe, making a fibrous soupy substance, which then ferments for at least three days. Once the fermentation is complete, the *jimero* rigs up a still, often a brick *horno* (oven) with a tube coming out of it leading into a copper coil. He heats the fermented mash and distills the liquor through a coil of copper tubing known as a *culebra* (snake). The finished liquid, collected in a jar is often distilled once again to remove any remaining impurities and increase the alcohol content to what must be approaching 100 percent. Howard Scott Gentry, the preeminent authority on agaves, makes the following observation:

> Most of the heads are still carried in from the surrounding mountainous slopes by mules and burros. Whether owing to this particular variety (of agave) or to the particular bacteria of fermentation, or to other unknown factors, this mescal has an outstanding flavor, even when tasted fresh from the still. [Gentry, *Agaves*, p. 15]

Bacanora production is not limited to the town after which it is named, however. Virtually every *serrano* town or settlement in the region has its *mescaleros*. Even a hundred miles away in Cucurpe, west of the Río Sonora, it's possible to obtain a drop or two of the precious elixir. Another seventy miles to the west in Tubu-tama or Altar the distillate is also produced. Anywhere where agaves grow, *mescal* is hardly far away. The best tasting moonshine I've found is in the hamlet of Buena Vista, far away from Baca-nora, where women weave hats and baskets from palm leaves. While I was waiting there one day for a weaver to return from a trip to the store, an old man offered me a sip from a small glass bottle. I found it to be a powerful but enticing brew and thought about buying up all of that year's production. Ignacio was his name. He explained to me the intricacies of *bacanora* production. I gathered from him that because work is hard to come by in Buena Vista, the only reliable source of income for some men is their sale of the forbidden liquid. Elsewhere in Sonora the moonshine is referred to as *mescal,* in other places, *lechuguilla.*

Agave numbers are down, the *jimeros* say. Some scientists say overharvesting has cut the production of pups, the young agaves. Others say that it has affected the food supply of the bats that pollinate the agaves: fewer bats to pollinate mean fewer agaves and fewer agaves mean fewer bats. Jimeros say they must go far-ther and farther from the town to find the agaves. The disap-pearance of the *mescalero* culture would mean a loss of vitally needed income in an already economically depressed part of rural Sonora, inevitably resulting in a migration of more Sono-rans to the cities and a loss of an ancient and fascinating art.

In 1994 the Sonoran government declared that, henceforth, the production of *bacanora* would be legal, provided that the producer register and purchase a license. *Jimeros* report scanty compliance.

CHAPTER 13

Arivechi: Home of the Governor

Fifteen dusty miles south of Sahuaripa, the town of Arivechi
(the name is an Opata term for a harvester ant) sits on a knoll
west of the Arroyo Sahuaripa, its skyline punctuated by the twin
spires of its modernistic church, perhaps the most unusual
building in all of eastern Sonora. The north-south road, paved
for a short stretch through the village, passes only a block from
the plaza after an arch welcomes the visitor and asserts that
Arivechi was founded in 1629. Actually it's much older than that,
for it was a *ranchería* when the Spaniards arrived. Only a crass
philistine can pass by the church without driving at least once
around the square, which is dominated by the most ornate
gazebo I've seen in all of Mexico. The structure is decidedly of
Mudejar design, reminiscent of the Alhambra, and the inside
ceiling is decorated with stained glass panels of the Muses, life-
size, in their full unadorned, shockingly alluring glory.

On the south side of the plaza is the elementary school, the
most modern in the entire state, I suspect. The plaza is clean as
a whistle, and the street is paved with concrete. How did this
small town ever come to be affluent enough to pay for the elaborate church, ornate gazebo, and modernistic school, I wondered?
I spoke with an ancient fellow sitting on one of the shaded
benches in the square.

"Sit down, young man," he said to me, pointing to the bench.
His name was Victorio. He professed to be ninety-five years old.

"My job is to make sure no one throws trash in the park.
Nobody does it while I'm here," he said solemnly. He recited to
me a long list of places in the United States where he had
worked: towns in Arizona, California, Oregon, and Nevada, but
he was born in Arivechi, and that was where he hoped to die. I
got the impression that if I had introduced myself again, he'd
have repeated the whole litany. He turned an ear to me as I asked
about the plaza but couldn't hear what I was saying. Another old

timer sat down and told me that former Sonoran governor, Samuel Ocaña García, founder and director of the Centro Ecológico in Hermosillo, is from Arivechi and in the early 1980s saw to it that his hometown had an urban renewal project financed by the state. Immediately I understood the affluent appearance of the plaza, the church, the school, and the *presidencia* (county office building). Sahuaripa also had one of its native sons elected in recent times, but they have little to show for it (he was booted out of office less than two years after being inaugurated). Nevertheless, Governor Ocaña did well by his townsfolk. I decided I needed to get to know Dr. Ocaña.

He had become director of Sonora's Ecological Center in Hermosillo, a job with which he's obsessed. He's a tall man with a nose rivaling mine in size. "It takes a good nose to make a good man, David," he told me. He walks with dignity and a sense that he is still an important political figure in Sonora. As he walks, he issues orders to aides, makes plans, and tosses out proposals. We walked into an Hermosillo restaurant, and several people greeted him with *abrazos*, while lesser folk, smiling in the background, waited. In a beer store in Bacanora the man behind the counter appeared to recognize him but seemed hesitant to greet him. Indeed, only after several other cowboys walked in and one of them said *"Eh, médico"* (sort of equivalent "What's up, Doc?") and slapped him on the back did the ice break and everyone present gather round to greet their old friend. Many of them recall him as a prominent pulmonary surgeon who administered a hospital in Navojoa for patients with lung problems.

I met him in Tucson. A reception for the Centro was held in a private home. He arrived, surrounded by aides who also translated for him. He looked ill at ease and bored with the party scene. I slipped through his aides and extended my hand. "I'm David Yetman, Dr. Ocaña, and I know your hometown."

His face lit up. "You know Arivechi?" he asked, astonished that any gringo would have an inkling where a tiny Sonoran town was located.

"Yes. I've seen the church and kiosk you had built. I talked with Victorio, visited the Agua Caliente, the Sierra de Las Conchas." His eyes misted over and he rhapsodized about the beauty of Arivechi. I agreed. A half-hour later, his aides interrupted to drag him away. Dr. Ocaña and I had become fast friends.

During the 1980s when Ocaña was governor, Sonora got its first major industrial manufacture, a Ford assembly plant. The ex-governor and I drove past the industrial plant that now stamps out a thousand Fords a day on Hermosillo's southeast side.

"Do you see this industrial park, David." He questioned dramatically. I nodded. "I did it." He made an emphatic gesture with his palm cutting a downward swath. "I had the park built. I guaranteed Ford land without taxes. I promised them sewers, electricity, telephone, highways, gas, railroad—*todo. Yo lo hice. Todo.*" (All of it. I did it all.) They were all set to go to Chihuahua. I showed them Sonora, the Sea of Cortés. I personally took them around. They went back to Detroit. The next day they called and said they had chosen Hermosillo instead of Chihuahua.

"The President of Mexico," he looked at me with a questioning look, "is a dictator. Nothing more. A dictator. He says, 'I want this done,' and *boom* it's done." Again he made a downward chopping motion with his palm.

"In your country you have the courts and Congress and the Legislature in the way. Ha! Here we have nothing to interfere. The President says 'Do it,' and it's done." Once again he made the forceful motion.

"I sat in the President's office. López Portillo was a friend of mine. I told him we needed Ford but had no natural gas. He said, 'Dr. Ocaña, you are a friend. I will do it for you.' He lifted up the phone and in a few seconds the director of the national gas company was on the line. 'Build a line from Reynosa (Tamaulipas, in northeastern Mexico) to Hermosillo. Right away.' He hung up the phone. *Boom.*" Once again the chopping motion. "'It'll be done,' he said. A few months later the line was finished. It even had to go for a little way through the United States!"

I expressed admiration for the speed and efficiency of the operation. "But it can be bad, too, David, as you know, too much power. We have no democracy here. It's a joke. When I was governor it was the same way. *Boom.* I had only six years, you know, no re-election here in Mexico. I had to do things fast, fast."

We drove in his pickup through the winding, mountainous terrain of eastern Sonora, crossing the deep Río Yaqui, ascending a steep mountain, then dropping into the Valley of Bacanora and from there up to his family ranch in the thorny mountains. As we ascended the mountain, a modest lake behind a reservoir appeared. He killed the engine and opened the door. "Come here, David. Let me show you the *presa.*" He left his pickup parked in the road, and we walked a few yards through the thornscrub to an overlook. He pointed out the reservoir with a sweep of his hand. "I built that reservoir," he said, matter-of-factly. "I had it built, others, too—nine of them in the state."

I expressed a general dislike for dams. He laughed heartily. "Yes, you're right, David. Take El Sumidero Dam in Chiapas (extreme southern Mexico). It's a crime it was ever built. No one did any environmental studies, and the dam destroyed thousands and thousands of hectares of wonderful land and wildlife. It's a crime.

"The same is true of the Miguel de la Madrid Dam in Veracruz. It flooded out some of the best farmland in Mexico—rich, productive farms. Forced the peasants to move out. What a crime!" I agreed. Both dams had become ecological disasters.

"But the dams I built—most of them, anyway—have helped. This one here controls floods. Most of the year the stream used to be dry. There was never any water for irrigation. Terrible floods during *las aguas.* Now the water is stored and we have more than a thousand hectares of irrigated land. Look at all the alfalfa." He gestured at the green fields below.

"There weren't any jobs in Bacanora. Now my friends have fields. They sell the alfalfa all over the state. During May and June they need alfalfa everywhere!" The green fields that framed the pastoral view of Bacanora I had admired for years were due to Dr. Ocaña's dam. The same was true for Nácori, Mátape, Bacadéhuachi, and Sahuaripa. I grudgingly conceded his point. The dams have created irrigation works for thousands of acres of alfalfa, alfalfa to feed cows. The dams actually reinforced the base of Sonora's cattle industry. (The fields do not yield food for humans, only feed for livestock.)

Ocaña's small mountain home overlooks a bowl-shaped valley. No cows graze there; the governor raises fruit trees. Fences protect an ever-faithful spring from trampling by cows. On the shelf in his small kitchen sat the five volumes of the *Historia General de Sonora.* The preface to each volume is written by Governor Samuel Ocaña García.

"How did the *Historia* come to be written?" I asked him. He was cooking onions on the stove. He turned off the heat, grabbed a volume and sat down at the table. "I ordered it written," he said. "We had no modern history. I assembled the best scholars and asked them to write a history. In only a couple of years it was done."

We sat at the table leafing through the books. "Friends tell me this is the best work of national history ever published in Mexico," I told him. "You deserve to be proud." He gave a smile of pleasure.

We walked over his lands, cataloguing plants and talking about ecology, education, and politics. How, he wanted to know, could President Clinton hope to get away with his position on abortion and homosexuals? I explained that the vast majority of North Americans supported him on abortion and nearly half thought he was right on homosexuals.

Ocaña was impressed. "But you know, David, your government has caused a disaster in my country with its policy on drugs.

"Everywhere you go here you find fields of marijuana. Everywhere. Why? Because there's a market for it in your country. Your government puts pressure on Mexico to crack down on drugs, so they create all these police, soldiers, *judiciales, federales*. You've created a huge police force in my country and in your own. What do they really do? Crack down on the Mexican people. Nothing happens to the drug lords, but the little people. *Boom.* If your government would make it not a crime to use marijuana, *boom*, things would change just like that."

We sat in the shade of a giant sycamore, staring into the clear waters of the stream that runs through his land. I asked him what he thought of the *federales*, the notorious federal judicial police.

"Hoodlums," he replied. "They do anything they want. They rob innocent people. They want to control the drugs themselves. They abuse their power."

"Why doesn't the president just get rid of them?"

He sighed. "Well, you see, it's written in the constitution that they shall exist. So they must exist."

"Couldn't the constitution be changed?" He shrugged and we moved on to other topics.

Back in Arivechi I spoke with the president of the *municipio* (county or township) of Arivechi, a tall handsome articulate fellow in his early thirties named Luis Flores García. He wore dress cowboy clothes and walked with a patrician air. Justifiably proud of the lovely square, he became most interested when I explained I was working on a book about Sonora and Virgil was taking photographs. "Please tell your readers about our town," he said. "Tell them we love to have tourists. We have a hot spring nearby with exotic plants seldom seen this far north. We have an Indian village—Pónida—only a few kilometers from Arivechi, and we're at the foot of the Sierra de Conchas, famous for its petrified shells." We talked about politics for a while. I explained that I had spent twelve years as a county supervisor, roughly the equivalent of his position. We both lamented the frustrations of politics, the ingratitude of the electorate, and the benefits of retiring. Shortly after we spoke, he joined me in retirement.

On his recommendation, I went to Pónida just across the river from Arivechi but significantly separated from the more prosperous town. It's the only known Jova village in existence. Jovas, mountain-dwelling folk, are closely related to Opatas, but spoke a somewhat different dialect and viewed themselves as distinct from the larger tribe. Although two hundred years ago observers pronounced them to have become assimilated into the Opata people, they retained some different customs. Today only one of them speaks any language other than Spanish, and she remembers but a few words of the old language. Still, their village retains clear marks of non-Spanish culture. The women still weave hats from palm, quite different from those of Buena Vista but of equal quality. In addition they produce tightly woven baskets and a delightful woven holder encasing a glass beverage bottle, appropriately called a *botella.* It makes a perfect container for stashing a couple of days' supply of *bacanora.*

Pónida lies on the east side of the river from Arivechi. The current is deep and the road deep in sand on the far bank. During floods the tiny village is isolated, although a suspension bridge provides all-weather access to pedestrians. The hamlet shows none of the affluence of Arivechi, but it is home to several superb weavers. One of the best is Carmen Guiriza, a woman in her eighties, hobbled by arthritis but still an expert weaver. She was sitting in the doorway when I approached. She rose painfully to her feet when I asked if she had any hats for sale. She hobbled away to fetch them. I bought them from her and watched, along with ten other Pónidans who crowded into her bedroom/workroom/living room watching me, as she "ironed" the hats (smoothed the brims with a flat rock by pressing hard on a table). The style is quite different from the hats of Buena Vista and their fame is not established as far as the Nácori hats, but they are a truly superb head-cover. They weave in *huuquis* just as in Nácori. The family were quite interested in my hat from Nácori. They examined the stitching carefully and pointed out that the Pónida weave is tighter than the Nácori weave. I agreed, of course.

The younger women seem less inclined to perpetuate the weaving than do the women of Buena Vista, but if demand is sufficient it will surely continue, for just as in Buena Vista unemployment for men runs high, and the weaving represents a steady, if meager, income. One of Carmen's granddaughters lives with her much older husband on Dr. Ocaña's farm. She doesn't weave, although she's convinced that a sufficient number of younger women know how to for the craft to endure. The extreme social isolation of the farm (five hours by horse) makes her homesick, even though she's economically better off where she is.

Pónidans regard themselves as *indígenas* but are ambiguous about their heritage. I sat on the lone chair in the room, while the rest of the family lounged on the bed and on the floor, discussing whether their heritage was Opata or Jova. An elderly man maintained they were Opata, while a younger fellow who spoke with authority asserted they were Jova. It doesn't much matter. Their days as a distinct people are numbered. In a few decades they will have been assimilated into the endless uniformity of things.

CHAPTER 14

Yécora

Sonorans often speak the name Yécora with a twinge of reverence. It's the town that represents the Sonoran Sierra Madre and all its associated romantic thoughts, like timber, bears, wolves, gold mines, snow, and wilderness. Yécora is the Flagstaff, Jackson Hole, or Durango of Sonora. On any given day it's a good twenty degrees cooler here than in Hermosillo.

I first made it to Yécora in 1974 when a couple of friends and I ventured across the Sierra Madre into Chihuahua. In those days the town was a jarring day's journey from Ciudad Obregón on a bumpy, narrow, one-lane dirt road. My companions and I felt a rush of relief when the rooftops of the village came into view after an eternity of steep mountain grades, canyons, forests, and creeks. We rumbled into the ancient town settled in a grassy valley surrounded by greatly thinned forests of pine and oak, the air sharply scented with the resins of freshly cut lumber.

Those many years ago Yécora gave the impression of being a town unconnected with the outside world. Ciudad Obregón was far away, and very little in terms of human habitation existed in between, just hamlets like Tezopaco, Nuri, Santa Ana, and Santa Rosa. Barely five hundred people lived there, most of them employed at the lumber mill or as small-time ranchers. Only a sprinkling of trucks was to be seen. The smoke from a hundred chimneys hung over the valley, for it was a chill February morning. We bumped along muddy streets, asking anyone we saw where we could get a meal. They directed us to a café that consisted of two small tables in a weathered clapboard house with a shake roof. We shivered as we sat in unfinished hardback chairs at the tiny wooden table constructed of roughcut lumber. A silent old woman in black served us breakfast. She rummaged around in a cramped kitchen, stoking the fire in her wood stove. As she brought us eggs, tortillas, fried beans, and coffee, she broke her silence and complained of the high cost of living so far away from the conveniences of the cities. She decried the lack of electricity and the failure of the government to address the needs of the people of the Sierra. "*Aquí todo caro. Todo. Caro. Caro.*" (Everything's expensive here. Everything). She grumbled on and on, even as she presented us with a steep bill for the breakfast. When we stepped outside, the sun was beginning to melt the frost and the old woman's mood. She smiled as we left. We drove around the town for a few minutes, then set out toward the east.

Yécora has expanded greatly since then. The highway is paved; the last forty miles or so are new and well engineered. Ciudad Obregón is now only about four hours away, Hermosillo not even five, although the road is not an easy one to drive. The first forty miles are grassland desert, but past the old Pima town of Tecoripa the terrain becomes hilly, and tropical forest gradually takes over. When the valley of the Yaqui River is reached, the highway descends through a series of sharp, steep turns into what looks like a different country. The drive from the Río Yaqui to Yécora provides scenery unmatched in all of Sonora. From the great river the ranges rise higher and higher as the road heads east. Tropical forest dominates at first: great kapoks, figs, *amapas, guamúchiles* and wild palms; octopus agaves drape sheer cliffs and raucous *urracas* (magpie jays) flaunt their foot-long tails at the traveler. The aspect of the vegetation gradually changes as the lowlands are left behind, then the highway plunges once again into a canyon, rises, and descends again. Finally, from afar, a white scar on the blue hillside shows the way. Oaks become the dominant tree, dozens of different kinds finally giving way to pine and cypress as the road begins the climb up the escarpment. Once the summit is crossed, the climate is different, the smell that of a forest. Yécora sits in a broad valley, a picturesque reward after a tough drive.

With the new highway "opening up" the Sierra, real estate dealers have moved into the area. They have begun offering vacation lots in the nearby Mesa del Campanero at steep prices to the affluent from Hermosillo and Ciudad Obregón who wish to flee the burning summers of the lowlands for the cool pine-scented air of the Sierra Madre. Offices of *buenas raices* (real estate agents) have opened in town. Dozens of pickups and cattle trucks bounce through the dirt streets. Most of the shake roofs have been replaced with corrugated metal, which is ugly but far more practical. Two bars, one called "The Office," provide alternative watering places and a couple of good cafés offer a more varied menu than any of the other *serrano* towns I've visited. I became nervous when I saw a man in a suit and tie leaving a building. Was he a lawyer, a real estate salesman, a right of way agent?

Buildings in Yécora are wired to receive electricity from a diesel-powered generator that's designed never to stop running. From where I camped a couple of miles away I heard the generator's roar throughout the night. Before morning I cursed it. Refrigerators are commonly available, and you can even buy ice from one of the beer distributors. Civilization can be measured by the presence of chilled beverages.

Nevertheless Yécora retains the atmosphere of a small remote village. Cows, horses, and burros still amble through the dirt streets. Men on horses are more common than men in trucks. At the creek that forms the east end of town women still wash clothes on rocks. At the south end, seated on a tiny pine-covered mesa, is Aldea, a *barrio* of huts constructed of rough-hewn pine where the Pima Bajo Indians live, *indígenas* (natives in a long-term sense) as they are called in Sonora. Originally Yécora was a Mountain Pima town. Gradually, though, *blancos* (whites or Mexicans) have replaced the Indians who were long ago driven from the heart of the valley and the best land.

What do the people do here? To answer the question I looked up Luis Guerrero, whose fame as a leather worker extends for fifty miles in all directions. I'd heard of Luis long before I came to Yécora. A grizzled lean cowboy repairing a fence near Guisamopa, fifty miles away, told me Luis makes the best *teguas* around. In the shady town of San Nícolas, perched on the side of a canyon an hour away from Yécora, I also asked where I could get good *teguas*. They referred me to Luis.

I found him sitting in the shady patio of a two-storey, plastered adobe house painted brilliant green. It was nearly seven o'clock in the evening, but he welcomed me like a long-lost brother and bade me sit down in his shady yard. When I told him the second time in a voice louder than was polite that I wanted some *teguas*, his face lit up. He peered at me through thick lenses. "Teguas, you say? Of course. Here, I'll open up the shop. What's your name."

"David," I told him, pronouncing it "DaVEED," as Mexicans pronounce it.

"Habib?" He asked.

"No, Daveed," I shouted.

"Ah, Daveed," he smiled, nodding. "Good name," and he puttered off.

While he was opening the shop, I engaged his wife, Zoila Jacobo, in conversation. She was a silvery-haired gracious woman, her hair in a bun, now content to let her children and grandchildren do the bulk of the work. She welcomed me to her home. What did she think of the changes that had come to Yécora?

"Bad," she said. "*Ahora es ruidoso, ahumado. La gente no le deja en paz. No se reconoce a todos.*" (It's noisy here now, smoky, with all the changes. People won't give you any peace. Half the people you see you don't even know.) She wished she and her husband—he was eighty-seven now, she confided—could go live on her ranch up north. There she had her own house. Even if it didn't have electricity, it was peaceful and clean. No garbage was strewn all over.

We sat at the table in her tidy kitchen. Their Yécora house has seen many changes, she told me. It was built in 1938. In those days it was a three-day drive to Tónichi where the railroad came. (Today it takes three hours; the railroad is long gone.) She offered me a cup of coffee and proudly showed me her wood cookstove of bright green enamel, kept spotlessly clean. "Luis brought it here by muleback in 1938," she said. "All these years it's worked perfectly. You see, it's American. They shipped it to Guaymas and brought it by train to Tónichi. Three days to make it up here! For fifty years I've baked pies and breads, and it's been perfect. Apple pies, peach, custard, *todo*, todo. All kinds! Nobody else has one like it here in the Sierra. Nobody. They all have Mexican stoves." She shook her head. "*Son corrientes las otras, corrientes.*" (The others are poorly made, poorly made.)

Zoila and Luis have many children and grandchildren. Their son owns the largest drygoods store in that part of the state, and their daughter-in-law manages it. In their kitchen is a calendar with the store's name in large letters. By Sonoran standards they share a good life, indeed.

Luis shuffled in and sat down. His wife helped him with his chair and set coffee in front of him. He talked in the loud monotone of the elderly deaf. He worked an antimony mine in Chihuahua during World War II—*La Guerra,* he calls it (the War)—hauling out the ore of the scarce metal on a team of twelve mules.

"*¿Entonces era arriero, también?*" (Then you were a mule driver as well?), I asked loudly. Zoila sat next to him at the table, making sure he heard my questions. She watched with a mixture of admiration and impatience. He smiled when I asked him, nodding vigorously.

"*Si, si, arriero.*" (Right. A mule driver.) "It took a lot of patience to keep the mules in line, but they were sturdy beasts, strong, patient. Never slipped, all the way to Tónichi and the railroad."

After the war the demand for antimony fell, and the falling price of the metal drove him out of the business. He worked his family ranch (added to that of his wife it's still a pretty good size at close to four thousand acres), but he preferred town life and began making leather goods, including *teguas.* He's been doing that ever since. Now the lenses of his glasses are thick and Zoila must stay near him to assure he hears what he needs to hear. He loves the social life of Yécora.

Luis's shop smelled of saddles, old leather, and history. He measured me for *teguas* and told me they'd be ready in a week. He'd been making them for fifty years, someone told me. He laughed when I shouted to him that he came recommended by people from far away. Half the men in Yécora must wear *teguas* by Luis, I figured, but I met two of his sons, and they didn't.

Most of the people in town still work in ranching, he told me, and at the mill, or at the government-owned seed storage factory. Yécora's high cool atmosphere is ideal for storing seeds to be used in lowland plantings. Neither he nor anyone else could tell me how long it would be before all the pines worth cutting around Yécora were gone.

Luis showed me how to get to his son's ranch, where he assured me I could camp. I found it a couple of miles, five left turns, seven right turns, three gates, and two stream crossings later. It was dark when I reached the house. No lights were on. I called hesitatingly from the yard. Presently a large man appeared at the door wearing only white underwear. "Who is it?" he called out in a booming voice.

I told him in the submissive tone I use when trying to defuse potentially bad situations and asked him if I could camp on his ranch.

"*Por supuesto, hombre*" (Of course), he boomed. He led me in the dark to a grassy flat spot under a couple of giant oaks, the kind they call *cusi* (*Quercus albocinta*) in the Sierra Madre. "This is a good place for you, David," he said. "Listen carefully, and you'll hear *guíjolos* (wild turkeys). I'm going to plow and plant in the morning, so I'll see you then. *Temprano.*" (Early.)

I told him I'd already heard *guíjolos.* "How about a beer before you go Luis?"

He couldn't have responded more positively had I offered him a bag of gold. He polished it off in a couple of pulls, washing down a bunch of cookies with it in no time flat. Then he took a handful of goodies for his family and set off across the field to his home. He needed no flashlight.

He was right about the turkeys. They gobbled far above on the hillsides all night, keeping me awake, making me think of abandoning my principle of not killing wildlife. Turkeys are the only wildlife that abounds in the heavily overgrazed mountains. Deer are scarce, and bears, lions, and wolves have long since disappeared under intense persecution by ranchers. Turkeys, however, thrive on the abundant acorns in the great oak forests.

Luis Jr. is a burly enthusiastic man married to a hefty healthy-looking woman, a native of nearby Mesa del Campanero. They have four children who attend school each afternoon in Yécora. Luis Jr. was a truck driver for years, hauling goods back and forth to Ciudad Obregón. In 1982 he moved out to his ranch when trucking work became scarce. He has lived off the land ever since. It's as fine a ranch setting as you can ever hope to see. Neither electric poles nor wires clutter the landscape. A house, a barn, and a couple of sheds sit tranquilly in the shade of big pines and oaks. Below the house is a permanent stream that empties on Luis's property into an even more permanent stream that sports a couple of swimming holes. He owns 109 hectares—about 250 acres. Over the years he and others have cleared about twenty acres for a cornfield. The rest he uses for pasture for his cows.

As is the case with most small farmers in the Sierra Madre, or in rural Mexico in general, Luis plows his land with mules (two in his case) and a steel plow. The soil around Yécora is rocky, but for years he's been clearing the stones off, making a rock fence or just piling them along the edge until the field is tolerably free of them. The slope is gentle, so in four days he can plow and plant the field.

The evening I camped on his land he told me he would plant early in the morning, so his wake-up call should have come as no surprise, but never have I heard a human voice of such power and penetration. "¡Levántate, David!" (Get the hell up!) he bellowed. His voice rang like a foghorn across a quarter-mile of field. I was up and out of my tent in a jiffy and walked across the field to watch him plow. He barked at the mules to keep them moving. The quiet, patient beasts looked to me as though they had been cowed into submission by his voice alone. A companion worked alongside him, feeding two kernels of corn at a time into a pipe with a funnel-like mouth that ran down into the plow and deposited, then buried the seed. He used a three-foot pole stuck in the ground at the edge of the field to guide his furrow. When the mules reached it, they split the pole, one passing on each side. Luis's friend moved the pole over two rows to act as a guide for the return furrow.

Just the thought of doing this for four days made my back ache. After an hour or so of plowing, Luis and his friend ambled over to my camp and asked me if I still had beer in my ice chest. At 7:30 in the morning? I thought, prying a cap off a bottle for him and one for his friend. He slammed the liquid down and wiped off his brow. The friend was more deliberate, savoring the expensive brew. "Well, back to work," he said.

I reached down and crumbled a clod between my fingers. It was dry as bone—dry enough that a small cloud of dust rose behind the plow as it tore the soil and that the mules' shoes raised little puffs as they plodded across the field. "Is there enough moisture in the soil for the corn to sprout?" I asked the big man as he handed me the empty beer bottle.

"Si, David. Hay bastante. Así germina el maíz y crece un poco y cuando vienen las aguas desarolla muy rápido, muy rápido." (There is just enough moisture for the corn to germinate and shoot above the ground. When the rains arrive, it'll grow like crazy.) I hoped for his and several thousand other dirt farmers' sake that the rains would be on time and abundant. Sonora has few temporales (dryland farms), and relying on rains is always tenuous.

With the corn he raises, Luis will feed his family and support his cows through the following drought seasons. Because he, like most Sonorans, runs more cows on the land than it can support, he must supplement their diet in the dry season. The corn does just fine, he says, to keep the cattle from losing weight, although he spends a lot of time grinding it. I couldn't imagine grinding enough corn by hand to feed a couple of dozen hungry cows. He and his family keep on grinding until the summer rains water the grass, and the cows get fat and are ready to sell.

It's a hell of a rough way to make a living. I don't know how many cows Luis can run on the two hundred acres or so of pasture, but it can't be more than twenty-five. His four young children ran out in the field to join him, along with their pet ram who pranced along with them. They gradually approached where I was camped and politely waited for me to initiate the conversation. I had no compunctions about asking them personal questions, so after precious few preliminaries, I got to the point and asked how many cows their father has on his ranch. After some discussion, they decided maybe twenty, maybe more. Luis is never going to get rich on that, but he has no hope of getting rich. He works hard, loves his land, and enjoys his family and his neighbors, although he denounced one of them to me as a *"huevón que no hace nada"* (a lazy good-for-nothing who never does anything). He has a distinct advantage over other dirt farmers in that his parents own a large (by my standards) ranch to the north of Yécora, which represents a hedge against economic disaster. His mother Zoila, a ranch owner in her own right, told me proudly that her son would never sell one centimeter of his land. I hope he never does.

I left Luis while he was still plowing and headed toward Maycoba, a Mountain Pima village to the east. I followed a vague track down a valley until I found an Indian family living in a hut well above a permanent stream in one of the most scenic canyons I have seen in all of Mexico. Virgil was with me, so I took him to the tiny farm. No road led to the peasants' hut, so we left the truck behind and plodded up the footpath in the direction of the building a half-mile away. Two children ran and hid as we approached, wondering what in the world two gringos were doing heading up their path, but their mother, whose name is Carolina Valenzuela, met us smiling and confident, a surprising demeanor for these people who have found the outside world to be mean and greedy and quite capable of stealing their lands. She's a slight woman whose cheerful face shows the signs of years of hard work and the struggle to keep a family fed.

The hut was built on a tiny terrace carved from a steep hillside. In the background giant pillars of volcanic tuff arose from the valley and jutted against the sky. Downstream the canyon curved out of sight. The gentle canyon sides were covered with oaks and small pines. Still puffing from the steep hike up the trail to her hut, I greeted her and asked if it would be all right for Virgil to photograph her home. She heartily agreed, and offered me a chair, smiling broadly when I promised we would send her a copy of the photograph. While Virgil set up his camera and tripod, her cousin, a nervous man in his mid-forties, appeared on the scene, and we chatted in the pleasant shade of the *ramada* that served as a porch for her tiny hut. A dozen or so flower pots with bright blooms decorated the edge of the porch. Chickens scratched in the dirt all around us.

She had been born right there of Pima Bajo parents. Her mother had come from Maycoba, and, she said without rancor, she had never met her father but heard he lived in Ciudad Obregón. (A colony of Mountain Pimas migrated there a couple of decades ago in search of work.) She had nine children, she said, the oldest just now able to work on the highway under construction a mile away. She didn't know how much he would earn for this work.

Carolina has enough land to have a couple of *milpas* of corn (called *magüechis* in the Sierra Madre) of maybe an acre each, an orchard of peaches and apples, a herd of goats, a pig, and a few cows. She hadn't planted her *magüechi* yet, because in late May there's not enough moisture in the soil to sprout the corn, and birds and raccoons will get the seed. (Her place is about a thousand feet lower than Luis Guerrero's ranch.) She leases her land from the government for a modest amount, and she is entitled to use it in perpetuity as long as she pays the rent, about seventy dollars a year according to her. How she would ever come up with this amount is beyond me. Carolina makes *guaris* (baskets) from time to time and was happy to sell me a couple for a price I considered embarrassingly low. Other than that, I couldn't figure out a source of income. Her daughters showed no interest in weaving, she lamented, so the craft will probably die with her. We chatted about her land, her house, the rain, gnats and mosquitos, and taxes. A cat was asleep in the sun on top of a clutch of eggs in a nest in front of us. I pointed it out to her. "Are you breeding cats here to sit on eggs and hatch chicks?" I asked her, unable to contain my laughter. She giggled and shooed the cat away, whereupon an indignant *culeca* (broody hen) leaped up to the nest and clucking a scold at the cat carefully lowered herself onto the eggs. Everyone laughed loudly. Chickens are ubiquitous in Mexico, even in densely populated *barrios* of the cities.

I noticed an itching on my exposed skin. Five or six bites began swelling on my hands and neck. Carolina noticed at once that I was scratching but said nothing. "It looks to me as though you have gnats here," I said, trying not to complain.

"Yes, there are a few," she answered politely.

"Don't they bother you?" I asked her.

She looked at her cousin, amused. "Not really," she answered, suppressing a giggle. "They like you because they can smell new blood. You're good food for them, not from around here." An entomologist tells me tiny gnats breed in cow dung. I think the gnats have gotten worse as more and more cows populate all of Sonora.

At one point Carolina noticed I was looking inside the dark room that was her house. "I have to fix the roof, you know," she said frankly. "It leaks." That was putting it mildly. The steeply shaked roof had gaping holes in it. A bathtub wouldn't catch all the rain that fell through those gaps.

"How will you do that?" I asked, curious, and suspecting she had no husband to do the work.

"Well, maybe I'll get some galvanized roofing." I noticed a bound pile of pine roof shingles behind the hut.

"Aren't *tablas* (shakes) better than *lamina* (galvanized roofing)?"

"Yes, they are, but I don't have the money to buy the shakes," she said without embarrassment or bitterness.

I knew all *serranos* made their own shakes by shearing off pine wedges from fifteen-inch pine logs. "You have to buy them now? You can't make your own?"

"No, we can't," her cousin interrupted. "The *pinche* government has let them cut down all the *pinche* pines. We used to be able just to walk up the hill and cut down a tree. That would give us enough wood to make all the *tablas* for every *jacal* (hut) around. Now all the pines are gone. We have to buy the fucking shakes. I don't know why the government lets them take away all our trees."

Now I understood why everywhere in the Sierra I saw homes that twenty years ago had been shaked, now roofed with galvanized metal. Granted the metal is more durable than the shakes, but everyone I spoke with agreed that the shakes are cooler in summer and warmer in winter. If no trees for making shakes are available, the people's only recourse will be to buy the galvanized roofing. This necessity will, of course, draw them farther from the land and more tightly into a cash economy, a fact the roofing manufacturers love. However, it will create an even greater necessity among the *serranos* for coming up with sources of cash with which to buy the *lamina* and will also mean the death of the once-thriving craft of making the roof shakes. It will erode just a little more of the beauty that once made the Sierra Madre one of the loveliest areas in the world. The village of San Nicolás, an hour west of Yécora, was as quaint and picturesque as I had ever seen when I arrived there twenty years ago, its steep-roofed buildings covered with dark brown shakes. Now the shakes are gone, replaced with functional, drab galvanized roofing. The village feels hotter and more sterile.

Carolina wasn't the only one to complain about the removal of the pine forests. North of Yécora, where thick oak forests predominate and pines are scarce, I came upon a handsome young rancher roping calves in a corral outside his home. I stopped and spoke with him in the shade of a gigantic mesquite. He had studied engineering at the University of Sonora but missed his father's ranch and had decided to come back and work on the ranch rather than continue in his studies. I asked him about the oaks.

He loved them, especially the *cusis.* He wished the government would not allow them and all the pines to be cut down. "We used to have pines all around here, but most of them are gone. They should cut down fewer and plant more," he asserted. "As it is, they just keep cutting, cutting, cutting, and soon all the pines will be gone." I thought of my own country and how my government's policy has allowed decimation of our forests, and I found myself intensely sympathetic with his viewpoint.

In Maycoba I spoke with a forester employed by the government, Ricardo Aguirre Péres. The variety of oaks and pines he enumerated is impressive. Twelve different pines and thirty oaks are species they regularly deal with in the Sierra Madre. Undoubtedly more oaks are waiting for botanical description. Aguirre and other government officials have been working with the World Bank, searching for ways to make Mexico's Madrean forests more productive and to limit overharvesting of timber. The problem is serious, he says. Government regulations on tree size are universally ignored. I saw numerous truckloads of trunks headed for the sawmill, the bulk of which were smaller than the required thirty centimeters in diameter. Rejecting North American-style clear-cutting of timber, Aguirre suggests that a goal of twenty percent removal of timber from a tract in any given cutting period could lead to sustained yield. The forests have been overlumbered, he told me, and the oak forests have grown up in response to excessive removal of pines. If they could thin the oak forests and plant pines instead, he believes the pines could come back. The oaks would be a valuable source of firewood, charcoal, and pulpwood, while the more commercially valuable pines grow.

Already the Madrean forests are under sustained attack. Pulp mills financed by international banks are chewing up vast wooded areas to produce paper products and plywood—for the export market, it appears. These are efficient factories, accepting all kinds of wood. The current practice of feeding them is to remove all vegetation, except for a few token seed trees, and feed the felled trees into the hopper. North American clear-cutting looks positively benevolent by comparison. Aguirre's figure of twenty percent removal seems to have been somebody's convenient fiction. The Madrean forests are poised to undergo the fate meeting third world forests the world over: extinction.

The pulp mills haven't reached Sonora yet, but if the owners and their bankers have their way it is only a matter of time. The World Bank folks can't have seen the magnificent oak forests growing east of Maycoba near the Chihuahua-Sonora state line, or they wouldn't classify oaks as a less-than-worthwhile species. On the north slopes of the rugged mountains grow patriarchs a hundred feet tall (*Quercus epileuca*), interspersed with stately, symmetrical *cusis* and massive Arizona cypresses. I walked up a narrow deep canyon, where sunlight seldom reaches the bottom.

Below me a tiny waterfall trickled, even at the height of the spring drought. I craned my neck looking upward toward the crowns of these great trees, their canopy of leaves utterly shading the canyon floor. I estimated the circumference of one of them to be six feet. I prayed there on the spot that they would never fall victim to the feller's saw. A rare black hawk darted from one of the oaks and glided below me, barely skimming the surface of the tiny stream. It was surely a portent from heaven, although I couldn't decipher it. A bewildering variety of birds, many with unfamiliar calls, serenaded each other and, I hoped, me as well.

At the state line that separates Sonora from Chihuahua the two governments have erected a sign commemorating the paving of the new highway. "To improve and speed up transportation and communication between the two states," it reads. It will certainly do that, but as is the case with new highways everywhere, it will bring new and different forces to the people of the Sierra Madre. Already restaurants are springing up, along with modest hotels. Trash litters the highways, and in places the road has split fields and ranches, making access difficult for the owners. In time, locals tell me, Chihuahuenses and Sonorenses with more available money will buy up the ranches, leaving those who now work the land with a dubious future. Already dope dealers have taken over most of the best ranches. These are not nice folks, *serranos*, say. They live behind locked gates with grim bodyguards and menacing dogs.

Of course, the road is a blessing to the traveler. Although it's still difficult, one can now drive from Chihuahua City to Yécora in ten hours or so, compared with the two days it used to require. Trucks will be able to move merchandise and goods between the two states far more quickly than by the old routes which either meant the interminable hours and axle-jarring bumps of the old road, or the distant and inconvenient route north to Janos and west to Agua Prieta. Progress truly is a mixed blessing, and nowhere is that clearer than in the Sierra Madre. It's a vast, rugged land, wild, but surprisingly tamed; it is big and brave, but fragile in its own way. For those gentle, quiet Mountain Pimas, for the resourceful ranchers, for the timber harvesters, and for all their families, I pray a way will be found to keep it beautiful forever.

Every student of the Sonoran pine forests knows that one day, a decade or so from now, all the pine forests will be gone, and it will be many, many years, before a new crop will be large enough to harvest. In the meantime Yécora may have to turn into a tourist retreat for affluent Sonorans who want their own summer retreat. The old Yécora is in its final days.

CHAPTER 15

From Nuri to Soyopa

At the time of the Spanish Conquest Pima Bajo Indians, who occupied lands along the middle Yaqui seventy miles upstream from the delta, found themselves squeezed between the expanding Opatas from the north and the obdurate Yaquis from the south. Their lands included the present-day villages of Movas and Onavas, several villages on the Río Nuri, including Nuri itself, and Yécora and Maycoba in the Sierra Madre. Their discomfort at being compressed between two great powers may explain why in the early 1500s one Pima village moved as a group to Sinaloa, where they requested baptism and settled on more peaceful lands.

Nuri, an ancient Pima village on the Río Nuri, a tributary of the Yaqui, is built on a terrace above the stream at the base of the *Lomas Las Cuates* (Twin Buttes), an imposing range covered with dense tropical deciduous forest, the dark pine-covered slopes of the Sierra Madre looming in the distance. Nuri seems unmoved by the paved highway that was completed nearby in the late 1970s. Someone from the village took advantage of the new route and maintains a fifty-foot-high painting of Our Lady of Guadalupe on a sheer cliff face so close to the highway that rivers of wax from candles left by the faithful have run onto the pavement. The new road has killed much of the town's commerce. Travellers no longer linger in the village to buy food and drink or stay in a rented room. Indifferent vehicles whiz by on the highway as Nuri declines into oblivion.

Many of Nuri's older buildings are crumbling adobes, magnificent in their senescence. I first visited here in 1967 after a summer of abundant rains. Grass was bright green in the valley, including the grass growing from the mud rooftops of the village. A goat stood atop one home, chewing away energetically at the rooftop pasture. The streets were rutted, with only a few cobbles to hold back the soil. There was no electricity. The men wore white *calzones*, the traditional white Mexican pants of the peasant. The girls and women all wore long cotton dresses.

The town's appearance has changed little, although the men now wear Levis, and the younger women and girls wear slacks. Electricity has arrived, but Nuri still has the atmosphere of a once-busy village slowly dissolving into history. No fence protects the plaza, and cows and burros have nibbled the pathetic vegetation to the roots and below. Virgil found the place starkly photogenic, as I had hoped he would. While he set up a giant camera, I ambled into a nearby general store and ordered two cokes. There must be fifty thousand such stores, known as *tiendas de abarrotes*, throughout the republic. Seldom illuminated with more than a bare light bulb, they always appear dark from the outside. Even at night, their source of illumination is a single sixty-watt light bulb. If the door is open, the store is open. If not, it's closed. It's that simple. This one was open. Conversation ceased among the nine or ten locals inside the store. Ten pairs of eyes stared at me soundlessly as the grocer, a stout fellow in his forties, pulled the bottles from an ancient, belt-driven refrigerator. I explained to him what we were doing. He nodded in approval. "Your town is a lovely place," I told him.

"Why don't you move here?" he replied, hope and curiosity in his eyes.

"That's not a bad idea," I confessed. "It's peaceful here, not as hot as Ciudad Obregón, plenty of open space. I might like it." I wasn't being completely sincere, perhaps, but it was a tranquil place, I thought.

"I can sell you a house—cheap," he offered.

"Ah," I said, lacking any response more articulate. "A house for sale!"

"Yes," he smiled. "I own eight of them here. From the top," and he pointed up the street to the base of the mountain that towers over the town, "to the bottom," and he indicated the river below.

I expected him to offer me a prospectus next. I assured him he would be the first person I would consult if I were to move here. Then I moved on outside with the cokes. What is it about real estate salesmen, anyway?

A block away, two white-haired old men were seated on the high curb, enjoying the pleasant afternoon weather. I sat down near them, and we watched Virgil adjusting his camera. I explained to them what he was doing. One of the men immediately launched into conversation. "*Siéntate, joven,*" (Sit down, young man), he said in an old voice. He was eighty-two, he said, and had had a serious fall a few months ago. Fortunately, he had dragged himself home and managed to undress himself, but he had broken several ribs and cut himself. Finally his children had come to help him.

He didn't feel comfortable living in Nuri any more, even though he had lived here all his life. He thought it had become very dangerous. He looked at me with expectant seriousness.

"Dangerous? In Nuri?" I asked.

"Yes," he nodded forcefully and pointed across the plaza. "Dangerous. That man down the street, there he sits right now, shot the school teacher to death. Just like that. He shot the school teacher to death, and they've let him go free. What a disgrace!" Maybe he had a point. I suddenly felt a desire to make sure the exits from town were unobstructed.

"So now you have no school?" I asked him carefully.

"No school. But all the rest of us in town have gotten up a petition to the Ministry of Education to send us a new teacher. That bastard!" He glared at the man seated along the plaza.

Well now, I thought to myself, I doubt if I'll apply to fill the vacancy. As a matter of fact, I'll just bet the list of applicants is rather short, especially once they become informed about the early retirement of the previous teacher.

It seems there's intrigue in Nuri I don't know much about. I decided I wouldn't stick around to learn more, even if it is a beautiful place, but just remember, houses are plentiful there— and surprisingly affordable. It is a place of undeniable charm, rich history, and small-town neighborliness.

In 1992 I found Onavas, on the Río Yaqui downstream on the Río Chico from Nuri, much changed from the first time I visited it in 1967 in a pouring rainstorm. I'd come to find Pima Bajo Indians who were said to be owners of an *ejido* near Onavas. I found none and learned that the *ejido* is made up entirely of non-Pimas.

The village sits on a gentle slope, green rich fields separating it from the river to the west. The ancient church, built in 1622 according to residents, was in a state of magnificent decay, the nave collapsed, the bell tower listing, but still resplendent. The town was peaceful and rural, my truck the only one to pass through there on that gray rainy day.

In 1992 the church was being restored. The bell tower stands upright, visible for several kilometers. The nave has a roof. The facade has been plastered and painted: the tower white, the nave yellow. Services, masses, and rites of passage are performed, although the interior is empty. There are no pews, no organ, and no piano.

A group of men sat on a bench under a grand *guayacán* tree. I chatted with them, while Virgil photographed the church. They wanted to know if Virgil is a professional photographer. I explained that he is a psychiatrist as well as a semi-professional picture taker. "He ought to come live here," one of the middle-aged men quipped. "He'd have plenty of business." They got a good laugh out of that, each of them pointing vigorously at the others.

An older man, thin as a rail, bowlegged from riding two thousand too many horses, wearing worn but expensive boots and a new cowboy shirt, wandered up to the group. He looked at me. "What the hell's a gringo doing here?" he asked the others. Some of the men snickered.

"He and his friend are taking pictures. He speaks Spanish," one of them told the older man, pointing at me. They all laughed as I grinned.

The old fellow sat down next to me on a low wall within the shade of the *guayacán*. "Well, gringo, my name's Lorenzo." His eyes twinkled.

"Mine's David," I said and held out my hand. He grasped it and laughed. "I suppose you want to buy some marijuana?" The others were expectantly silent.

"No," I said slowly, trying not to burst out laughing. "I don't use *mota* (slang for marijuana)."

The crowd murmured. This was fun. "You got your hat in Nácori, didn't you?" he asked, pinching the brim, verifying its double weave.

"Close," I answered with a compliment. "Buena Vista. A few kilometers down the road."

"You want to buy gold?"

"How much."

"Ten grams. It's all I can afford to hold onto."

"No, I mean, how much do you want for it?"

"200,000 pesos. That's all."

"Nuggets or dust?"

"Dust, of course."

"I think I'll pass, but tell me, were you born here?" and we lapsed into other conversation. He told me of gold mines in the area, of Texans hoping to strike it rich, opening up old mines.

"Strange folk, those Texans. Didn't speak much Spanish. Spoke funny English, too." His body shook with a cough as a truck sputtered by. He hopped in. Another fellow walked up, carrying several *caguamas* (liter bottles) of Tecate beer. The gathering dispersed and headed for the local pool hall.

COLOR PLATES

Photographs by Virgil Hancock

Roadside Shrine between Imuris and Cocospera

Children outside Jacal at Agua Salada, Alamos

Alamos Looking East toward the Sierra Madre after the Summer Rain

Jacal in Los Pilares near Yécora

The Beach at Huatabampito

Guaymas

Pinacate Lava Fields with Cerro Colorado

Painting a House in Huatabampo

The Gulf Coast

The Mayo Village of Teachive

Bacanora

Boojums in the Sierra Bacha

Nuri Street Scene

Casa de Pepe Terán in Moctezuma

Street Scene in Alamos

Guaymas Street Scene near the Harbor

Row House in Guaymas

Cemetary in the Yaqui Village of Pótam

Hermosillo Street Scene

PART THREE

The Hot Country

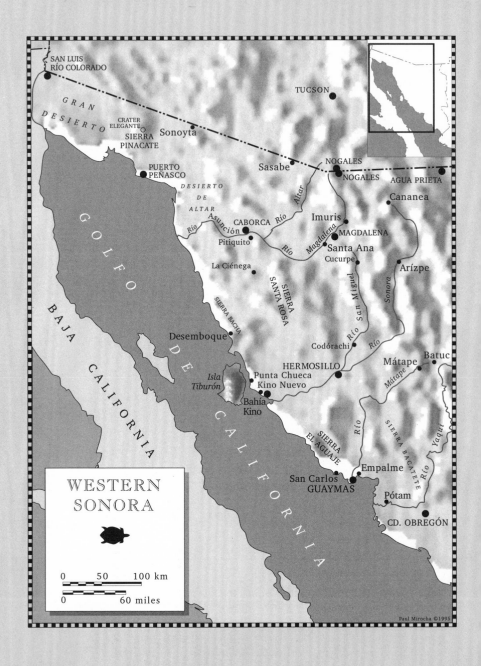

SAN LUIS
RÍO COLORADO

TUCSON

GRAN
DESIERTO

CRATER
ELEGANTE
SIERRA
PINACATE

Sonoyta

Sasabe

NOGALES

NOGALES

AGUA PRIETA

PUERTO
PEÑASCO

Cananea

DESIERTO
DE
ALTAR

Altar

Río

Imuris

Asunción

CABORCA

Río

Río

Magdalena

MAGDALENA

Santa Ana

Cucurpe

Arízpe

GOLFO

Pitiquito

La Ciénega

Sonora

Río San Miguel

SIERRA
SANTA ROSA

DE

SIERRA BACHA

DESEMBOQUE

Codórachi

Río

Mátape

Batuc

CALIFORNIA

BAJA

HERMOSILLO

Mátape

Isla
Tiburón

Punta Chueca
Kino Nuevo

Bahía
Kino

CALIFORNIA

SIERRA
EL AGUAJE

Río

SIERRA BACATETE

Yaqui

Empalme

Río

San Carlos
GUAYMAS

WESTERN
SONORA

Pótam

CD. OBREGÓN

0   50   100 km

0   60 miles

Paul Mirocha ©1995

CHAPTER 16

Coast and Desert

In the summer of 1968 a friend and I set out for the Sierra Madre east of Yécora to spend a couple of weeks roughing it. In those days the primitive road was a rough dirt track. We ran into flooded streams, impenetrable mudholes, and had Jeep trouble to boot. We had to return to the coast long before reaching Yécora. My friend suggested we change our plans and visit the Seri Indians on the Gulf Coast instead. I'd made numerous trips to Alamos, a couple to the Bavispe River, and a few forays into the Sierra, but had never been to the Seri lands.

On that trip I met the Seris and became an instant convert to the Sea of Cortés. During the next six years, I made a good hundred trips into the Gulf Coast area, most of them visiting the Seris. What ecologist Forrest Shreve labeled the Central Gulf Coast Region became my favorite part of Mexico. It's where the Sonoran Desert, the real Sonoran Desert, meets the sea. The prototypical Sonora is desert, and the soul of the Sonoran Desert lies along the Sea of Cortés.

It's a small narrow band, extending from a little north from Puerto Lobos where the desert mountains and hills extend to the edge of the Sea of Cortés, southward two hundred miles to where they end just north of the delta of the Río Yaqui. It's as different from the rugged Sierras and the Río Mayo region as any two areas can be. It's a long sweep of irregular coast, of intimate coves and broad bays, of sandy, gravely, and cobble beaches, of sheer cliffs overlooking the deep blue of the Gulf, of desert islands, cactus forests, and offshore rocks. It contains Sonora's most important port, Guaymas, its most popular resort, San Carlos, its most graceful inlet, Kino Bay, and its biggest island, Tiburón. Nowhere does the region extend more than twenty miles inland, no farther, that is, than the maritime influence on dews and temperatures that in turn alter patterns of plant growth and speciation. Apart from the city of Guaymas at the extreme southern end and Kino Bay, its principal inhabitants are Seri Indians, fishermen, and cowboys.

I came to know the southern part of the region long after I had spent countless hours among the Seris. They had told me the area was wild, so I went looking for wilderness. There is none in Mexico, no area where human presence is officially temporary. There's not even a word in Spanish for wilderness. The concept is difficult to explain to the Spanish speaker. Everywhere that can be inhabited is or will be.

The closest I could come to wilderness was along the Sierra el Aguaje on the coast of the Sea of Cortés north of San Carlos. In 1974 I took my family—my wife and two young children—on a kayak trip that skirted those mountains, from the quiet inlet of Tastiota south to the bay of San Carlos, a distance of about fifty miles. My children were young (ten and five years old), and I must admit to having some hesitant feelings about taking them.

Two friends joined us. Our kayaks were almost capsize-proof, and the Seris had taught me the habits of the Gulf. We stuffed the hulls full of waterproofed bedding, food, and water bottles, and off we paddled. My wife and I propelled the large boat with my daughter tucked inside the hull, just barely able to see over the top, while my son paddled the smaller kayak, attached to me with a length of nylon rope.

We were blessed with nearly perfect weather. For four days we paddled south at leisure, often on waters smooth as glass, past beaches, rocks, cliffs, caves and intimate coves. We found a spring in a large cove and replenished our water. We watched dolphins, sea lions, electric-colored fish. I sang to my wife and daughter and chatted with my son as he paddled alongside. When he tired of paddling, I would give him a tow. The nights were cool and fresh on the soft sand under the brilliant sky of the Sea of Cortés. The lapping of the waves on the isolated shores became a part of my existence.

Only on the last day did we begin to see boats, yachts, and fishermen plying up the coast from San Carlos. Once a black object reminiscent of the Creature from the Black Lagoon sprang from the depths next to our boat, leaving us gasping. It was a scuba diver. On the last morning we paddled around the *Tetas de Cabra*, the peak that marks San Carlos Bay, worked our way through the passage, and buried the prows of the boats in the beach among sunbathers who looked at us curiously. Never since have I had a trip like that. I was now permanently hooked on the Gulf Coast. I began exploring the area by land.

After I was elected to public office, the Gulf became a refuge from the dirt and hate of politics and a place to nurse my wounds from a painful divorce. Isolated coves were only a few hours south of Tucson. I went there often, usually with my children, sometimes alone, sometimes with a lover, always with Chess my little black-and-white terrier. He came to know the Gulf so well that when we were close to the ocean, even if we couldn't spy it yet, he would whine with excitement and jump into my lap while I was driving. Once on the beach, he was indefatigable, sniffing, climbing on rocks, hunting lizards and dead fish, chasing birds, and wandering in desert. He's long since dead, but the Sea of Cortés was in his soul when he died.

In the solitude of that timeless sea I became absorbed in the life and death of the great margin between land and water. I stared for hours at dolphins, sea lions, frigate birds, ospreys, and pelicans, was lulled to sleep by the gentle lapping of the Gulf's quiet waters. My friends the Seris wondered why I came so seldom to their lands far to the north to visit. The men understood when I explained how I found the rough coasts to the south good for my soul. They had seen the coast, too.

I was first elected to the Pima County Board of Supervisors in 1976 and was re-elected in 1980 and 1984 by wide margins. It was widely assumed that I would run for the United States Congress. Indeed, I went through the preliminary motions. I established a campaign committee, worried about the excessive informality of my appearance, and began talking with political mucky-mucks. My initial campaign was building the right kind of momentum. Political writers were taking notice.

In the spring of 1987 I spent a few days with the Seri Indians. A month later I took Chess to my favorite cove on the Gulf coast. As we sat on a hill and watched the golds, reds, purples, and blues of the sun setting over Baja California, I realized that a career in Washington would remove me from Sonora, from this coast, from the Seris, from Bacadéhuachi to the east, possibly forever. I shook my head and decided then that I could never be involved in any enterprise that took me away from Sonora. The sun set. Chess wagged his little tail furiously, and that was that. The campaign committee never met again.

Thirty years ago only a few roads led anywhere besides Guaymas and Kino Bay. Even in 1974 the coves were nearly empty. There were no roads by land, and it was too remote and rough even for cows. Today, dirt roads, some of them primitive, criss-cross the whole province, at the cost of trampling some sensitive terrain. Coves once accessible only by boat are now crowded on holidays. Cows and burros frequent the roads and have invaded the coves. Fishermen have built permanent camps and piled the sand high with bottles, plastic, and tin cans.

A decade ago an architect from Guaymas named Hector parked his pickup next to my tent in an isolated cove up the coast from Guaymas and set up his gear just far enough away to face the next tiny cove to the south. It was too beautiful a place not to be friendly, and we found ourselves chattering away swapping stories almost at once. One of us offered the other a beer then the other returned the favor, and before long Hector, Chess, and I were sitting on a rock high above the coves, exalting the Central Gulf Coast in the most eloquent Spanish, a language noteworthy for its flowery turns of phrase. Hector lamented the loss of quality on this part of the coast. "Mexicans always soil their beaches," he fumed, pointing at the accumulated trash above the high-tide line. "They never appreciate the beauty around them," he railed. He tossed a beer bottle in the direction of his truck (he picked it up later). Then he took heart when I pointed to a peak to the south and reminded him that on the other side lay a cove that at least at that time had not been pene-trated by a roadway.

"Don't let them build a road there, Hector," I pleaded.

Our conversation ended inconclusively when one of his bud-dies called him to go fishing. "David," he said, pronouncing my name with the English, not the Spanish, accent, "be sure you come back here again." I often have.

The *smell* tells me when I'm in the Gulf Coast region. I figure it's a combination of aromatic desert herbs in the salt air, per-haps *Bursera microphyllum* or elephant tree, known for its incense-producing sap, or maybe the decaying of desert plants in the surf. Hector pointed out wild oregano (*Lippia palmeri*) to me as he tramped off into the bush carrying a bag to collect a few branches for his wife's kitchen. Just a couple of its leaves crushed between the fingers make for an arid land's perfume.

It's not just the smell and the air that set this place off from the rest. The plants assume a peculiar aspect, and the mountains have a certain grim richness unmatched anywhere. It's all there for the viewer to see, for deserts abhor camouflage. Plop a peak down where its sides will be attacked by the relentless action of the sea and its insides will one day be revealed. Some people find this desert barren; I find it a source of unending variety. If any one part of my life stands out in aesthetic richness it is the thousands of hours and hundreds of days I've spent in this region, transfixed by the sea and its teeming life and by the desert creatures, scorpions and snakes included (the latter are present in ample numbers, I assure you—I once spent three days on Tiburón Island and encountered seven rattlesnakes), plus the incomparable variety and richness of desert plants. When the sun disappears into the sea or over Baja California, there's no question that it's dropping to the other side of the world.

Humidity swings in the region are astonishing: from four or five percent at midday in May—almost absolute dryness—to saturation at sunset only a few hours later. Lunch left out in the sun is desiccated in a matter of seconds. Clothing left out after sundown is wet in just a few moments. It's all part of the mystique of the Central Gulf Coast.

The defining plant of the area should be the *cardón* cactus, *Pachycereus pringlei*. The many-armed giant grows as tall as fifty feet and dominates the varied and numerous flora of the region. *Cardónes* extend almost to Puerto Lobos and become the dominant columnar in many areas. In small pockets in the Guaymas area they form dense forests and then abruptly cease a few miles south near the delta of the Yaqui. They need a frost-free, moist-night, sun-drenched, aromatic atmosphere, I guess, but they can't take more than about ten inches of rain or a lot of competition from other plants, either. Somewhere at the southern edge of the *cardón's* range, fifteen miles south of Guaymas, the last of them makes its stand and is replaced by its genetic columnar cousin, the *etcho, (Pachycereus pecten aboriginum)*, which then flourishes well south into the tropics. For a kilometer or so the two meet; then, abruptly *cardónes* end and *etchos* take over.

At the northern limits, *cardónes* seem to grow best on flats, even in poorly drained soils, and preferably within sight of the sea. On the other hand, they cover a couple of steep islands in Guaymas Bay with a seeming impenetrable jungle of specimens. They've made a secret agreement with the giant saguaro cactus whereby they divide up the territory and one doesn't grow profusely in the same area as the other. Although individual saguaros may grow taller, the *cardón* is a bigger cactus overall. I know of individuals whose trunk at ground level is more than twelve feet in diameter. Fifty arms are not an unusual number. Plants this big provide welcome shade in the desert, an unexpected boon from a cactus. One individual *cardón* I have met became so overwhelmed by the heavy rains of fall and winter of 1990 that it could not sustain its own ponderous weight, and about a third broke off and fell to the ground. The remainder lives on, and the place where the huge branch broke away forms a sort of tree house seven or eight feet above the ground where I love to sit. The shade remains till midday.

The cactus grows very fast in response to available moisture. I know of one that in six years has grown from three feet tall to eleven feet tall with three huge arms. It would take a saguaro fifty years to grow that much. In parts of this region ospreys find *cardónes* especially to their liking for nests. Every few acres of desert finds a *cardón* with a huge, crude osprey nest taking advantage of its height and strength. Some of the nests have been continuously occupied for decades. One year I watched ospreys raise a family in three different *cardónes* all visible from my campsite.

Cardónes are as important a food source as saguaros, even though their range is far more limited. Their fruits are full of seeds, rather bland compared with the moist, juicy sweetness of the saguaro fruit, but for nutrition they can't be beaten. For centuries Seri Indians have harvested the fruit and stored it for use as a principal source of protein and oil in their diet. Seris so honored *cardónes* that some individual cacti came to be identified with individual Seri Indians. One day I came upon a huge *cardón* with an ancient baby stroller dangling from a crooked arm. A Seri child had died, someone said, and the child had loved that cactus. Seris once loved to decorate the giants by hammering a clamshell into the tough skin of the cactus where it would remain for decades as a monument. Individual cacti in Seri country today exhibit the shells, which are now almost impossible to extract, so powerful is the scar tissue formed around the incision.

So far *cardónes* seem to have withstood the hammering of soils around them by livestock. While other desert plants may suffer from the desperate gnawing of goats, burros, cows, and horses set loose to gnaw every possible plant molecule from the ground, *cardónes* are not edible. I still find babies issuing from the ground.

Guaymas, the quaint little city I stopped in back in 1961, has become a metropolis of 150,000 people. Since it has one of the world's most sheltered harbors (and now one of the most polluted), its significance as a port was recognized in the sixteenth century. In 1539 Francisco de Ulloa, possibly the first European to venture into Guaymas, found the site to be "a fine port with two entrances separated by an island." More appropriate terminology would be "a magnificent port." Nowhere in all the rest of the Pacific is so fine a natural bay to be found, sheltered from storms by a row of high hills, separated from heavy waves by all of Baja California. It's an intimate bay, with waters so still and hills so abrupt it was possible for boats to anchor immediately off the shore and for sailors to jump to the ground.

Over the centuries Guaymas has flourished and languished, depending on many factors: the status of international trade, the political situation in Mexico, the availability of transportation to other cities from the port, and so on. Now, however, it seems destined (or damned) to become a major trading center. Already its population has exploded, and its trade volume has jumped. Gone is the quiet town where the hottest topic was the coming and going of the shrimp fleet. Vendors still hawk bags of cut limes and shrimp purported to be freshly boiled, but Guaymas now bustles with the energy of international commerce. An aqueduct across Yaqui lands to the Río Yaqui imports water, necessary since the Guaymas area has only a modest aquifer incapable of sustaining a large population. Not surprisingly, Yaquis were compliant when the government requested the use of their lands and appropriation of their water for the aqueduct. They've learned over the centuries the cost of bucking the government. A Sonoran government official tells me proudly that the aqueduct must be expanded.

Squatters are building on hillsides, and ubiquitous trash builds up on fences turning a serenely beautiful landscape into an ugly, cluttered dump. A power generation plant spews a heavy brown plume over the entire basin. Freighters are common, and rusting, aging oil tankers caked with corrosion stop by to assuage Sonora's thirst for gasoline and oil. A major oil spill would be catastrophic. The quiet waters of the Gulf lack the energy to clean and dissipate oil scum.

The shrimp fleet crowds into the harbor, looking quaint and colorful from a distance but rusting and worn out up close. From Guaymas used to come many of the shrimp consumed in the western United States and much of Mexico as well, along with a prolific quantity of fresh fish. Each year in November the shrimping season began with a great fiesta replete with rituals and prayers to the patron saint of the shrimp fleet and ample Tecate beer and tequila. The government supposedly regulated the harvest and the season, realizing on paper that a sustained yield requires a certain degree of restraint. All the world seemed hungry for Guaymas shrimp, and if there were always to be shrimp, the resource must be managed. That was the spoken policy. Even so, between 1984 and 1991 the number of boats increased from two hundred to five hundred. Then the catch dropped precipitously, by as much as eighty percent. Overfishing and destruction of the Gulf's bottom habitat appear to be the culprits. Our taste for shrimp and fish is killing the Gulf just as our deification of beef threatens rangelands and forests. The great shrimp trawler nets scrape the Gulf's bottom, dredging up myriad vibrant organisms. All except the shrimp die and are unceremoniously dumped back into the Gulf. One net load may produce five hundred pounds of sea life yet but one kilogram of shrimp. The rest of the life is considered a bothersome byproduct. In 1992 Sonoran shrimpers brought in over four thousand tons of shrimp. The amount of other sea life sacrificed for the shrimp is dismaying.

In mid-1993 Mexican President Carlos Salinas de Gortari took the unprecedented step of declaring the northern Gulf of California a "Biosphere Reserve," closing it to all commercial fishing. His decree was both environmentally and economically necessary, for it afforded immediate protection to a rare dolphin and the great totoaba fish but also promised to give the fisheries of the northern Gulf a chance to recover after decades of superexploitation. His move was applauded by small-time fisherman whose traditional livelihood has been almost eliminated by commercial overfishing. The Gulf near Guaymas was unaffected.

San Carlos, only a few kilometers from Guaymas, is a virtual city as well. Until recently the bulk of the vehicles on the highway in winter months bore North American and Canadian license plates. San Carlos abounds with fancy homes bearing tile nameplates like "The Brandons, Harriet and Bob, from Oak Park, Illinois" or "La Casa de Los DeWitt"—sort of a transported Sun City, Mexico style. Nearly all signs are in English, as are restaurant menus. Nowadays North Americans are fewer, scared away by tales of robbery and intimidated by expensive toll highways, convoluted customs regulations, and astronomical prices.

Signs of the boom and bust economy abound. Near the highway approaching the bay an unfinished luxury hotel, some fifteen stories high, incomplete because of some scandal or other, stands as a monument to financial transience, a quixotic Beirut Hilton, resembling nothing more than the bombed-out remnant of some ghostly war. Its stark decaying concrete and rusting steel stand as an ugly mute reminder of greedy attempts to milk profit from the timeless beauty of the blue Sea of Cortés and the brown of the desert hills.

The original San Carlos Bay was one of the most enchanting places in the world. The blue-green water was still and so clear the bottom was visible thirty and forty feet down. Myriad schools of brightly colored fish glinted like underwater confetti. In 1961 I visited that very bay and was the only person there, overwhelmed by the magnificent solitude. The still waters of San Carlos Bay were so quiet, so rich, turquoise, blue, azure, malachite in their colors, that as the sun set, turning all to gold, I felt myself merging into their color. However, the bay was not big enough to accommodate the all boats and yachts needing shelter from the *nortes*, so bulldozers, cranes, and heavy earthmovers went to work and removed an entire hill to expand the bay and create a marina.

Toward the end of my 1974 kayak trip we paddled to a small cove at the base of the landmark peak Tetas de Cabra (Goat Teats for the tall rock spires that seem poised to squirt milk into the heavens). Not another soul was to be seen. We spent the night next to a sea so calm that not even a slight lapping of waves was to be heard. Stars were reflected mirror-like on the bay's surface. The only light came from an occasional shrimp boat passing by, far out to sea.

If ever a lovely place was killed for its beauty it is San Carlos. Today tacky condominiums line the base of Tetas de Cabra. A new road, dynamited from the hillside, gives access to the secluded cove, but it remains quiet, fenced, walled, and protected, the private beach of the wealthy and influential, access controlled by a guard shack staffed by an unsmiling sentry. Those lacking economic power needn't bother to stop.

Thousands of trailer and recreational vehicle spaces now fill the shoreline of San Carlos. On the Gulf side of the desert hills, the beach where the movie *Catch-22* was filmed in the later sixties now hosts a Club Med. Friends tell me that the filming destroyed one of the *tetas* on the mountain. Next door is Howard Johnson's. Real estate signs are in English. Inland, numerous non-Mexicans have built homes ranging from simple bungalows to opulent castles. Plush homes are stacked on the stark mountainsides. Trailer parks, walled and protected by guard shacks, expand into the desert. In the tourist season gray-haired joggers and well-tanned tennis players fill up the cafés. Glitzy restaurants and pretentious and deceitful boutiques line the streets. Mexicans hustle to cash in on North Americans' desperation for active retirement and denial of age. The Mexican government plans to double, triple, quadruple the tourist facilities of this splendid desert-sea environment. Until recently only a handful of Sonorans has raised so much as a murmur of protest. Now their voices are being heard.

The best conversation I could make was with a gasoline station attendant. At first he was submissively polite, trying to act efficiently, speaking in broken English, assuming he needed to put on his proper behavior for another *norteamericano*. Gradually he opened up as he leaned on the hose. Yeah, the place had grown. He lived in Guaymas, not able to afford life in San Carlos. The gringos bring jobs with them, but the jobs don't pay well. Yes, the retired gringos all look alike. Maybe if the new resort was built he'd get a job there. Otherwise, he might go north to the United States. Did I know if there was work in Phoenix?

I spoke with a developer, owner of a large block of condominiums. He asked for suggestions as to how he could build a rustic development up the coast that would be attractive to North Americans. "We have Mexicans filling San Carlos all summer," he said, "but the North Americans aren't coming as they once were in the winter. We need to attract more down here." I looked around at the amount of pristine area that had been sacrificed to attract North Americans and wondered if many Mexicans would benefit if they attracted more.

CHAPTER 17

Life on the Waterfront

Kino Bay, some seventy miles to the north of San Carlos along an irregular and mountainous coastline, consists of two separate towns: Old Kino and New Kino. The old town is a bustling, crowded Mexican and Indian village of a couple of thousand that lives on products of the sea and ironwood carving. The streets are unpaved, the dwellings small, the people brown. Many of the inhabitants are Indians, only lately arrived from Oaxaca and Chiapas in the south to seek their fortune in the more affluent north. Most are involved in producing carvings of sea animals in ironwood (*Olneya tesota*), which they hope to sell to tourists in Kino Bay or elsewhere. While they are certainly not affluent, they seem to have fit into the village, which is not at all unpleasant except after a big rain when the streets are transformed into one horrendous mud puddle.

A few years ago I watched a classic Mexican drama unfold in Old Kino. A parcel of land, perhaps twenty acres near the highway at the edge of town, sat unused. One day I saw dozens of men busy erecting shacks, digging roads, and marking off plots. A group of peasants and workers had organized an *invasión* (a takeover). Under Mexican law (since rescinded), lands not being put to beneficial use could be taken over by people who choose to live and work them. The scuttlebutt was that the PRI, the ruling party, organized the event as a punishment for a wealthy landowner who lacked the proper attitude. Several months later the lots were occupied by a dense community, which survives to this day.

Cruz Matus is a forty-five-year-old Kino Bay fisherman, the owner of a small fishing boat. He and his brother eke out a modest living using the boat to fish, ferry supplies to shrimp boats, and rent out to occasional sports fishermen. It's gringos, he says, that give him the most business. From time to time the brothers also work as laborers when there's a demand. The boat

shows signs of wear, and the motor is old, but it must keep going. A new one would cost a couple of thousand dollars. Gasoline is expensive, and the cost of repairs to the motor is outrageous. Cruz is unhurried, affable, optimistic, and appreciative of
his environment. He seldom wears shoes, of course, since Old
Kino is a sandy place and hopping in and out of his boat would
just mean getting footwear wet. He was born near Guaymas and
moved to Kino when he was young. He has been here ever since.
It's fishing that keeps him employed. On a couple of occasions
Cruz took me and some friends to camp for a few days on an
isolated desert shore far from Kino. On the seemingly endless
ride in his boat when he was ferrying me and my companions to
our campsite, he broke out into song, his pleasant baritone voice
rising above the droning of the motor. Only a happy man could
sing with such enthusiasm and accomplishment.

New Kino is separated from Old Kino by a high dune, so neither is visible from the other. It's a resort city dominated by
North Americans, and rumor has it that it will soon be invaded
by wealthy Chihuahuans now that the highway across the Sierra
Madre is completed. The landowners are light-skinned; the
streets are paved. Homes are large, located on one side of the sea
drive or the other, often ostentatious luxury dwellings. High
walls, iron gates and grills, and impenetrable fences protect
them. Signs are written in English. In the few cafés menus are
printed in English as well, often with quaint typographical er-
rors. The biggest house in town, located, strangely enough, several blocks from the beach, stands frozen in time, only half-way
built, occupying an entire block. It rises three stories high, and
there are two stories underground. It was commissioned by one
of Sonora's most prominent drug lords with the intention of
making it into a palace worthy of a Saudi sheik. Mid-way
through construction, however, the owner ran afoul of Mexican
authorities. He was captured while hiding out on San Esteban Island and tossed into the clink. His future remains cloudy at best,
and his castle remains unfinished with little prospect for improvement. The opulence of the finished part, with its poured
columns and lofty porticos, states clearly that drug dealing can
be profitable. The permanently unfinished portion—toppled
concrete forms, exposed reinforcing bars, and crumbling
plaster— suggests that it can be hazardous as well.

Kino Bay's sea drive, called Mar de Cortés, runs for nearly five miles along a crescent beach of light sand, ending at a dark red hill called Cerro Prieto. For the most part it's only one dwelling wide on each side. At night, from atop a sand dune it's possible to see the long arc of lights of New Kino and the softer denser blob of illumination from Old Kino. The new part is a white-hair ghetto in winter, a playground for retirees from Dubuque who stay the season in their motor homes. They go fishing in the morning, play cards at the *Club Deportivo* in the afternoon, and bounce around in square dances after "happy hour." They're a happy bunch. In summer the North Americans leave, finding the bugs and heat unappetizing. Their homes are watched over by Mexican caretakers, their mobile homes carted fitfully northward to the United States.

Chapo Gonzales is one such caretaker. He was born in the south and grew up in Old Kino. His wife Chapita is a short, se-rious, Indian-appearing woman with a no-nonsense attitude and wry sense of humor. They live with their three children in an ag-ing trailer in the compound of a house owned by Americans. Chapo is a gold mine of information. Prematurely old, aged by hard work and the effects of the maritime sun, he is still lithe and strong. He has it better than most, with access to a washing machine, electricity, an evaporative cooler, a refrigerator, and a regular salary, but he is realistic enough to know he has reached the peak of his earning power. Mobility in Mexican society is more sharply limited than in our own and most lower-income folks accept their fate with resignation. Chapo and his family never mix with wealthier Mexicans. The barriers are permanent.

One day Chapo mentioned that he needed to go to Her-mosillo. A generous friend was with me. "Take my car, Chapo," he offered. "You have a license," he offered.

"No thanks," Chapo replied, sadly. His nervous, thin face almost twitched with regret. "The *federales* will stop me for sure."

"Why?" I asked. He explained that the rich never get stopped by the hated *federales* because they have connections, and the *federales* might get in trouble. The poor never get stopped because they have nothing to cough up for a bribe. However, middle- and lower-middle-class drivers are an easy target for police thugs.

"If they find me in your car," he said to my friend, shaking his head, "they'd throw me in jail as a car thief, and I'd never get out without a huge *soborno* (extortion payment)."

In the mid-1980s Cruz Matus took me to Tiburón Island, visible from Kino Bay to the northwest. It is separated from the mainland by a narrow channel called *El Infernillo* (Little Hell"), a strait that narrows to barely more than two miles at its most constricted point. Tiburón is a nationally protected area, called a natural park. It's a large island of just under five hundred square miles and shows very little sign of human habitation. It has never been grazed by livestock, a rarity indeed, which makes it an incomparably valuable natural laboratory. Knowing this, the Mexican government has made the island off-limits to the public without specific permission, although Mexican fishermen have places they regularly camp. On the shore we found the remnants of a camp, trash strewn everywhere, and more beer bottles than a fisherman could ever afford. "Deer hunters, David," Cruz stated without rancor.

"How do they get to hunt here?" I asked, getting more indignant by the second.

"Well, you see, they're important men, pretty rich, and so they come here each year to hunt. They get special permission. Sometimes they shoot deer from the boat." I was indignant. Cruz was calm and matter-of-fact.

CHAPTER 18

The Seri Indians

Tiburón Island was for centuries part of the homeland of the Seri Indians. In fact, this region was their country. They ranged from Guaymas (named after a band of Seris) north to Puerto Lobos and inland as far east as Ures, east of present-day Hermosillo. They liked living in the coastal mountainous areas just as some of us do. The Seris shaped the history of this region of Sonora as Yaquis did the coast and valley farther south.

Seris have inhabited the coast for eons, roaming the deserts and mountains, gathering, hunting, adapting, manipulating their environment. It's a tough place to live. The only live stream in all their lands runs for approximately one-fourth of a mile. The rest of their water came from seasonal waterholes and scattered and infrequent springs. A friend and I once brought the people of a village a big canteen full of water from one of the distant springs. When the first woman took a sip she crowed something in Seri. A happy crowd gathered around and shared sips of the sacred water until it was gone.

I came to know the Seris in the late 1960s, visiting them many dozens of times. I have no explanation for my deep affinity for them except to say simply that they are the most extraordinary people I have known. For years I knew their lives and they knew mine. I knew their children, they knew mine. They gave me a name, as they do all Americans whom they get to know well. *Aajsh coopool acait* was my name (father of the black dog)—a reference to the black Afghan hound who accompanied me before Chess became my regular companion. The Seris were terrified of the Afghan, believing he was part bear, but they loved Chess.

They were baffled by my varied career, knowing me first as a philosophy professor, then as a camp manager, later as a politician, then as a peripatetic researcher. One dear friend, inured to my erratic career changes, took to asking me when I showed up in the village, "Well, David, what are you doing now?"

Linguists have linked the Seri language to that spoken by Yuman Indians who live on the lower Colorado River. Some Sonorans maintain, whimsically, I assume, that Seris are actually descendants of Polynesians who ventured eastward across the Pacific. Seris were one of the last Mexican Indian groups to be contacted by Spaniards. I asked one of them about origins, and he shrugged. "I don't have any idea where we came from," he said, grinning, and proceeded to sell me a wood carving at an inflated price.

They resisted conversion and never took well to the discipline of mission life, refusing to take missionaries as seriously as the latter hoped. When less-persuasive measures failed to pacify the Seris, the Crown resorted to military intervention. In the face of Spanish imperialism, Seris became adept and elusive fighters, attacking villages at will and evaporating into the wilderness or taking refuge on Tiburón Island when pursued. During the uprisings in the mid-eighteenth century, they survived for years in the labyrinthine canyons of the Sierra Libre south of Hermosillo, a craggy, rugged, ravine-filled desert mountain range. The Seris frustrated all Spanish military campaigns against them and frequently inflicted terrible wounds on their attackers with poisoned arrows, which they unleashed with uncanny force and accuracy. In 1767 a force of seven hundred uniformed soldiers, the biggest force of armed troops ever to campaign against an indigenous population, failed to dislodge them from the Sierra Libre.

Continued military attacks finally wore down their resistance, and they were forced by the Church to relocate at Pópulo on the San Miguel River near present-day Hermosillo, far from the coast. Over the decades, however, all either ran away or were killed. Still they resisted, rebelling against the Spanish practice of stealing their lands and wives, viewing pacification by Spaniards as interference in their way of life. Over the years they developed a reputation as warriors second in ferocity only to the Apaches.

Of Sonoran Indians, the Seris alone were never converted to Catholicism. They retained their nomadic lifestyle well into the twentieth century. The first family I got to know vanished overnight from its shack while I was camped nearby. Grandparents, parents, and children hopped in their boat and moved for a few weeks to another camp where the shellfish were more plentiful. That family had five places it called home at various times of year.

In the mid-twentieth century some Seris were converted to a fundamentalist Protestant sect. The proportion of the tribe adhering to the tenets of that religion varies with each year. Whether from the influence of the church's teachings or the pervasive influence of the dominant Mexican culture, in recent years the men have abandoned their traditional long, braided hair and the apron-like mantles they wore over their trousers. Women still sew the traditional colorful dresses and blouses that made them visible from far off, although it seems to me more and more of the younger women wear common Mexican-type clothing.

The Seris were actively persecuted by Spaniards and, after them, Mexicans. As ranching gradually spread through Sonora, Seri lands were invaded by cattle, and the inevitable skirmishes with ranchers began, invariably leading to government involvement on the side of the ranchers. The Seris' fondness for the newly savored beef was not viewed favorably by the ranchers whose cows they rustled. Repeated government-sponsored programs of extermination became cumulatively successful, and by the early part of this century fewer than two hundred Seris remained, less than ten percent of their original number. Since then they have become established at two villages north of Kino Bay, Punta Chueca and El Desemboque, where they live in conditions that tend to frighten first-time visitors. The villages are an apparent chaotic mass of trash, rusted cars, tarpaper shacks, prefabricated but antiquated houses, and sand, with ample animal dung mixed in. Nevertheless, they weave a magical order out of this topsy-turvy arrangement, knowing where everything is and where everything ought to be.

Seris have never managed to survive for long away from a view of the Sea of Cortés. Their numbers have increased to a figure of nearly six hundred today. From having been demoralized hangers-on by 1942, they have done rather well economically in the last thirty years, especially after one of their number, José Astorga, began producing hand-carved sculptures of rock-hard ironwood which became a sensation among native art collectors.

José had a way of startling me. I spent many hours by his side, reflecting on his work as he reflected on mine. He always wore a policeman's cap, even at night, and gave me lectures on carving, tending goats, loving women, and mining for gold. As he grew old he told me of many buried treasures, relating exactly where one was to be found—right under the floor of a neighbor's hut. His late wife Rosa polished his carvings with enduring and uncomplaining patience. She was coming back from the bushes one evening when she scared up a baby javelina. I don't know what had happened to its parents, but she brought the little thing home. It imprinted on her and never strayed more than a few feet from her heels.

The little javelina was snoring loudly one day as I squatted next to José. We passed the afternoon gabbing easily, time long on our hands. He was in his late sixties then, still a skillful carver. Out of the blue he stopped and pointed to Rosa his wife. "*Muy caliente, esta,*" he said, "*como la gallina.*" (She's a hot one, just like a hen.) Everyone got a good laugh at that, including Rosa, who said not a word but kept on polishing, a happy smile on her ancient face.

That's how they are: an independent, earthy, jovial, resourceful people whose culture is being pulled out from under them.

By the late 1960s most of the Seris were involved in carving and, until the craft spread to non-Seris, Mexican and North American markets absorbed all the carvings the tribe could produce. Since that time, however, the market has been flooded by non-Seri carvings, mass-produced with power tools. The Seris cannot compete with the rest of the industry, and many of the male carvers have returned to fishing, where they can make a better living. One of my closest Seri friends has given up carving altogether. He's rustled up a diving rig, and he and two brothers spend hours clawing along the floor of the Gulf harvesting the shellfish from which scallops are made.

Even as ironwood carving is declining, basket making is resurging. Nearly every house has a carefully protected pile of the raw materials. Seri handmade baskets are a collector's dream. Seri women produce the best baskets in the world, period, woven from a native plant called *torote* (*Jatropha cuneata*). The baskets are a marvel of color and style, strong, graceful and highly decorative. Wealthy buyers from all over North America snatch up the baskets as they are finished, sometimes getting into altercations among themselves as to who has the right to buy them. Seri women find the bidding war amusing and profitable. Top-quality baskets bring thousands of dollars. Chances are, if you find a basket, it is either already commissioned or will cost more than you ever dreamed. One woman offered to trade me an extra-fine basket for a pickup truck.

The procedures involved in making baskets have been elaborately described, but no mere description can match the richness of the experience of following the women through the intricacies of basket making. Years ago when I visited the Seri lands monthly, I became a resource for them. I had a Land Rover and seemed incapable of refusing to take the women and their children on *torote* gathering expeditions into the bush. Many times I stuffed the Land Rover full of Seris, and we bounded into the hills until one of the women would give me the order (in the Seri language) to stop so they could gather *aaat*, the basket making plant. The women always wore old skirts on these outings, not the brilliantly colored garments that were their everyday apparel. The *torote* branches ooze a sap that stains any garment it comes in contact with, so old clothes were the order of the day.

The women gathered large bundles of the bush, and I pitched in, tossing the heavy burdens into the rack on the Rover. I also learned to be of some help by gathering dead pieces of *cholla* cactus, which they burn to roast away the bark.

Back at the village the real work began. I sat and watched. Conversation was not easy, though. Seri women only spoke to me in Seri. They are either embarrassed by their poor Spanish or consider speaking Spanish the mark of a floozie. I understood some of the Seri language, but not enough to follow their conversations, so I hunkered (chairs were scarce), and they sat comfortably on the ground, their legs spread to one side. They roasted the branches to remove the bark, split the long branches in two, then split the halves in two again, then began soaking the splints in water or in the dyes they make from various plants. Only after all this work and a lot of gnawing at the splints to get them down to the right size could they begin the actual weaving.

The finished products are marvels. One especially fine basket I purchased for a friend had twenty-two stitches to the inch and a design of diamonds and dogs in a breathtakingly symmetrical pattern. Two months of work went into making a basket only slightly more than seven inches high.

Older women have made fine baskets for decades. Elvira Valenzuela, who was born in the 1920s, first wove when she was in her early teens and has made scores of baskets in her many years. Some stand several feet high, so big they will only fit in a full-size pickup. She also knows full well what they're worth and won't come down a penny. When a gringo offered her about twenty percent of what she was asking (and what the basket was worth), her face curled up into an indignant sneer. She pulled her scarf down over her eyes so no one could see her face, and continued to work. She finally got her asking price.

Much of the Seris' future depends on Mexico's ability to manage the Sea of Cortés. The Gulf of California was, until recently, a remarkably productive body of water. However, over-harvesting has depleted the supply of fish and green sea turtles, once a mainstay in the Seris' diet. Destruction of wetlands, mostly through construction of dams on the Colorado River and other Sonoran and Sinaloan rivers has eliminated prime habitat for fish and other wildlife. Years ago I'd ride out in Seri fishing boats and watch men snag a few fish for supper. On more serious trips they'd land hundreds of pounds of huge fish. That seldom happens now. The big ones are gone.

Mexico is learning what the United States has learned, that the price paid for building dams is always higher than the contractor's bid. Mexico's more modern farms, irrigated with impounded waters, apply agricultural chemicals that are highly restricted or forbidden in the United States and whose residues wind up in the Sea of Cortés. The long-term effects on wildlife are discouraging, and the specter of a Sea of Cortés becoming a watery desert is no environmentalists' poppycock. Controversial plans for expanding resorts in San Carlos and Kino Bay, if executed, will destroy additional estuaries that are the basis for the marine food chain. Fortunately, Mexican ecologists are raising the right kind of clamor.

The Seris are a boundlessly resourceful people. Psychologically they're still hunters and gatherers, and their ability to adapt to new conditions is admirable. I've spent twenty-five years among them and continue to be amazed at their ability to absorb some changes in the world and reject others. Their culture and language are strong, their spirit is unbroken, and their enthusiasm for life is unaffected. Young women still paint their faces on special occasions, fiestas still feature *pascola* dancers, and the people still have an uncanny knowledge of desert plants and creatures. Still highly conscious of being *congcaac*, as they refer to themselves, they prefer to associate with other Seris and express a desire to have their lands free of outsiders. Another Seri friend commented on a robbery that occurred in the desert not far south of Desemboque. "I'm leaving here, David," he said emphatically, chipping away with a machete at a block of ironwood.

"Why would you want to leave?" I asked him, puzzled by his remark.

"Too many *guachos;* too many *yoris* (Mexicans). It's not safe here any more. We need to get the *yoris* out of here."

In early 1994 Mexican squatters began invading the Seri *ejidos* with their cows. As of this writing the government refused to take action against the invaders. Bulldozers also began leveling hills and putting in roads at the south end of the Seris' lands. A seaside resort and "recreational community" are scheduled for construction.

During the Chiapas uprising of 1994 the Mexican government stationed troops in the Seri lands—a precautionary measure, I was told.

CHAPTER 19

The Boojum Forest

The boojum tree: Seris avoid it, cows ignore it, and botanists ogle over it. Wind and drought don't faze it. It is weird, bizarre, scrubby, contorted, irreverent, disrespectful, defiant, and outrageous. It is enchanting and a marvel to behold. How to describe it? Try inverting a thin parsnip and sticking toothpicks up and down the stem. Then magnify it a hundred or two hundred times. Now imagine it bent, twisted, split and deformed. That's a boojum.

Fouquieria columnaris is its scientific name. Mexicans call it the *cirio* (taper candle)—not a bad comparison. One botanist has called it the most unusual plant in the world, a point hard to argue. The most undebatable thing one can say about the boojum is simply that there is no other plant like it. Taxonomists classify it as a relative of the ocotillo, but the two plants are so different, their kinship is barely recognizable at first. The tallest is taller than a tall pine, but few aspire to such heights, each preferring instead to plod through the ages with individuality.

The name *boojum* seems appropriate, and we know exactly how it came about. In 1922 Godfrey Sykes, explorer, astronomer, and naturalist, was standing in the Sierra Bacha in Sonora, looking through a telescope in the company of a group of scientists in quest of the *Fouquieria*. According to his son, he spied one and exclaimed, quoting Lewis Carroll, "Ho, ho, a boojum, definitely a boojum." Thus, the plant was named.

There are millions of the strange trees in Baja California. Robert Humphrey, "Boojum Bob" as he is often known, has measured the tallest boojum there at eighty-one feet in 1990. The plants are far less common in Sonora, where they grow only in a narrow belt of desert mountains between El Desemboque del Río San Ignacio and Puerto Libertad. They also grow smaller and in less profusion in Sonora than in Baja, but they're still big and plentiful enough to be wildly impressive. Not long ago I slept next to one that was about thirty feet high and a good two feet in diameter near the base. Boojums are also very, very old. Studies by Ray Turner and the late Rodney Hastings indicate a maximum age of boojums of between seven hundred and eight hundred years, three times the age of a saguaro cactus! Their longevity shouldn't surprise us, for up close the boojums exhibit a decidedly ancient look. They also exude a certain, well, *wisdom*.

I had seen a lot of photographs of boojums, but I was not prepared for the actual experience of seeing one up close back in 1972. A friend had described how to get to where they grow, and my family and I set off across the rocky scrub desert in search of the mythical plant. The trip required a ride by Jeep from the Seri Indian village of Desemboque where I had been visiting the Indians, followed by a hike of a mile or so. I was prepared to see a large plant even in this dry desert. Good-sized desert trees abound. However, I wasn't prepared for the shape. Neither was my son Chris, seven years old at the time, who giggled when the first boojum came into view.

Up close it was just as strange as from a distance. Twenty feet tall, it grew on a steep slope facing slightly north. For all its appearance it could be an unidentified flying object come to root in the earth. Thick, sharp thorns protruded from the sides, protecting the greenish-gray bark. Short, spine-covered branches seldom more than a foot long, jutted from the trunk all the way up. The spring rains had been generous, so it was covered with a profusion of bright green leaves. It split near the top into three branches that pointed vaguely heavenward in three different directions as if unable to make up its mind which way was really up. The shimmering Sea of Cortés in the background made it look even more exotic.

We spent an hour or so ogling the unearthly creatures, then bounced our way back to the Seri village. Odd, I thought, but the Indians, usually bubbling with information about the desert, showed no interest in discussing the *cirio*. Even more remarkable was the fact that few of them had ever been near a boojum, despite their uncanny familiarity with almost every other plant in their environment. Seris would hike for miles in the burning desert to gather special plants. I was routinely astonished at the sophistication of their knowledge of their environment. They know and use at least some part of every large plant, except the boojum, that is. They'll have nothing to do with them. Oh, well, we had plenty of other things to talk about, and I forgot the subject.

It was years later that I learned from an ancient Seri man that the people view the boojum as a plant of great power. In fact, boojums once were giants, they say, who fled northward from Seri country to escape a flood. It caught up with them where the boojums are now found and transformed them. Short, fat boojums were females, tall ones were men. Only ten years ago an old Seri man warned me, his rugged lined face a study in seriousness, that if you harm a boojum in any way, a great destructive wind will spring up. A bold Seri once took me and a friend by boat to where a grove hung onto steep, rocky slopes above the ocean. He examined it as a surgeon looks over someone else's incision and left only when his comrades whistled from below that a fierce wind was springing up. Before long, six-foot waves were slapping at the plank boat. We barely made it back to the village.

It's no wonder the Seris viewed the boojum with skepticism and distrust. The plant has an air of mystery about it, and there are mysteries that surround its behavior. It transplants well and grows throughout the Sonoran Desert, even in Arizona, but it resists reproducing its kind away from its home in the Sierra Bacha. One growing in my yard in Tucson is more than fifty years old, but sterile. Nearby in the tiny cactus garden on the mall of the University of Arizona, three individuals more than fifteen feet tall seem to prosper, but nary a baby is to be found. They're sterile, too.

Humphrey has given a lot of thought to the Sonora population of boojums. They grow in that narrow, mountainous belt scarcely thirty miles long and three miles wide, he theorizes, because once, eons ago, an intense hurricane blew across Baja California during the time when the boojums were flowering. Powerful winds carried the light seeds clear across the Sea of Cortés, which, at that point, is more than eighty miles wide. That same storm moistened the soil in the Sierra Bacha, providing ideal conditions for the seeds to germinate. Subsequent rains nurtured the seedlings, allowing them to become permanently established. It was a one-shot deal, he thinks—a combination of events that occurs once in a score of millennia and hasn't occurred since.

If anyone should know, Bob Humphrey should. He's made a career out of studying boojums. However, he acknowledges that he can't explain why the boojum won't migrate to other ranges. They won't grow on their own anywhere else on the mainland. To the south the mountains receive slightly more moisture, frosts are fewer, and growing conditions are kinder, but boojums will not reproduce there.

Studies by Ray Turner and Tony Burgess of the United States Geological Service have shed light on the boojum's finicky behavior. At the Desert Laboratory in Tucson, Tony described for me what they'd found. In addition to boojums, at least ten plants in the Sierra Bacha are more typical of Baja California than of Sonora. Furthermore, they observed, the Baja boojums never grow close to the Gulf coast of the Sea of Cortés, suggesting they need the influence of the Pacific to survive. An oceanographer perchance mentioned to Tony that not far from the shore where the Sierra Bacha meets the Gulf, deep waters well to the surface, producing local climatic conditions typical of the Pacific side of Baja California, so just the Sierra Bacha has an environment more like the Pacific than the Sea of Cortés. As Tony says, this small mountain range has been preserving a host of plants on the Sonoran mainland since the retreat of the last glacier, ten thousand years ago. When the next one comes, in a few thousand years, those plants will be there, ready once again to expand and populate the earth!

In 1988 a Seri youth told me he had found a cave in nearby mountains with paintings inside it. Within a couple of weeks my wife Lynn and I and another friend had my dear Seri buddy Santiago Astorga as a guide along with his twelve-year-old son, Santiaguito. Santiago is tall and lean, as are most Seri men, with sharp, insightful eyes and a gentle handshake. In my Volkswagen bus we parked as close to the mountain as we could and walked the rest of the way, a good four miles in each direction. The day started off cool but got warm fast. At first we plodded across smooth desert pavement, but as we approached the mountains the going got rough. When we arrived where the boojums grow, we had to duck under brush, push through thorny ironwoods and acacias, hop jagged boulders, and dodge myriad cacti. *Chollas*, especially, seemed to lie in wait for a chance to spear us with their needle-sharp spines mounted in detachable balls, which for all practical purposes spring up from the ground at the passer-by and lodge in the skin, a garment or the shoes.

Then the going got steep. We crawled up a loose slope of talus on hands and feet, then scrambled up boulders and solid rock, our way always made slower by thickets of thorny scrub and cactus. Finally we arrived at the top, a thousand feet above the Sea of Cortés. A small cave lay in front of us. Inside, several faint but definite designs had been daintily painted on the rock face. Santiago had no idea how old they were, but I saw a close resemblance to paintings made in the Sierra Libre, more than a hundred miles away, while the Seris were holed up there in the eighteenth century.

It was time to go back. Santiago and his son drank water, the first they had consumed since we left the vehicle. The three of us had drunk up a couple of canteens, but Santiago told us Seris don't drink much during a hike. We slid and tumbled down the mountain, marveling at the boojums in full leaf after heavy spring rains. Santiaguito kept up bravely all the way back, not complaining, even though a *cholla* stuck to his foot. The desert was downright hot by the time we got back to the *bajada*, the flat slope we had to pass over for a couple of miles before we reached the Volkswagen and snatched up the beer we had stowed away for the occasion. We congratulated ourselves for a successful expedition and congratulated Santiaguito as well. He had made the entire hike, ten miles of punishing, hot desert, crossing sharp stones, burning sand, thorns, cacti, punishing rock—barefooted.

Recently squatters have moved into the Sierra Bacha where the boojums grow. Fuelwood cutting has begun, and burros have been released to fend for themselves. They are hardier than cows and can survive in desert landscapes, climbing steep peaks to nibble at forage. They are also fiendishly destructive of native plants. The slopes of the Sierra Bacha and the delicate habitats of the boojum are, for the first time, experiencing the gnawing of the burro. The trampling of burro hoofs, their removal of vegetation on the steep slopes, and their indefatigable appetites portend an end to the pristine beauty of the Sierra Bacha. Gully cutting, erosion, and a decrease in plant and animal life are not far behind.

CHAPTER 20

Yaquis

The Seris know Yaquis well. They still purchase dance parapher-
nalia from them. Far back in history they fought against each
other. In other battles they fought on the same side. Sonora's
most important river is appropriately named after its most important indigenous people. The headwaters of the vast and complicated Yaqui River include tributaries in southeastern Arizona
and southwestern New Mexico. Most of the flow originates in
remote Sierra Madre canyons in Chihuahua. Sonoran geogra-
phers pronounce the river to be 858 kilometers (535 miles) long.

A few years ago I camped for an evening at the artesian ponds
of the Slaughter Ranch in southeastern Arizona. It dawned on
me then that if I were to spill a bottle of ink into those ponds
east of Douglas, the dark liquid would soon enter the San
Bernardino Creek, empty into the Bavispe River, pass through a
dam, join the Yaqui, pass through another dam, stain the homelands of Opata and Pima Bajo Indians, pass through yet another
reservoir and dam, and dye some silt in Yaqui lands before tint-
ing the sands of the Sea of Cortés.

Other tributaries of the Yaqui are longer than the Bavispe. In
Chihuahua, far from the Sea of Cortés, rains and melting snows
of the deep Sierra Madre trickle into rivulets that form a thousand streams pouring into the Río Papagóchic. It meanders
through deep canyons, past cliff dwellings abandoned a thousand
years ago, along *milpas* (cornfields), tilled for centuries, first by
man alone, then by ox, then by horse or mule, until it empties
into the wild and rugged Río Aros. Winding its way northwest,
this river cuts through rock and sand in tortured gorges till it
merges with the Bavispe to form the Río Yaqui and the new
river, too, is tamed by a dam.

On the Río Yaqui Spanish conquerors met their first stout,
organized resistance and their northward advance was held up
until the Yaquis requested and received missionaries. Along the

river's tributary waters lived Yaquis in the lower portion, Pima Bajos in the middle portion, Opatas in the northern portion, and Tarahumaras in the far eastern tributaries. Two hundred years ago Apaches roamed the northern headwaters as well.

The most significant dynamic in the history of Sonora has been the struggle over control of Yaqui water and Yaqui lands, a conflict that was already ancient when the Spaniards arrived. The Yaquis' historic position concerning their lands has been, and continues to be, that the river valley was for the Yaqui and no one else. Yaquis occupied the lower fifty miles of the river, the delta portion with deep, rich soils and a reliable water supply. Their fierce determination to protect their lands against usurpers led to bloody warfare, which continued into this century. Yaquis fought against Mayos, Pimas, Opatas, Spaniards, and Mexicans. They sided with the Maximillian regime during the occupation of the 1860s, believing the French would honor their historic land claims. They resisted Mexican plans to tax their lands and later schemes to divide them up among *latifundistas* (wealthy land barons) and, finally, to divide the lands and parcel them out among individual Yaquis, steadfastly maintaining that *"Dios nos dió a todos la tierra y no un pedazo a cada uno."* (God gave the land to all and not a piece to each.) This was the Yaquis' position three hundred years ago, and it continues unchanged into the twentieth century. When uprisings have occurred, the Yaquis' demands have been simple: a free Yaqui River and non-Yaquis off their lands. Yaquis to this day define their lands by a series of landmarks, desert hills, sharp peaks, arroyos, simple crosses imbedded in the earth. Their fear of losing lands is as real today as it was three centuries ago, and their vows to protect it are just as uncompromising. Recently I received an urgent message from Sonoran Yaquis: Mexican drug lords, with support from the government, were terrorizing Yaquis, taking over their fields to raise marijuana. "Please, David, help us" was the request. I made phone calls to the few contacts I had and could only hope they would have an effect.

Yaqui *barrios* in Tucson, South Tucson, Marana and Guadalupe, all in Arizona, testify to the land battles in the early twentieth century. Yaquis fled to the United States during the rule of Porfirio Díaz and later fled from his successors. They sought refuge from political and economic persecution, whether in the form of forced relocation and enslavement on plantations in distant southeastern Mexico, or death at the hands of the dictator or his allies in Sonora. Yaquis are now settled in the United States, some living on their own reservation. Most live in old *barrios*, still carrying on the ancient ceremonials, working at menial jobs on the margin of our affluent society. For the older Yaquis in Tucson the *diaspora* is still a reality. "David," an old leader told me as he sat in the shade of a ramada on Tucson's north side, "I just want to go back and live on the Río Yaqui." The promised land still beckons.

In spite of the ongoing historical persecution of Yaquis, Sonorans today honor them, at least officially. A Yaqui deer dancer is the official state symbol and imitation dancers are found in festivals throughout the state. Indeed, Sonorans are proud of the numerous *Cahita* (Yaqui and Mayo) terms in their vocabulary. Some authorities claim Cahitas are descendants of Aztecs. Historian Fortunato Hernández says the Cahitans derive from the Toltecs. Others currently favor a theory that they are a mixture of Toltec and Chichimeca with a trace of Aztec. While these are undoubtedly romantic fictions, their existence shows that some historians hope to aggrandize Sonoran aboriginals by linking them to the heroic civilizations of Middle America. The great leader and military commander of the uprising of 1886, José María Leyva, better known as Cajeme, is now a state hero, in spite of the savage Sonoran campaign to defeat his Yaqui forces. The government forces won. Cajeme was executed. The man who directed Cajeme's execution, future Governor Ramón Corral, wrote a flattering book about him.

The waters of the Yaqui are the lifeblood of the Yaqui lands. In the early 1940s the dam on the Río Bavispe far upstream at Angostura was completed, regulating the river's flow and forcing the Yaquis into accepting irrigation waters on a schedule determined by non-Yaquis. If any one incident sealed the Yaquis' fate, it was the completion of the dam. The addition of dams at Novillo and Oviáchi have further forced the Yaquis into the grasp of "modern" agriculture. Yaquis now occupy the only official Indian reservation in all of Mexico, on the north bank of the Río Yaqui. Their eight towns, part of Yaqui legendry, endure through the eroding influence of mass culture. The lower Yaqui Valley is one of the most densely populated areas in northwest Mexico.

A few miles south of the ancient bed of the Río Yaqui a gigantic aqueduct directs the bountiful waters of Sonora's most important river east and south to fields of astonishing productivity owned by men of astonishing affluence who became rich through astonishing circumstances. Nearby, to the north, a far smaller ditch conducts irrigation water in the opposite direction to Yaqui farmlands. Thus reads the current history of the Yaqui people. They live on the north bank. The wealth of the south bank is derived from what belonged to Yaquis and from water derived from the declining eastern part of the state.

Just above where the Río Yaqui enters its delta, it has been dammed again, this time at a place called Oviáchi. From this huge reservoir the Yaqui's waters are diverted, to be deposited on the vast fields of the lower Yaqui Valley. The great city of Cajeme, now known as Ciudad Obregón, nearly as large as Hermosillo, rose from the plain, built on wealth wrested from former Yaqui land to become Sonora's most affluent city. In the fields surrounding this metropolis, Norman Borlaug, funded by the Rockefeller Foundation, experimented with newly developed strains of hybrid wheats, intensely responsive to fertilizer and high-tech farming methods.

The successes were breathtaking and thus was born the Green Revolution. Average yields of wheat grew from 750 kilograms per hectare (about 700 pounds per acre) in the 1940s to nearly four tons per hectare (about 3,000 pounds per acre) in 1980. As dramatic as these improvements have been, the benefits have been bestowed upon a relatively small group of affluent, private planters, for only they have had the resources, the credit, and the political influence to install the sophisticated irrigation and land management equipment necessary to take advantage of the modern plant varieties of the Green Revolution. For the most part, the small producers and the *ejidos* (and Yaquis), their crop yields being far smaller, remain impoverished.

Ciudad Obregón is new, wealthy, cosmopolitan, and modern. Its streets are paved, its residents well dressed, and its homes modern. Some are mansions designed by Mexico's most distinguished architects. The Yaquis live in poor, dusty, quiet villages mainly on the north and west bank of the river, little changed in two hundred years. An open sewer brings the rank discharge of affluent Obregónenses close by Yaqui homes on the way to discharging into a Yaqui bay.

Eight towns form the center of Yaqui culture. The people are clearly Indian. The villages are made up of homes built in classic Yaqui wattle-and-daub construction with a *ramada* built outside. Each village has a church that becomes the focus of all Yaqui life during Holy Week.

Pótam is one of the villages. It was originally a port when the waters of the Yaqui were high enough to admit ships of low portage. Since then it has become a large town of crowded Yaqui homes where ancient traditions hang on but seem doomed by the forces of acculturation and impoverishment. It is not much different from other Yaqui towns—Vícam, Tórim, Huírivis, Bacum, Cócorit, Raum. In all of them some Yaquis fiercely hang on to their proud tradition, while all around the silent forces of absorption into the international economy and its grinding uniformity slowly wear down their resistance.

The ancient brick church, massive but poor, rising from a barren plot of land, was empty inside as I stood in the apse. There are no pews and no softening altar decorations. Outside a sea of white crosses fills the cemetery that nearly surrounds the church. It's a hundred yards to the nearest house, a vast, open, lifeless desert separating church and people. At Easter, though, the whole place comes alive. Yaquis decorate it. They bring palms, cottonwood branches, and flowers. Deer dancers, *pascolas, matachines,* coyote dancers perform all night and all day, on Maundy Thursday, Good Friday, and Holy Saturday. The many dancers still express the strength of the Yaqui people; Yaquis from as far away as Chicago come to watch and participate, to renew their Yaquiness. The Yaqui language predominates. However, television, the great equalizer, informer, and destroyer, has come to the pueblos, and their demise as places of Yaqui nationalism can only be a matter of time.

CHAPTER 21

Of Firewood and Dust

Pitiquito, on the Río de la Concepción, and a two-hour drive
from Nogales, is a gateway of sorts to thorny desert scrub covering a thousand square miles of land to the south of Mexico
Route 2. I passed through the town many dozens of times heading south or north to and from the Seri village of Desemboque.
One cool Sunday afternoon as I was passing through, when the
rest of the world lay torpid, I heard music blasting out of the
cantina in an old adobe row house. I experienced a sudden thirst
and soon was pushing my way through the double doors. I sat
down at the bar self-consciously and in a low voice ordered a
beer, painfully aware that no matter how inconspicuous I try to
be, wherever I go in Mexico I look, walk, and move like a gringo.
The room was dark, and I could barely make out the couples
dancing to the *ranchera* music. Somebody went to the jukebox and
summoned up a *tapatía*. By now my eyes were accustomed to the
dark. I leaned over the bar, pulled on my beer, then gripped it
tightly. The couples were men dancing with each other. This was
not a gay bar. These were healthy, lusty, inebriated males, mostly
cowboys from poor ranches to the south, in a bar where women
never came, feeling a need to dance and stomp around with whoever happened to be there. One glared at me. "*Gringo,*" he
sneered. I left the rest of my beer on the counter and was gone.

Pitiquito is a streamside oasis, a sunburned northern outpost
of some tough desert scrublands. South of the old, tired town
of five hundred, a mean dirt road penetrates the rough arid cattle country of the Santa Rosa Mountains, winding over hills of
exposed limestone that cannot be graded and will never be sur-
faced. That rock eats at tires the way a butcher tenderizes meat.
The road goes south for a hundred miles till it runs into the Sea
of Cortés, passing through a half-dozen ranch headquarters before it arrives at the Gulf.

This hilly, seemingly endless scrub desert is crisscrossed with woodcutters' roads. Since most poor families in Sonora cook exclusively with wood, Sonora has an army of woodcutters. Wherever firewood is more than a few minutes' walk from the house, they will have a market. From horse-drawn carts to big cattle trucks, vehicles are pressed into service to provide fuel for the ever-growing *barrios* of the cities. On highways near the larger cities the large trucks appear every day, crammed with wood the thickness of an arm, cut into two-foot lengths. The woodcutters have developed to perfection the art of stacking firewood so as not to lose any space.

Almost anywhere within thirty miles of a city, the woodcutters will have lopped off every available dead branch. Sometimes they even cut down live trees. Mesquite is the preferred wood nearly everywhere, but in northern Sonora ironwood is highly touted. While mesquite grows quite rapidly, ironwood is a slow grower, so supplies of it for firewood are more limited. It's almost impossible in the scrub of Pitiquito to find an ironwood tree that has not been hacked for firewood. Ranchers everywhere place locks on their gates to keep out woodcutters and rustlers. I must confess that I'm mystified by the continuing ability of woodcutters to locate new sources of firewood. In some cases they've cut down vast groves of mesquite, but usually the cutting was done as preparation for leveling and planting.

The woodcutters develop routes where they sell to customers almost as newspaper deliverers have fixed routes in the United States. They drive through neighborhoods selling one stick or ten. The *barrios* come to rely on the woodcutters, without whom they could have no cooked food.

In recent years woodcutters have established more or less permanent charcoal-manufacturing sites. Charcoal is more compact, lighter, and easier to transport than wood. It is the cooking source for the many hundreds of *taquerías* (taco stands) in Sonora. Tens of thousands of sacks are also exported to the United States. The charcoal manufactures have prospered with the proliferation of pasture clearing for buffelgrass planting. Bulldozers pile up serpentine mounds of uprooted trees. The woodcutters scavenge the mounds, called *chorizos* (sausages), for all available fodder for the charcoal pits. The sale of the charcoal often more than offsets the cost of the *desmonte* (the clearing of the vegetative cover). Buffelgrass expansion has spawned a prosperous charcoal industry in the same way the slaughter of bison on the Great Plains produced a short-lived slug of buffalo robes.

When I first visited Mexico in 1961, I would smell mesquite cooking fires before anything else in each Sonoran town. I could tell by the scent of the air when I was near a town. This has changed somewhat, for the areas through which the paved roads now pass are more affluent and most of the kitchens along those routes have gas cooking stoves. Away from the highways in the poorer neighborhoods, however, the sweet, nostalgic aroma is still there.

I've found woodcutters to be resourceful and helpful fellows. More than once when I've been hopelessly lost without a soul in sight for miles, a woodcutter has appeared on the scene and helped me locate the place in question. I came to rely on them greatly, preferring not to stop in some towns to ask for information. Bámori was one of those places I'd always avoided.

Bámori, a gathering of dying huts, is south of Pitiquito, a large open space of pounded, muddy clay in the rainy season and clouds of powdery dust in the dry. It's a tiny farming oasis, a huge, ancient stock tank that plugs a spring and irrigates a few pastures and corn fields. The erosion of the heavy soil is as bad as any I've seen in Sonora. I stopped here one day and knocked on the warped sagging door of an ancient melting adobe, intending to ask directions. A mangy cur of a dog ran out and sank its fangs into my leg. The owner appeared behind. He was a sallow, thin man with a filthy shirt and three days growth of beard. He said nothing to the dog. Rubbing my bleeding leg, I asked him about the road. His reply was an angry mumble that set the dog to growling again. With no sign of a woman anywhere, I backed away from the door, nursing my wound. I never stopped at Bámori again. I'd stick to woodcutters for guidance.

I drove thirteen grueling miles to the southeast, across ancient lake beds lined with a clay that makes a superfine dust capable of flowing into ruts like water and making a dust cloud that clings and lingers for hours. At the end of that ordeal sits an odd hamlet called La Ciénega where artesian springs feed a tiny pond, a centuries-old oasis. A derelict mining operation still extracts lead in dwindling amounts. Fewer folks live here now than twenty years ago. It's hours away from the nearest electricity, from any refuge in blistering heat in the summer. Two hundred years ago seven thousand people crammed the area as *gambusinos* (prospectors) grubbed for gold in the mining city of Cieneguilla. In 1969 I counted eight families in the village, two tiny stores, a bakery and tortilla store, and a fellow who sold gasoline from barrels. Twenty years later most had gone; there was no way to scratch a living from that place. It's the same all over Sonora. Tiny rural desert towns depopulate as the cities explode.

Over a period of several years in the late 1960s, I came to know some cowboys who lived in isolated ranches in the rolling desert country south of Pitiquito. They were humble, polite men, asking me how my family was if I didn't happen to have them along. I feared to ask how their families were, so desperate was their poverty. Their job was to manage cows for absentee landlords who lived in Caborca and Hermosillo. As time passed and overgrazing caused range conditions to deteriorate, I could see the cowboys getting poorer and poorer. One by one the adobe ranch buildings, already scores of years old, were abandoned.

The last time I visited the area, around 1980, most of the homes were empty, the windows broken, doors caved in, adobes dissolving under the elements. It's the same at La Ciénega, a microcosm of the fate of much of rural Sonora as overexploitation takes its toll. The cowboys do their best, and quiet heroes they are, seeming to be thinner each time I saw them, but they cannot do the impossible, cannot squeeze increasing profits from deserts when nature refuses to tolerate the burden placed on the lands.

The woodcutters (often a father accompanied by his sons) pick over even these abused lands. The penetrating dust covers them as they drive along, hoping to spot a dead tree or enough dead limbs to make cutting worthwhile. When rains come, they may become hopelessly mired in mud and be forced to wait, often with limited food, until the road dries out enough for them to make it back to the nearest highway. Even worse, the weight of the wood (ironwood is the heaviest wood in the region) often leads to tire punctures. Changing a tire on a heavily loaded wood truck is no picnic, and since the spare is usually as bad as the punctured tire, getting back home may take far more time than anticipated.

The woodcutters are a hardy lot. Often they'll camp in abandoned ranch buildings overnight. Theirs is hard, dangerous work, physically exhausting and only meagerly profitable. Without them urban riots would surely erupt, but as easily harvestable wood becomes scarce and the cutters are forced to drive farther and farther from the towns, invariably escalating the price, the cost of cooking rises. At some point the government will have to intervene. Otherwise, Mexico will find half her population without the means to cook. Raw beans and corn are decidedly unpalatable.

CHAPTER 22

Lumber Country

Another kind of woodcutter struggles with the earth to the east
and south of Nácori Chico in a rugged semi-wilderness inhabited by only a few ranches and numerous cattle. This is the hard-
core Sierra Madre, where roads are mere trails and speeds over
ten miles per hour are usually excessive. The roadway rises
abruptly to the crest of a ridge in the thornscrub east of Nácori
Chico, then plunges precipitously to a crystal-clear stream in the
bottom of a deep canyon only to rise once again out of the
canyon. The white gash of the road against the blue backdrop of
a peak towering far to the east marks the route. Up, up, up the
rocky trail rises from 3,500 feet elevation to 8,000 feet in the
space of ten miles, finally creeping over the top. On the way
scrub growth of mesquite, organ pipe and *mauto* gave way to oak,
yucca, and agaves and then to a thick coniferous forest of pon-
derosa, Apache, Chihuahua, and white pines, and Douglas fir, or
at least what was a thick forest until the tree fellers got to it.
This line of high mountains extends almost unbroken from the
United States border to the Mexican state of Nayarit and is the
source of most of Mexico's timber. In two hours' time I encountered only one vehicle, a pickup.

In the high mountains old, ponderous lumber trucks are the
biggest users of the roads, rumbling monsters piled dangerously
high with logs. The drivers cut and load felled pines and haul
them to the high town of Mesa Tres Ríos, thirty miles and three
and a half hours northeast of Nácori Chico.

Virgil Hancock, a Tucson psychiatrist and photographer, was
with me the first time I entered the village and breathed the
crisp, cold mountain air scented with pine smoke. The town
spreads out over a broad area on a rolling plateau, still forested
except where fields have been cleared for crops—corn and potatoes. No power lines enter the town, yet here and there are
houses sprouting television antennae. Later we found the entire

community has a satellite dish operated by solar power and the individual sets are powered by car batteries! The houses are separated and spread out, unlike the valley towns. Some are built of wood, some of adobe, and some of dressed stone, still bearing the shake roofs that once made mountain villages so picturesque. For the most part the dwellings are new, built for lumber mill workers.

The industry in Mesa Tres Ríos, apart from the subsistence farming of the five hundred or so inhabitants, is a cooperatively owned sawmill. The cooperative's treasurer is a man named Miguel García. A large, friendly fellow with smiling eyes, he occupies the office at the entrance to the mill. On the wall was a poster of Carlos Salinas de Gortari, then president of Mexico. When I asked Miguel if we might visit the mill and take pictures, he smiled broadly, saying, "You take all the pictures you want of those monkeys down there!"

He told me that the mill employs thirty-eight men, including the truck drivers and tree fellers. The cooperative owns the mill and the trucks. The drivers unload their cargo of twelve to fifteen logs into a pile. Six men work outside using long hooks to feed the logs into the hopper of the diesel-powered mill housed in a building about a hundred feet long. Inside, an operator sits on a sled, operating the controls that move the vehicle's massive blade back and forth, slicing the logs into boards with a high-pitched *"yeeeeeee."* The cut logs are fed into a jointer by other workers, and the resulting wood is tolerably smooth. Other workers sort the cut boards into stacks of similar sizes and carry out the waste wood, which is piled and burned during the rainy season to protect against forest fires. Still others load the stacks carefully onto the trucks that once or twice a day carry a huge load of cut lumber eastward to Chihuahua.

I sat on a log and watched the operation, while Virgil photographed it, much to the glee of the workers. One of them sitting next to me, safely out of the range of Virgil's lens, told me the work is dangerous but good. He had a large scar on his forehead and chain smoked as we watched the saw operator swing back and forth in the sled. The problem, as he saw it, was that there was nothing to do in winter when deep snows cover the logging roads and during periods of heavy rain when some roads are washed out and mud clogs others.

"What *do* you do in the winter, then?" I asked him.

He thought for a moment. "Eat and sleep, and . . . ," he said, with a sly look on his face.

The wood goes to Chihuahua, he reported. The road to Sonora is too steep and the cities too distant for the markets they need. Some of the wood is made into furniture and some is shipped directly to the United States.

Logging practices in the Sierra Madre have increasingly been the subject of public discussion. According to a young, knowledgeable forester, a clean-shaven, earnest fellow I spoke with, reforestation efforts to date have been minimal, although the government hopes to change that rapidly. He ticks off forest facts: The Sierras have twelve species of pine and thirty species of oak identified so far. Regulations limit logging to pines in excess of thirty centimeters in diameter, but he conceded sadly that the rule is not enforced. The government hopes to thin the oak forests that have taken over since the initial removal of pines by making the oak available for fuel, always in a chronic shortage in the cities. Once the oaks are thinned, they hope to plant a desirable mix of species, leading to a mixed ecosystem. Clear-cutting is out, he said, proudly. Unlike the United States where as much as eighty percent of vegetation in an area may be removed, they intend to limit removal to twenty percent and monitor revegetation carefully.

At least that's the government's line. The forest lands owned by *ejidos* are being denuded as quickly as any other. Most *ejidos* are starved for cash and each tree they fell will bring a few dollars. The ground will produce more grass without trees, they say, and more grass means more cows and more bucks. The young forester's claims were based upon some lofty ideal. The reality was grim.

The forests are vanishing, and even though the destruction wrought by logging does not appear as bad as that I have seen in national forests in the United States, environmentalists on both sides of the border have sounded alarms. Some areas have become reforested, others remain devoid of pines fifty years later. The absence of expensive heavy equipment like bulldozers prevents the creation of wastelands such as the clear-cut areas in western United States forests. Logging is often still carried on by cross-cut saws and mules. The local men who cut the logs seem to recognize that removing all the trees will leave them with no future. Even so, the logging goes far faster than nature can produce new trees. Logging roads are everywhere. Areas where pine forests once whispered in the breeze now support dense stands of small and medium-sized oaks and alligator junipers—or nothing at all.

The lumberjacks raise much of their own food, growing potatoes, beans, and corn in the high, rocky fields around Mesa Tres Ríos, but all the cash they have is a result of their hard work. Were the timber harvesting to be curtailed or eliminated, they would have to find work elsewhere, probably in cities where the rate of unemployment is already high, and another small town would become depopulated. It probably will be, anyway, for the unspoken reality in Mesa Tres Ríos, according to a source in Hermosillo, is that in a few years all the harvestable pines will be gone. Sonora's timber industry is not of huge economic importance. According to government statistics the entire coniferous timber industry produced about three million dollars' worth of lumber in 1992. Nonetheless, in a nation plagued by heavy unemployment, the loss of one job is a tragedy.

While Virgil was photographing in Mesa Tres Ríos, his tripod standing in the middle of the local cemetery to get the best shot of the town, an older man walked by. He introduced himself. "Rafael Burgos, a sus órdenes." I did likewise. He was twice widowed, he said, his second wife's grave lying nearby where Virgil was photographing. He had stopped by the cemetery to visit her grave, as he does every day, inspecting the fence around the cemetery to insure that livestock don't trample the hallowed ground.

Rafael seemed delighted with the opportunity to chat with a gringo. He smiled broadly, showing off his only tooth, as he told me he was born and raised in Nácori Chico. He came to Mesa Tres Ríos forty two years ago, he informed me proudly, his grizzled stubbled face a study of delight. There were only eight houses then. Now there are a couple of hundred. Then there wasn't a road, only horse trails. He showed me a plant, a low-lying composite called *cuchaca*. He said that people all over México use the plant as an herbal cure. You boil it and drink it. What did they use it for? He wasn't quite sure; he just knew it worked.

Rafael is especially enthusiastic about the climate of Mesa Tres Ríos. At 6,800 feet there are four seasons. He lists them as if reciting a poem: the cold, the dry, *las aguas* (rains), and the pleasant weather. Cold, he says, is December through mid-April with snows deep enough to cover the mounded graves in the cemetery. Dry is mid-April to July when it is dusty and windy and the fire danger is high. (If ever there were a serious fire the entire town could be destroyed.) *Las aguas*, he says, is July, August, and September when the rains come. It rains every day, and the countryside turns lush and green and deliciously cool, but the roads are muddy. The pleasant weather is September through mid-November, sometimes later, when the days are warm but not hot and the evenings cool but not cold. He showed no desire to return to the *tierra caliente* that is Nácori Chico.

Rafael was fascinated by Virgil's large-format camera. "It looks like the old-time cameras," he said, and he was right. Many times Virgil drew laughs and excitement when he covered his head with a blanket to view his subject inverted in the large glass window of the camera. He always drew stares when he set up the huge camera in view of people. When we urged Rafael to take a look for himself, he found the view fascinating, although he was short enough that he had to totter on the top of his toes to see the upside-down, reversed view.

Following Rafael's advice, I decided to follow the road the lumber trucks take to the Chihuahuan frontier. It was only an hour, possibly less, to Rancho Tres Ríos, people told us, not far from the border. It's where the Río Bavispe is joined by two major tributaries, forming a deep and swift-moving river. I wanted to see it and the wooden bridge I'd heard about. The ranch lies 1,500 feet below the mesa, under ten miles away. A few miles to the east of it lies the Chihuahua border and the towering mountains deep inside the Sierra Madre. It's a six-hour drive to the other side, a rancher told us. He lives above the bridge and is caretaker for the ranch's owner who lives in Colónia Juárez in Chihuahua.

The bridge stands fifteen feet above the fast current of the river. On July 13, 1990, a flood covered the roadway, he related excitedly. How the bridge survived is a great mystery to me, although the piers are of concrete the superstructure is of wood. I walked across and found piles of jetsam still covering part of the plank roadway. I'd have let others go over the bridge ahead of me after that flood. Virgil took photos, I chatted with the rancher.

Ignacio was his name. He was a rugged, short man with bad teeth, and dirty tattered clothes. He'd been there thirteen years with his wife and some foster children. He punched cows, sheared sheep, did a little gardening, and I suspect kept an eye on who came by. He didn't mention drugs, but I felt that he took Virgil and me for drug agents of some sort. Sometimes four days went by without a single car passing, he said. In the height of timber season, however, a truck stacked way beyond capacity with cut lumber came by at least once a day and usually a couple of cattle trucks as well.

Ignacio was a nervous, multi-talented individual, touting his abilities at sheep shearing as well as punching cows. He often fished in the river, he said, and caught trout, catfish, and a special delicacy, blacbás (black bass). He had just finished shearing a sheep when Virgil and I arrived. From the looks of the bedraggled sheep, this talent will require perseverance and inspiration.

I waited for him to invite me into his house that sat on a knoll overlooking the river, but he made no move. Instead he poured forth his life history. Ignacio had been a Mormon at one time, he confided to me. "Lots of Mormons around Colonia Juárez. Oh," he paused, suddenly concerned. "Are you a Mormon?"

I could have had some fun by claiming to be LDS, but thought better of it.

"No, I'm not," I answered, laughing to calm his fear.

"Well, the Mormons came down to Mexico a hundred years ago to live where they could have more than one wife, but they don't do that anymore." His voice contained a note of regret, and he looked away toward the mountains. If his wife was in the house he kept her well hidden. All I caught a glimpse of was a fleeting face in a doorway. "Mormons don't practice polygamy any more," he reminded me.

"One woman's enough." I agreed.

"Do you have one?" he looked at me, skeptical. I assured him I did and was very much in love. In fact, I wished to hell that Lynn could have seen that beautiful river with me.

He didn't want to hear about my wife. "I've quit being a Mormon, David," he confessed, not at all sadly, looking off at the sparkling river. "You don't have to go to church to be religious, do you?" He looked at me expectantly. I mumbled something that sounded profound and backed out of that conversation as soon as I could. I'd seen the blue peaks of Chihuahua where Sonora's trees, now transformed into logs, disappear. It was time to go back.

CHAPTER 23

Land of Fires from Heaven and Hell

In Northwest Sonora, Pinacate Region, it's almost noon in early February. Virgil and I are alone. There is no one else for miles around. We trudge up the steep path, panting. Perhaps a hundred yards above is the top of the hill. From the base it looked like nothing more than a long, flat ridge, maybe an extended mesa, although such a uniform plane would be unusual in the tortured, convoluted land of lava flows, cones and hills, washes, and sand that we had bounced over to get here.

The climb is steep but not especially difficult, no more than ten minutes from Virgil's four-wheel-drive pickup, now looking like a Matchbox toy below. The only clue in the landscape that this is different from an ordinary hill is the grayish volcanic ash we're climbing on. It gives the hint that this particular hill does not have a routine, natural origin.

A last push and we're at the top, which is suddenly flat. We relax, both breathing hard. Virgil's face is flushed with sweat in spite of the chilly weather, a little redder, matching the color of his beard, which contrasts tastefully with the straw color of his hat. Another five steps and we both stop, left without words.

Before us yawns an immense crater. The sides are so steep it looks as though no one could possibly descend. On the bottom, saguaro cacti resemble green matchsticks. The view is dizzying, the hole immense and beckoning, the other side far enough away to appear hazy in the sharp wintry desert air. The floor appears to be of dirt and sand, strangely out of place, as though some mischievous demon packed a false bottom into the crater, and anyone who set foot on it would break through, fall another thousand feet, and be swallowed into the bowels of the earth. The ash rim slopes sharply down toward the bottom. A third of the way down the sides are of stratified, sheer rock—gray, red, purple, and white. Below that forbidding cliff, a steep layer of ash drops more gently to the crater floor. The whole thing looks so abrupt and slippery I wonder if it could be descended without rope.

This is Sykes Crater, just one of ten or so big craters plus many cinder cones that pock the twisted, tangled face of the desert in the Sierra Pinacate, southwest of where Sonora borders Organ Pipe Cactus National Monument in Arizona. Nowhere on earth is there a landscape quite like that displayed by the Pinacates. Rising from sea level at the nearby Sea of Cortés to nearly four thousand feet, this jumble of sandy desert and volcanic devastation packs lava flows, tubes, caves, craters, archaeological treasures, sand dunes, rare desert plants and animals, and scenery rugged beyond description into an area roughly twenty by thirty miles. The terrain is so rough and desolate that it suited NASA as a site to train the Apollo astronauts for walks on the moon. Some lava flows are so fresh they could have cooled off last year, although no one will give me an age of less than two thousand years for the youngest flow. Other flows are in excess of 200,000 years old. The place has been restless on and off (mostly off) for the last quarter of a million years at least.

Indians have frequented the area for millennia—perhaps as many as forty thousand years, according to archaeologist and Pinacate expert Julian Hayden. Julian's still tough in his eighties and happy to talk about the Pinacate and the moonshine he once got a hold of from eastern Sonora. *Sotol de víbora* it was called (rattlesnake hooch) because the Chinese gentleman who brewed the yucca-based firewater dropped a rattlesnake in the keg to give it a slightly rougher edge. "I just drank a couple of tablespoonsfull and damn if it didn't cause my finger and toes to go numb," he chuckles, his handlebar mustache twitching. Julian traipsed all over Sonora, devoting most of his spare time for a few decades to the Pinacate. "I've got tools—human tools with desert varnish on them dated forty thousand years," he says, his muscular, thin frame strong with conviction. "The academic archaeologists just can't fit my facts into their theories." Almost nobody else will give humans much more than eleven thousand years in the New World.

In February and March of 1991 a series of cyclonic storms, unusual for so late in the year, swung from Alaska down along the coast of Southern California and into Arizona and Sonora. None of them left huge amounts of rain, but the total amassed by all the storms was impressive. I camped alone in the Pinacates immediately after one of the soaking rains. The smells and sights of exuberant plants were incomparably fresh. At Crater Elegante the only sound to be heard was the occasional explosion of a bomb in the Barry Goldwater Bombing Range forty miles to the north. After that the silence was nearly absolute, the air clear, but misted with a dew that made the opposite rim of the crater appear to be miles away when it is actually less than one mile.

I drove from there to Cerro Colorado and hiked the easy climb into the bottom of the crater to stare in wonder at the oranges and reds that surround the observer for 360 degrees. Not a soul was to be seen from the rim, only the specks of buildings at a cinder mine four miles away in the lava flow.

Refreshed and excited by the rough majesty of the craters, I returned to my truck and took a short cut in the direction of the highway, wondering how I would describe what I had seen. After about half a mile, the road, smooth and fast on a bed of ashes, degenerated into two deep ruts filled with standing water. *Don't slow down,* I warned myself. *Keep your momentum going.* I tried, gunned the motor, steered frantically. Slowly, agonizingly, the truck lost speed and came to an excruciating, sloshing halt in a lake of mud and water the consistency of thick oil.

After an hour of sloshing around in the slimy clay, digging away at the sodden mass, trying to force branches of dead mesquite and creosote under the wheels to gain a little traction, I had gained about ten feet. The trough looked as though it went on forever.

I set off on foot for the distant mine, hugging the edge of a massive lava flow all the while. The towering, jumbled shapes of the lava were a powerful consolation, and I found myself actually enjoying the walk. It took better than an hour, half running, half walking, for me to reach the mine. The two gatekeepers at the mine were uninterested in my plight. They looked at the sky and at the ground, but not at me. They demanded more money than I had to drive me out to the highway. I had exactly seventeen dollars, and they wanted all of that to take me four miles. When I asked them to take me for less, they both rolled their eyes heavenward. I turned my back on that hope and set off walking the four miles to the black ribbon that curls across the desert.

At the highway I hitched a ride to Sonoyta with a wealthy

Mexican who eyed my muddy clothing with suspicion and disdain. He ordered me to lie down in the back of his pickup. "I go fast, fast," he said condescendingly and made the thirty-mile drive in less than twenty minutes. I prayed all the while and held on to a spare tire for dear life. In Sonoyta I hopped out of the pickup and hitch-hiked to the border. Four hours later a man named Henry Gray, from Ajo, Arizona, arrived at the border to give me a hand. Two hours after that I was back in my truck, heading for Sonoyta and the border. I wasn't ready to get stuck again.

Henry grew up in the Pinacates. He was born in Sonoyta, though he now lives in Ajo, Arizona. His wife is a descendant of the Celaya family that founded Sonoyta, and most of his life he has ranched in the Pinacate area. His brother still runs a few cows at Los Vidrios Ranch in the northeastern part of the range. I sat between him and his son, who also works for the county highway department. Henry drove carefully and at moderate speed, the heat of youth apparently defunct within him. When he was young, Henry recalls, his brother ran cattle all the way from the ranch to the Colorado River, a trip of more than a hundred miles. They planned the route carefully, so that each night they would camp at a *tinaja* (tank) or spring. But now there are too many fences, and, he says without bitterness, the country has become too dry to raise enough cows to make a living. "Used to be plenty of *galleta* grass, (a hardy perennial). Cows could live on that when everything else was gone. Now there's less *galleta* and not much else, either."

Henry turned off the highway and drove tranquilly south into the Pinacate. I pointed out Cerro Colorado. Had he been there? "Hell yes, when I was young." I urged him to take his son by to see it. The man was in his late twenties and hadn't been to any of the craters.

"It's only a quarter-mile detour." Take him to Elegante Crater, too," I urged. I pointed out the flat mesa that rimmed the gigantic hole. It was no more than a fifteen-minute ride. Henry nodded but wasn't impressed. He told me more stories, alternating between English and Spanish. One day when he was a teenager he walked from the ranch to the *tinaja de los papagos* (Papago Wells), a good thirty miles. The walk took him by numerous craters, cinder cones, lava flows, and mountains, he remembers.

At that time there was usually good water at the *tinajas*, but now it's become scummy and undrinkable.

Country's dryin' up," he said. Then he lapsed into Spanish to relate another story.

Henry and his son pulled my truck out from the muck in ten minutes. I sped out of the Pinacate, suggesting before we parted that he had ample time to take his son to see the craters. The desert was too beautiful not to spend just a little time there. When I got to the border an hour later, Henry was right behind me. I waved to him as he passed me.

As arid as the west side of the Pinacates may be, cattle nevertheless manage to survive. Veteran Pinacate watchers tell me numbers are increasing, even though it has been designated a Mexican national park. On the occasions when I visited the west-side craters, I checked in with the rancher whose cows nibble out a tough survival on the low grass and browse.

He's a cheerful, stocky fellow, only there part-time. His ranch house is, well, rustic—an ancient, listing trailer and a few walls of whatever was lying around. There are a few rusting truck frames, a broken windmill, fading equipment, peeling plywood, aging steel barrels, and dust a foot deep that becomes a clingy mud in the infrequent rains. The ranch has an air of poverty and drought, as though it had been transported from the Kansas dust bowl in the 1930s. "Make sure you go to the *tinajas de los papago*," he told me, leaning on his aging GMC pickup, "and see Mac-Dougal Crater while you're in the area." He stepped inside the rickety trailer.

A mile from the tanks a small herd of cows trotted by. I wondered if they were real or phantoms, wandering around in this fierce desert, but fresh dung proved they were real enough. Soon afterwards we found the tanks, huge hollows carved out of solid rock by the pounding action of water. The hollows held a couple of hundred thousand gallons of a green, viscous liquid. Probably it had once been water but had since been so nourished with cattle urine and feces that algae were staging a population explosion. No creature would want to drink from that glop. Early explorers had described the tanks as a dependable source of *fresh* water, but that was in the pre-cattle era.

On my return I stopped by to chat with the rancher. He held an axe in his hand. "How many cows did you see?" he asked.

"Eight, I think," I replied.

"Brangus or Zebu?"

I told him. "Are they yours?"

"They're mine," he smiled. Of course they were his. Nobody else runs cows in there, nobody. A quick calculation explains their existence: a cow on the hoof is worth about two hundred and fifty dollars. If he sells six a year, that's fifteen hundred dollars, a pretty good chunk of cash for a marginal farmer whose gross income probably doesn't exceed five thousand dollars. If he can manage to produce just a couple of cows more he may be able to buy that refrigerator. His cattle truck is pretty well worn, too. Was he bothered by the drug dealers who frequented the area during the drug season? No, he said, they don't bother him at all, not at all. They leave him alone. Maybe so, but stories abound about bullet-ridden bodies with bound hands found in the southwest Pinacate.

West of the Pinacates lies the Gran Desierto. This is hard-core, no-nonsense desert with active sand dunes, scorching temperatures, desiccating windstorms, alkali flats, and an almost total absence of water. It's seventeen hundred square miles of shifting sand, the largest dune field in the hemisphere. Temperatures in the summer exceed 125 degrees. The more gentle parts of the Sonoran Desert in which I grew up seem verdant and lush by comparison. The almost total absence of water, the ferocious, unceasing winds and the relentless march of sand make the Gran Desierto repel settlers. The area from the eastern Pinacates west to the Colorado River has the lowest population density in all of Mexico. Almost nobody can live there. Past attempts by the Mexican government to relocate landless peasants from the south into *ejidos* on the margins of the Gran Desierto have uniformly ended in failure as the relentless fire from heaven and dust from earth suck the spirit from even the most dedicated of wills. Maps and road signs mark former human habitations. "Ejido Benito Juárez" or "Ejido Miguel Alemán" are names the traveler sees on rusted, bent signs shot full of holes.

All that remain are the skeletons of rude huts, bits of faded plastic blown along the parched earth by unending burning winds, and an occasional rusted car or truck body half-buried in sand telling a grim story. When the government brags about land distribution, citing so-and-so millions of hectares made available, they don't mention that most of it was on lands as poor as these. I think of the abandoned *ejidos* and wonder what those poor *ejidatarios* would ever have done for a living.

In 1993 President Salinas de Gortari proclaimed the Pinacate and Gran Desierto protected areas, part of an international biological reserve. His edict came after many years of hard work by researchers from the Centro Ecológico in Hermosillo and from Mexico's National Autonomous University. The principal researcher for establishing the preserve was Dr. Alberto Búrquez, a Cambridge-trained ecologist who has memorized the Pinacate's physiography in the course of studying its myriad organisms and how they interact with each other.

Alberto, a child of the 1950s who has conducted intense ecological investigations all over Sonora, is a handsome fellow speaking English with a Cambridge accent and sporting a professorial beard. He has watched with despair the gradual disappearance of Sonoran vegetation as rangelands are torn up and replaced with buffelgrass. To a great extent the Pinacate has been unaffected, both because it is too dry and because the few cows it supports would hardly be worth the enormous effort to plant the grass.

As of mid-1994 the protection granted the Pinacate was still on paper only. I spoke with Alberto after he had just spent a week tramping around the Pinacate, venturing into areas that few had ever seen—sand dunes, lava flows, cinder cones, and vast middens of sea shells. I asked him what the government should do to "manage" the area.

"There is nothing it should do," he answered. "The Pinacate needs to be left alone. It doesn't need to be like your Grand Canyon with hotels and stores and traffic. It needs a few *vigilantes* (rangers) to see that the wood that is left after all the woodcutting doesn't get trucked off, that the Sonoran pronghorn antelope and bighorn sheep aren't poached, and that the lava flows aren't plundered, but that is all. So far, we don't even have that."

A week before I had been in the west end of the Pinacate. I heard a rumble from a cinder cone I had used for years as a landmark. The sound was the diesel engine of a huge loader that was excavating great bites of cinder from the base of the hill and dumping it into a semi tractor-trailer rig, which then hauled it off to the United States.

Land of Fires from Heaven and Hell 197

So this was how the new national park would be managed, I thought angrily. Why even bother going through the motions if in a newly protected area North American economic interests can still exploit an irreplaceable resource? It was as though Lassen Volcano was being removed, bit by bit, right under the government's nose.

Alberto shrugged unhappily when I told him about the mining. "I guess it's on private property," he muttered. "Maybe they've decided that it's just outside the Pinacate. Oh, I don't know. It's just a peripheral cinder cone."

We ended our conversation with a hope he expressed that the promised protection would come soon. His disillusionment with government was beginning to match that of many of my countrymen.

CHAPTER 24

Crowds and Crowding in Nogales

Poor Sonorans flee to Caborca, Hermosillo, or Guaymas. Poor southerners stream into the tiny valley of Nogales, the principal port of entry into Sonora from the United States. Unlike most Sonoran cities, it can't boast a varied and colorful history. Before the construction of the Nogales-Guaymas railroad in the 1880s, it was only a ranch, a sleepy, quiet narrow valley with a bottom land shaded by walnuts and cottonwoods, the hills softened by great Emory oaks. The United States–built railroad put it on the map. When I first visited Nogales, its population was around twenty-five thousand, mostly involved in curio shops and the import-export business. According to the Mexican government's census, Nogales had a population of a hundred thousand in 1990. The real number was about three hundred thousand in 1994. The precious few flat places were built upon decades ago. The only direction growth could go is up. The steep hills for miles around teem with shanties or small homes. Higher and higher they go, until at some point they will reach the crests of the hills. The dense, frail-looking housing ends abruptly at the international fence, posing a dramatic and symbolic contrast.

Most of the shantytowns, slums, *colonias*, have no utilities. Providing pumped water to these *colonias* clinging to the steep hillsides would tax any urban planner. A root of the problem is the *maquiladoras* (foreign-owned assembly plants) that have proliferated in the last couple of decades (there were nearly two hundred in 1990). These factories hire Mexicans at low wages to do assembly work. The finished product is exported and a duty is paid only on the value added. Foreign companies, predominately from the United States, have thronged to border cities to cash in on the bargain wage rates.

To attract factories and jobs, local governments, with full backing from Mexico City, offer tax incentives. The foreign plants pay no local or Mexican taxes. The result is that the flood of new job seekers arrives on the scene with no money, and the city of Nogales has no tax funds to provide urban services. Immigrants arrive ready to work, but have nothing with which to buy or rent housing. The pay at the *maquiladoras* is low (three to five dollars a day). Workers can never afford to build or rent, and the city has no funds to provide housing for them. They must construct their own shelter. New *colonias* (shantytowns) creep up the hillsides like strange growths. No sewers, water, or electricity are available. Often they never arrive at all.

In spite of the poverty of the *colonias* the residents are surprisingly well organized—by themselves. Mexico's top-down democracy functions slowly at times, and participatory democracy is unknown. Governments operate by official edict and in utter secrecy. Mexico has no open meeting laws. Decisions are made by the elite in Mexico City or Hermosillo and announced in Nogales. No public discussion is involved.

In response to this authoritarianism, a tradition throughout the Republic is the takeover or direct action by organized citizens. Members of a shantytown will organize a demonstration or a takeover of a building or area until their demands are met, sometimes for water, sometimes for a school, often to protest official inaction or police actions. Such confrontations between authorities and the police on the one hand and residents of the *colonias* on the other, are ongoing chapters in the history of modern Mexico. The poor people win an occasional battle, but invariably lose the war.

In the few decades I've been visiting the Republic of Mexico, its population has zoomed from the high thirties to nearly ninety million people. Mexico's population density now exceeds that of the United States and is increasing its lead rapidly. An educated and environmentally sensitive Mexican friend and I were discussing population concerns over dinner one evening. I asked him what size family he came from.

"Oh, ours is a small family. I have only six brothers and sisters."

"My God," I answered, "What's a *big* family like, then?"

"Oh, twelve, thirteen children. That's big."

He wasn't kidding. Seldom does one find a family through the childbearing years with fewer than four children. Couples with three or fewer are decidedly small in number. In the countryside an additional child may make some economic sense, for another hand to help scrape a living may be a positive asset, but in an urban setting and in a cash economy another child in a poor family is usually an added burden. Most of Mexico's population is under twenty-one and as they come into reproductive age, their expectations for large families will make the population problem even worse. The crowding, the problems of sanitation, health, and education, and plundering of natural resources, can only worsen in the face of such numbers. While Mexican women are often aware that alternatives to constant pregnancy do exist, men seem inclined to keep the birth control alternative out of their reach. Poor young women have it worst. Their culture finds open and frank discussions of sex embarrassing and shameful. Young women expect to be a mother again and again. They dream of opulent, fashionable weddings, romantic sighs, precious babies. Little more. Few other options exist. Professional women in Sonora, as in all of Mexico, are as scarce as seat belt users.

In the 1980s I spent a few days in a small Río Sonora town with some friends, a wealthy family from Hermosillo, who maintained a big house that could have been designed by a Dutch architect. My children and I were served *comida ranchera* (ranch-style food) by a motherly woman who waited on us as though a servant, hovering over us, filling our plates in the morning with *machaca* (jerked beef sautéed with tomato, onions, chiles, and spices), *frijoles* (pinto beans that have been boiled, then fried in lard), eggs, and flour tortillas. Where was my wife, she wanted to know. How could a man be raising children? The notion is peculiar enough to Mexicans that I was met with curious stares whenever I mentioned that I was divorced and was raising my children.

Their perplexity shows how Mexican society, and Sonora is no exception, is male-dominated to an extent difficult for many Americans to comprehend. Men overwhelmingly command all dimensions of Mexican society. Women's expectations are culturally limited to mothering and nurturing roles. No society in which women lack political power will offer women reproductive choices. In Mexico women with higher expectations have a hard time of it, indeed. I was present at a barbecue in a Sonoran city when the host introduced his family to other guests. He presented his youngest daughter, a biologist working on a master's degree, as "My daughter who isn't interested in marriage."

Men have most of the fun. They gather in great numbers in bars, at sporting events, at political gatherings, at fiestas, at popular hangouts, around pickup trucks, and at truck stops. In most of these places respectable women are absent or, if present, are under the "protection" of their man, preferably their husband. In these situations men feel compelled to drink heavily, generally a conspicuous beer like Tecate, which is also outrageously expensive. Unfortunately, drinking Tecate has become a compulsory male ritual. A high government official complained to me one day when we saw some youths ostentatiously displaying cans of Tecate as they lounged against a wall in a Sierra Madre town. "Look at that, David, their mothers encourage them to do that. They tell them, 'Get out there with a can of Tecate so people don't think you're a sissy.' No wonder we have such a problem with alcoholism."

CHAPTER 25

The Río San Miguel

West and south of Ures the Río Sonora opens into a broad
plain as it approaches Hermosillo, where the arroyo of another
historically important river, the San Miguel, joins the Río
Sonora. In Father Kino's time the San Miguel bustled with mission activity among the Opatas and Pimas Altas and the riches
of a dozen or so mines. In the eighteenth and nineteenth centuries several San Miguel villages flourished. For a while the
town of San Miguel Horcasitas was the capital of Sonora and
politically the most important town in the western half of the
state, but that was when Spain was conquering Indians, converting and protecting the heathens, and whipping them into piety.
Today the villages on the San Miguel linger vaguely, quiet empty
shells of their former selves, nurturing a nostalgia for more
prosperous days of long ago, before a combination of Apaches,
Spanish politics, the demise of the mining industry and, ultimately, the advent of the automobile deprived them of the commerce that was their life's blood. Their young men leave for the
cities in search of work and fulfillment.

The river itself is the north-south highway. It detours at
rapids and pools. At the northern end of the San Miguel lies
Cucurpe. The name is derived from an Opata word imitating the
sound of a dove. Cucurpe is in a different world from the towns
along the modern highways. Its narrow, steep, shaded streets create reminiscences of colonial times as it sits on the east bank,
well above the flood-prone river. Cucurpe, as the other towns of
the San Miguel, lives on the raising of cattle and crops, including marijuana, I was informed. It has changed little since I first
visited it in the early 1970s. The ruined church sits starkly on a
terrace above the village, its naked brick arches content to wait
out history. Not ten yards away is a rusting machine foundry. Its
metal is decaying faster than the rock, bricks, and mortar of the
church. Cucurpe's current chapel, a mythical religious shrine

from a surrealistic de Chirico painting, looms solitary atop a bare rocky knoll culminating a long, narrow staircase.

Tom Sheridan, an ethnohistorian with the Arizona State Museum, first visited Cucurpe in the 1970s. He became entranced with the place and made it the center of his book *Where the Dove Calls.* Knowing he was as familiar with northern Sonora as any American I know, I asked him one day, "Tom, where's the best place in Sonora to be on *el día de San Juan*?" St. John's day is June 24th, the fiesta commemorating the summer solstice and the day when the summer rains traditionally begin. (They seldom do.)

"Cucurpe." He said without hesitation. "They have a great fiesta. People come from all over. Hell of a party."

My wife Lynn and I headed to Cucurpe on June 23rd. It was 107 degrees in Tucson that day, and Curcurpe was baking under the same summer heat, but on the San Miguel the sun's power was tempered by the trees that shade Cucurpe's streets and the temperature was tolerable. For a village in the middle of a fiesta, Cucurpe was surprisingly composed. I flagged down an old cowboy on a horse to find out what was happening. There would be no action till the next day, he told me, without enthusiasm. He looked as though he felt dreadful. The town was quiet because people were already "tired" from a weekend of fiesta. They needed to catch up on some sleep. The night was reserved for *vísperas* (private vigils and processions held by each family). There was hardly a party atmosphere.

Lynn and I headed east over the mountainous road to an old hacienda on the Río Saracachi, one of the tributaries that merge upstream from Cucurpe to form the Río San Miguel. From the old, sprawling estate we drove up the stream, which flows through a narrow, densely forested canyon. On the steep, rocky sides grew dwarf fig trees, clinging heroically to the rock. They never become actual trees this far north, for they're frost-sensitive and die back every few years. The stream is permanent, and the canyon walls provide enough protection that plants normally found only well to the south have made a foray into this south-facing gorge. In the canyon bottom the stream is crammed on both sides by great, white-barked *guerigos*, Sonoran cottonwoods, spreading ash trees, graceful willows, massive canyon hackberries, stately walnuts, ancient rugged mesquite trees, dense grabbing catclaws, whitethorn acacias, box elders, and Emory oaks. High on the steep slopes a profusion of desert plants appears, magically clinging to the sheer sides: agaves, saguaros, organ pipes, tree ocotillos, dense thickets of poison ivy, coral-bean trees with fiery red spears of blossoms, Spanish daggers, and *palo verdes*.

Well up in the canyon, in an ancient ranch hut that merges into the side of the canyon, lives Carmen Sinohui de Palafox with her youngest son. Her husband died in 1987, and she has stayed on. She was born at the *hacienda* downstream, as was her mother before her and her grandmother before her. Carmen has become the area's resident expert on the curative properties of plants. We sat on her porch and listened to her describe how she used herbs to keep her thirteen children well without having to take them to the doctor in Magdalena, a long drive away and expensive to boot.

She sat in a rickety chair describing in the exquisite voice of the Mexican Indian *viejita* how she used herbs like *malaquete, gobernadora, yerba buena, mariola,* and a dozen more. She brewed teas, fashioned poultices, pills, powders, syrups, and aromatics. She showed us a root from which she carved small pieces, ground them in a *molcajete* (grinding stone), and pressed them into a sort of tablet. She placed a couple of pieces in the circular rough stone vessel and ground away with the pestle. The resulting powder was especially good for curing stomach aches and as a poultice for eye problems. Carmen's son Larencio, twenty-one years old and appearing healthy, looked on while she described her pharmacopoeia, occasionally nodding with approval.

She wore a simple cotton dress and sat under her *ramada*, talking with animation as the sun boiled the roof. Her daughters showed little interest in the herbs, she said sadly. Her children have spread over a wide area of Sonora and live, it sounds to me, in areas where they are unlikely to have access to the necessary plants to carry on the medicinal tradition. *Curanderas* need open, undisturbed space. When Carmen dies, her knowledge will die with her, unless someone spends the time to work with her on writing it down.

Carmen was able to attend school only through the second grade, because there was so much work to do in her home. When she married, she cared for thirteen children and a husband, which, so far as I can tell, amounts to forty-five meals a day. Those years of drudgery have taken their toll, yet she remains talkative and optimistic, perhaps, dare I say it, relieved. Her husband worked as a rancher and a miner, working local placer deposits in search of gold. He was the unofficial greeter of the Saracachi; his house was the place where wanderers stopped for orientation and coffee.

I assured Carmen that Lynn and I would be back and would ask her to give us a guided tour of medicinal plants. She heartily agreed. Driving down the canyon we talked about the value of Carmen's knowledge in a world where potent, expensive, and potentially toxic medicines are used too casually. There are not enough people like Carmen around to help us use nature as a part of healing.

At five o'clock, a cowboy had told me, the race in Cucurpe would be sure to start. I believed him because riders on horseback were thronging toward the town flanked by more pickups than I thought could possibly exist in such a sparsely inhabited area. Lynn and I drove back to the village, slowly at times, waiting for horses and riders to clear the road. A man in a huge cattle truck told me the race would take place on the local *pista* or airstrip. We followed another cattle truck out of the town to the *rancho* where the event was going to be staged. A couple of kilometers away the road became clogged with vehicles, horses, and pedestrians, all of whom raised clouds of fine, sifting dust. A man halted us and held up five fingers, then mentioned delicately that the entry charge was five thousand pesos each (one dollar and sixty-five cents) to attend the race, funds to be used to support Cucurpe's school. That's what he said.

Trucks of every possible breed were parked perpendicular to *pista*. Under a spreading mesquite tree a family had set up a table and was selling *tacos de carne asada,* roasting pieces of beef and scallions over coals. For three thousand pesos (about one dollar) you were given a flour tortilla with meat and onion piled inside. You spooned salsa on top and had Sonora's most famous culinary innovation, ready to be washed down with beer. The taco operation was in competition with another family who sold hot dogs from a portable stand across the strip. A troupe of girls paraded back and forth on horseback, one of their number seated side-saddle, as used to be the custom. An older fellow wearing new Levis, boots and shirt, some sort of official, informed me that years ago a parade of *muchachas* would file up and down the track before the race. Now only a dozen or so did so. However, he cautioned, I needed to remember that when the holiday fell on a weekend, many more people would show up. Nowadays, most of the people had to work.

Cowboys by the dozen milled about the area, all clad in Levis, colored cowboy shirts and light-colored straw hats, a reddish-silver can of *Tecate* beer in hand. Small groups of men huddled secretively, their billfolds in their hands, taking or receiving bets from their compatriots. Young people, some of them under ten years of age, sporting brightly colored new shirts, pranced back and forth on their horses. The younger ones jauntily carried cans of Coke; the older ones casually sipped on beers held in one hand while they held the  reins or in the other. Little puffs of dust arose by the thousand as hundreds of horses pranced. Not a donkey was to be seen.

Lynn and I sat on the rear roof of my pickup's camper, where we could see the racecourse and the parade. Next to us a cattle truck had backed up to the edge of the *pista*, and a large family enjoyed the view. I struck up a conversation with one of the men standing in the bed of the truck. The race would be short, he told me, no more than 250 meters long, between two of the best locally raised horses, ridden by boys in their early teens. They were paid a set amount by the owners to race the horses,—not much, he thought—maybe a million pesos (three hundred and twenty-five dollars). These weren't the best horses; those come from America, he said. Some of the local horses don't get the best nutrition and aren't carefully bred the way prize horses have to be. Manuel Arvizu was his name. His family had been in Cucurpe for many generations, but he and his brother, seated next to him, both worked in Southern California. There are no jobs in Cucurpe or anywhere else in Sonora, he lamented.

Finally, around seven o'clock, Lynn nudged me. The race was about to begin because cowboys had so filled the racecourse that we could barely see the finish line, even though we were standing on top of the camper. Besides, almost everyone was drunk. The ground was littered with spent Tecate cans. The crowd watched the starting point expectantly. Excited shouts from up the course told us the race was underway. We strained to see, heard the staccato of pounding hoof beats, and the two horses thundered by the finish line, one leading by a full two lengths. The winner was cheered lustily, but by the time the horses and their riders returned to parade around the course, the cowboys were back to nursing their beers and counting their winnings or losses.

Shortly after the race, began a series of *chiruzas*, races between various young men to see who had the faster mount. These drew apt concentration from the crowd, since each of the riders was related to roughly half the people there. One pair of horses thundered by, then another, then a third, each race preceded by noisy voices, shouts, whistles, and an occasional obscenity. Manuel explained to me all that was happening. Beer followed beer followed beer. Out of the blue he challenged me to a foot race.

"David, *no quiere correr conmigo?*" he said. I nodded, stupidly, for I immediately noticed how young his mustached face looked and his lean figure, with only a slight paunch. We walked to the middle of the dusty *pista.* Manuel measured off the course—only thirty meters. I was cooked. A cowboy shouted in English, "Wan, tooo, thdee," and we were off. Manuel, running in his stockings, his boots lying on the track, flew down the *pista* and won by four lengths, to the unimaginable joy of the crowd. Local boy made good, burying the gringo in the dust. Lynn told me later she was much relieved that I had lost the race.

Far down the San Miguel, past somnolent towns with intrigu-ing names—Tuape, Merésechic, Opodepe, Rayón—only twenty miles or so north of Hermosillo, the remnants of a fading hacienda slowly erode, one of many that graced the state in the late-nineteenth and early-twentieth centuries. This one is called Codórachi. It greets every traveler up and down the San Miguel with its mute testimony of past glory, the flour mill standing as big as a church, brooding over the river valley. Its history mirrors the history of the state. Jesús Uribe, a relaxed Hermosillo archi-tect with smiling eyes and a keen sense of irony in history, took me there. He's taken a fancy to abandoned *haciendas,* their form, and their social and political history.

A hundred years ago Codórachi was part of the huge estate of a rich and powerful Hermosillo family, he said. Thousands of hours of labor went into constructing the massive mill and the adjacent home of the *hacendado* (the hacienda's owner) where the ceiling beams still hold up the roof (although insolent and intolerant wasps have built a city of nests within), and the plaster outside remains intact. Jesús pulled out the original plans, which he had gotten from state archives, and spread them on the ground, pointing out the structures. He, his young daughter, and I stared into a deep, stone-lined ditch. Workers constructed a ten-foot-wide diversion canal up the San Miguel, Jesús said. Water flowed through a rock-lined channel down to the mill where it tumbled along a raceway, pouring into a turbine that supplied the motor force to the mill. The mill ground wheat into flour for inhabitants for miles around, even supplying some to Hermosillo. How well did the owner fare? I asked Jesús. "He prospered," the architect answered. "He added income from the mill to the harvests from the fertile fields in the adjacent floodplain, and the rich pastures where hundreds of cows fattened on the nutritious grasses. He did fine, until the 1930s when the government of President Cárdenas expropriated the mill." The twinkle in his eye showed his approval of Cárdenas's act.

The succeeding administration of President Avila Camacho saw to it that the facility once again wound up in private hands, but the handwriting was already on the wall. New electric or petroleum-powered turbines generated far more power than the primitive water-powered mill. More precise grinding equipment was invented, capable of producing ten times the amount of flour from a machine of the same size. New mills appeared in Hermosillo. Codórachi could not compete. Transportation costs to the populated areas were too great. The nail in the coffin was driven in the 1940s with the opening of vast new irrigated fields west of Hermosillo where mechanized harvesting of wheat produced a rapid decline in the price of grain. The traditionally harvested, smaller fields around the *hacienda* could not compete with the government-subsidized, mechanized production of the newly irrigated areas. Wheat production in the area of Codórachi fell, and the mill finally fell into disuse. Today its antique machinery lies rusting inside the roofless building. The once bustling *hacienda* is quiet, the silence marred only by an occasional horseman or a truck and the mooing of cows in the pasture below.

I flagged down a cowboy as he rode by the abandoned mill.

He stayed in the saddle as he introduced himself as Gaspar
Bueras, sixty-one years old, born and raised right there at
Codórachi. He wore a tattered shirt and thick chaps, necessary
in that brambly country, thickly overgrown with mesquite, ironwood, and catclaw. Two small dog companions seemed to welcome the pause and lay panting in the shadow of a melting
adobe wall. "We left at five o'clock this morning," Gaspar said,
pointing to the dogs with a nod of his head. "They're pretty
tired by now." Home was nearby, where he could be out of the
hot noonday sun and rest till the heat slackened later in the afternoon.

"Yes, I work right here, for Sr. [_____]," and he named a
prominent Hermosillo politician, absentee landlord. He offered
me a cigarette, then lit one for himself. "I spend a lot of time
breaking horses. That's my specialty." I noticed three of the
fingers on one hand were twisted grotesquely and imagined them
being caught and broken in a lariat holding onto a bronco.

It was near the end of July and the rains were late. We looked
to the eastern mountains where summer storms originate.
"When will it rain, Gaspar?" I asked him.

His face lit up. "Well, I tell you it will rain on July 28, five
days from now."

"Excellent!" I answered. "This country needs the rain, all
right."

"Yes it does," he agreed. "Right now things are very bad.
Many cows have little to eat. It's very bad, but I know how to
predict *las aguas* (the rains). You see, my grandfather and grandmother taught me how to look at the stars at night and the sun
and other things during the day. So I know. The 28th. That's
when it will rain."

It did.

Gaspar spoke matter-of-factly, patting his horse who waited
patiently as we chatted. His mount's name was *Hilo de Oro*
(golden strand), after its golden mane. The cowboy proudly ran
his fingers through the horse's ample mane. I asked myself if this
gentle beast had been a fiery-eyed saddle bronc before Gaspar
had managed to break him of his anti-social ways.

The cowboy took his leave, raising his hat slightly, as all
polite cowboys do on bidding *adios.* I wondered if he would see
any of his three children or two grandchildren that evening.

Gaspar was a happy man, utterly without pretensions, content to live out his few remaining years of hard work helping an absentee landlord manage an estate from which the landlord extracted money, while a few cowboys and farm workers did all the work. He exemplified the uncomplaining stoicism I've seen all over rural Sonora. He had a family and a horse, would probably survive drought and famine without great scars, and would never see his children living nearby because the land could not support additional people. He accepts Mexico's rigid class system without question, having no pretensions or ambitions to be anything other than he is. "*Con el favor de Diós, nos vemos,*" (God willing, I'll see you again), he said. The same parting is invoked a hundred million times a day in Mexico. It's God's will, not human action, that determines events.

CHAPTER 26

Hermosillo

Hermosillo is the state's capital and its most important city. Its people consider themselves the most important of the state. They're probably right. The *machos* of Hermosillo strut far more than the real cowboys of the countryside. Expensive, plush automobiles, flashy new pickups, and cellular phones are the signs of the new Sonoran male. They're hurried, frantic fellows whose wives demand social status and whose children crave possessions. "*Papayos*, that's what we call that kind of kid," a lawyer friend told me, "because they're always saying '*Papa, yo quiero este,*' y '*Papa yo quiero ese.*'" (Daddy, I want this, and Daddy, I want that.) They're the new men of power in Sonora.

"*Zeroteros*, big turds, that's what we call them," said a friend of mine from a smaller town with a working-class, rural orientation. He says it with a bitterness that underscores the profound class differences that permanently divide the Mexican population. "They get away with everything. The police never stop them. They're rich, in bed with politicians. They do anything they want and shit on the rest of us."

In the exploding city a new breed of motel is being built with a garage next to each room. A client's car zips into the garage, and an attendant pulls a curtain over the entrance. The license and make can't be seen from the outside. It's far more discreet that way. Business is booming—all day.

Sonora's capital, with a population of over five hundred thousand is named after José María González de Hermosillo, who died fighting to liberate Mexico from the tyranny of Spain. Only in this century has it become a major city. Originally named Pitic (place where two rivers meet), it has been Hermosillo only since 1828. Many locals agree that Pitic is a nicer name. Only in the last fifty years has Hermosillo become big.

The city has spread on both sides of the Río Sonora, now dry most of the year due to the dam and reservoir on the city's

east side. The lake makes a pretty backdrop for the city, but feed
lots ring it and until recently drained their offal directly into the
water. I stay away from the foul liquid, as does nearly everyone
else.

I met an engineering student on one of downtown's busiest
streets that was a riot of color and high-rise buildings. I asked
him about the massive flood-control project being constructed
through the middle of the city along the watercourse of the Río
Sonora. Martín was his name, he told me respectfully, and
launched into a proud and comprehensive explanation of the
project. He said that the reservoir behind the dam is silting up,
so its capacity has dwindled over the years, increasing the danger
of flooding downstream. As a flood-control measure, the Sonoran government has completed what they call the *El Megaproyecto*
(the Megaproject), a concrete-lined ditch that extends for six
kilometers in the center of the floodway and is intended to discharge any excess flood waters into the old channel of the river
well west of the developed area of the city. This will free up a
good amount of land, Martín pointed out: areas formerly subject to flooding, now rid of that menace. The government has
sold off lands where a huge mall and medical/industrial complex
have risen.

Martín spoke with great earnestness and enthusiasm for the
massive project, the biggest in the history of Sonora, he thought.
I didn't have the heart to ask if he'd had an opportunity to
review the history of similar projects in my country. In the end,
especially since the channelization was about complete anyway, it
would be mean to dampen his enthusiasm with jaded observations about projects by the Army Corps of Engineers or the
Bureau of Reclamation in the United States, how they wound up
benefiting only a small number of people of influence. Nor did
I inquire as to his familiarity with the history of the Presa
Rodriguez, the dam that impounds the reservoir at Hermosillo.
The story, as narrated in the excellent *Historia General de Sonora*
published by the Sonoran government, tells how governor
Abelardo Rodríguez made a killing for himself and his buddies
by constructing the dam that shouldn't have been built, using
concrete from a plant they owned. He and his friends gobbled
up choice lands for affluent suburbs and gained title to lands
below the dam now freed from the danger of flood. I thought

about lending Martín a copy of the *Historia,* but his generous attitude, his eagerness to be of assistance, his idealism made me ashamed even to think of such a cynical maneuver.

The highway enters Hermosillo from the north along a graceful, busy boulevard shaded by large trees and interspersed with *glorietas,* traffic circles in the middle of which a statue commemorates one of several Mexican heroes so honored. Drivers seem to careen around the statues by habit. Hotels, motels, and shopping complexes rise up amidst tropical trees flaming with proud colors. The central plaza, located between the *Palacio de Gobierno* and the burning white cathedral, is strangely aloof from the rest of the city. Graceful old trees protect against the desert sun, while in the background high-rise office buildings and hotels dominate the landscape. Shoppers pack modern supermarkets, increasingly crammed with United States products. Women drive automobiles, even a few trucks, something unheard of in the countryside. A rocky hill called *El Cerro de la Campana* in the center of town has a cobbled roadway in terrible condition built up to a *mirador* (lookout) from where on a clear day you can get a good idea of the size of the city. Some days the smog is so bad that visibility is limited to only a kilometer or two, but at least you can get a good idea of the smog.

There is old and new. An electronic sign flashes news headlines to heavy stop-and-go traffic only a few blocks from the old municipal market where vendors hawk their wares, and foods and merchandise of every conceivable variety can be found in stalls, kiosks, and shops. Cowboy apparel is just as fashionable as in Scottsdale, and the rate of authentic cowboys per capita is probably about the same in the two cities. Hermosillo merchants capitalize on the cowboy image. Shoe stores feature an astonishing array of boots at reasonable prices, and from the looks of the men in the market area they do a land office business. At the eastern entrance long rows of stools on either side of the aisles are filled at lunchtime with men dressed as cowboys. They drink coffee and eat *cocido* (a meat and vegetable soup) or some other meat-based dish. Viewed from the outside their lineup takes on an almost comic aspect, a sea of straw cowboy hats.

A wholly different city is to be found a few blocks away near the government offices. The new technocrats, yuppies, lawyers, bureaucrats, and politically well placed, drive fancy cars, dress in

suits, frequent United States–style restaurants, and head for San
Carlos condominiums or Tucson hotels on the weekends. They
listen to an FM radio station that plays exclusively popular
songs in English.

Political intrigue occupies most of the time around *El Palacio
de Gobierno* and now around the huge new high-rise government
office complex on the Río Sonora. One case symbolizes the system. A Sonoran friend of mine, whom I'll call Miguel, gradu-
ated from the University of Arizona with an M.B.A. Also a
lawyer, he had a robust business in real estate around Hermosillo
and an inside track at a big stack of clients. However, he despised the PRI, the ruling party that has controlled Mexican
politics for sixty years. He aligned himself with the PAN, the
opposition conservative party, to protest government corruption.
He became a prominent PANista. Unfortunately for him he
found his business enterprises falling on lean times. Deals requiring government approval languished on bureaucrats' desks. Documents disappeared. Partners pulled out from deals. Government
inspectors found problems with his business operations. His career was going nowhere. Then one day Miguel had a sudden
flash of inspiration. He switched from the PAN to the PRI.
Miraculously, his business fortunes picked up, papers zipped
through bureaucrats' hands, and the skids were greased. Prosperity followed in short order. Today he is a loyal PRIsta, available
at the beck and call of the government to carry out the governor's will. His career is insured.

The city expands, bloats, and grows again. Each time I visit,
new *barrios* of poor people appear on the south and west sides
and new subdivisions for the middle class spring up to the north
and east. The streets are crowded; the traffic is intimidating.
Hermosillans have no comment on the growth, just fatalistic
mutterings about the bad roads and the difficulty of getting
where they want to go.

For those who must deliver urban services, the explosive
growth is more than a mere technical problem. In thirty years the
city has grown from less than 100,000 to 500,000. I've seen less
explosive growth in Phoenix and Tucson, and I know that local
governments there have been stretched to provide services to the
newcomers. More important, the newly arrived inhabitants of
those Arizona cities are, for the most part, educated, employed,

and more or less affluent. The immigrants to Hermosillo have neither education nor employment nor money.

Hermosillo is hard-pressed to handle the growth. "The problem, David, is the all the *guachos* who come here," a yuppie Hermosillan told me. It's an unflattering term used to denote southerners, especially poor ones fleeing economic desperation in the south. Sonora is full of *guacho* jokes, racist slurs that stereotype southerners as dumb and illiterate (also largely dark-skinned), as opposed to the erudite and educated Sonorans. *Guachos* eat corn tortillas and pork. *Sonorenses* eat flour tortillas and beef.

"Sonorans aren't poor," an affluent, well-educated woman told me. "We don't have poverty here. It's caused by *guachos.*" It could equally be caused by Indians. Even though the state symbol is a Yaqui deer dancer, Indians are looked down upon. To be called an *indio* is an insult. Dark skin is a curse. Light skin and light hair (preferably blonde) are virtues. Models on television, in magazines, and on billboards are light-haired and light-skinned.

Hermosillo is hell-bent on imitating the appearance of United States cities. American-franchised business are everywhere—McDonald's, Blockbuster Video, Dominos Pizza, Kentucky Fried Chicken—patronized because they symbolize America (and because the service is better, most say). Drive-ins, salad bars, automatic teller machines, photomats, all spring up every day. A country club with a microscopic golf course teeters on the shoulder of a hill. No crowds pack the scarce bookstores, and only an occasional newspaper, thin at that, crosses my path. Sonorans don't read them much. They get information from TV, plots from comic-like pulp thrillers, social analysis from the radio, headlines from the *Hermosillo Flash* electronic marquee.

The technocrats and their large families drive Ram Chargers (the symbol of Hermosillo yuppies) to Tucson to do their shopping, returning with vehicles crammed full of (ironically cheaper) American merchandise. Their appetites are stimulated on the drive north by a long series of billboards luring them to shops in Nogales and Tucson. Each year more billboards appear on the northbound lane. Not one is to be seen driving south.

All the fellows who have abandoned the jobless countryside seem to have collected in Hermosillo. Jobs are scarce, so many hang out near the market. Curious, surprisingly polite, modest and unmacho, the recent arrivals contrast sharply with the city slickers and hustlers, who are crude, vain, insecure, immature punks. The immigrants arrive at the huge bus terminal, a vast warehouse filled mostly with men waiting endlessly. The new arrivals are obvious by their look of wonder and confusion, the oppressing intimidation of the big city reflecting in their faces. Those waiting assume the stoic expression of one resigned to economic pain.

Everybody is from somewhere else. Few seem to have original family roots in Hermosillo. My friends come from families that migrated from some little town or ranch out in the sticks somewhere. A connection to a ranch is a mark of distinction; the cowboy mythology is as important to Sonorans as it is to Arizonans. Wealthy businessmen buy ranches to establish their roots, even if they only visit them once a year.

Somehow, in spite of the hustle, the plastic veneer, the sleaze of rank imitation, the city overcomes the superficialities and retains something genuinely and legitimately Sonoran. Part is the deep pride Sonorans take in being Sonoran. They produce first-rate historians and sociologists, incisive social critics. They subject themselves to endless social criticism.

The city is livable (aside from its smog, lack of sewers, and dubious water supply). When its residents stick to Sonoran building motifs, what they create is enchanting. Businesses, shops, and homes, merge quietly and tastefully together into an urban whole. The city converges on the cathedral, the Palace of the Governor, and the University of Sonora. Original Sonorans built with common walls, emphasizing courtyards and patios, not wasted front lawns. (Cynics remark that they used common walls to prevent the riff-raff from sleeping between their homes.) Colors help divide the varying landscape. Streets curve through *barrios*, each bend producing a new form. The sidewalks are a pleasure to walk. Music pours from every home. In the older city each house is designed for life, not for show. Even late at night, pedestrians pass without fear. One evening I caught a half-moon illuminating the north transept of the cathedral and felt an ethereal glow that couldn't have come from Anglo culture.

Even the poorer parts of the city teem with vitality. The old neighborhoods are just that, full of neighbors. One night I searched a street for a friend whose house number I didn't know. I stopped at a home with lit windows and asked if anyone knew where the Padillas lived. *"Pues, creo que sí, conozco ese nombre,"* (I think I've heard the name), said the middle-aged woman who answered the door. She was quickly surrounded by children who pointed down the street. I drove; they ran. We tried three more houses, four and five blocks away. At each stop the crowd of house locators increased. By the time they found my friend's house, a band of twenty folk of all ages waited at the front gate, pointing inside the gate where the family was seated on a porch, chatting with their neighbors.

Part of what makes Hermosillo work is the ubiquitous presence of food stands, cafés, and restaurants serving tacos de carne asada A stroll through the more popular areas any evening is accompanied by the fragrant aroma of roasting beef and onions. Sonoran cuisine is dominated by the delectable dish, scorned by southerners, venerated by local patriots. Vendors set up grills everywhere, slicing up narrow slabs of meat, which they roast over mesquite coals alongside giant green onions. They slap this mixture on tortillas, making a dish that brings misty eyes of pleasure to the consumer. Sonora introduced this food to the world, and Sonorans know best how to prepare it.

Tacos may be followed by a sweet called the *coyota,* said to be invented by a poor tradesman in a working-class neighborhood. It's a sweet pancake with bits of brown sugar baked into the middle in a wood-fired oven. Several bakeries now turn out the delicacy and vendors hawk *coyotas* at gasoline stations for miles around. Only Hermosillo makes them.

Hermosillenses welcome North Americans as though the United States had never gobbled up most of Sonora. Hundreds of North American tourists file through the city each day heading south, hardly any speaking a word of Spanish. Hermosillans view them with an amused tolerance. "All retired Americans look alike, David," a friend confessed after his second beer," but at least they're nice." Giant motor homes, Airstream trailers, and big cars stack up at gasoline stations. The retirees emerge—gray-haired men in golf shirts and baseball caps and fading women in polyester pants. They stretch to stare at Mexicans. They fill their tanks, empty their bladders, and plod on toward the golden ghettos of the Gulf where the money they spend is vital to Sonora's economy.

West of Hermosillo thousands of acres of irrigated farmland

have transformed a flat, desert plain into one of the most productive agricultural areas on earth. The lower Río Sonora Valley is a major producer of grains, poultry and eggs, citrus, and grapes. Walking in the huge, mechanized croplands, it's impossible to tell whether one is in Sonora, the Salt River Valley, or the San Joaquin Valley, so vast are the plantings and so flat the land.

As is the case with irrigated desert in the United States, problems of a falling water table and heavy use of agricultural chemicals are increasing. Cotton, once a boom crop, is gone, replaced by wheat or other grains, themselves now of marginal profitability. The dazzling green of the fields contrasts with the blue of the sky and the browns of the desert, as water makes the desert blossom.

In the coastal area the fields depend entirely on pumped groundwater. When the farms were first created in the mid-twentieth century, promoted by fat government subsidies for leveling, drilling wells, and installing sophisticated pumps, mining of groundwater commenced at a rate that would have exhausted the aquifer in a few years. Since then, the government has begun to regulate the pumping, and the rate of depletion has slowed.

Jesús Flores Lara is a technical secretary working for the federal department of water and hydraulic resources. Startlingly young, with an earnest face, he's fluent in the sometimes arcane world of agriculture and agribusiness. In his crowded office in Hermosillo we chatted about the future of agriculture in the Río Sonora, his countenance calm in the face of news that promises long-term problems.

According to Flores Lara, urban sprawl from Hermosillo and increased use of stored waters by city folks have combined to decrease the amount of acreage irrigated by waters of the *presa*, the dam on the Río Sonora. As for farms nearer the coast, "Well," he smiled philosophically, "some areas have gone out of production completely; others have had to change the crops they grow. Cotton, grains, alfalfa, once mainstays of the immensely fertile soils, are no more. It costs too much to pump the water for irrigation, and aquifers were pumped so quickly that the overdrawn wells sucked in salt water from deposits near the Sea of Cortés, which rushed in to ruin the water supply." Flores Lara's department is helping farmers change crops. Vegetables that bring quick cash are doing fine, although growing them means the fields will lie empty a good part of the year. Grapes use less water, and if the market holds up, bring better returns than grains.

"The future of grains like wheat, rye, and corn, is not bright," he adds, shrugging. Mexican farmers who must irrigate (only ten percent of the acreage in Sonora is capable of dry farming, and that must rely on often late or scanty rains) cannot hope to compete with American farmers who are blessed with fertile soils and rainfall sufficient to grow their crops without having costly irrigation. Agriculture in the lower Río Sonora will be around for a long time, if, that is, things are done carefully and scientifically.

In the long run, however, no hope exists for replenishing the aquifer. No new waters will be available for the fields. As Flores Lara knows, over the next few decades the fields will become fallow, tumbleweeds will move in, and over the eons, desert growth will slowly reclaim its domain.

In 1994 a group of city boosters announced plans to construct a water pipeline to the Río Yaqui, seventy-five miles to the east. The river is already overallocated, but Hermosillo has the political power.

CHAPTER 27

Where the Jesuits Gathered

Mátape is a quiet town in a quiet province. I remember it most because a ferocious argument was going on between some neighbors the first time I passed through. I heard their shrill voices a block away on the shadeless plaza where I had stopped because a cow was blocking the way. Only in a quiet town can you hear shouting that far away. The only soul to be seen was an old man, seated on a wall in the shade of the *presidencia* (the city hall). I chatted at length with him. Jesús Hurgos was his name. He was born in Mátape and spent his life here, except for those periods when he was working as a *bracero* in the United States. Jesús now spends his retirement working as a dispatcher for the Secretary of Water Resources, reporting weather data by radio on a daily basis to nearby Mazatán. He's a mild-mannered chamber of commerce gentleman, a widower whose children had all moved away.

He tells me that it's a good bit cooler in Mátape than in Hermosillo, even though it's only a few hundred meters higher. The mountains send down cool breezes, he figures, pointing to the dark blue Sierra de Agua Verde to the northeast. Summers are hot here and not much goes on after the processions of Holy Week with their *matachines* and *pascolas,* remnants of Easter fiestas of long ago. When the rains come, bugs are a problem, he warned me, even though the *municipio* arranges for spraying. Mosquitoes are a nuisance, and a further problem is a gnat that breeds in the fruit of the *pochote* (the kapok tree). When they hatch, they can make life miserable until the authorities spray. A truck comes around and sprays the streets and inside the homes. After that, he smiled. No further problem, just the heat. A voice called to Jesús from the door of the *presidencia.* He excused himself. It seems that he had been called to the radio to make another dispatch. When he left, not a soul was to be seen from the plaza.

It's a fine small town, set in an intimate valley between blue mountain ranges. Most of the outsiders that villagers see are only passing through Mátape on their way to the village of San Pedro La Cueva on Lake Novillo, where fishermen and water sport enthusiasts congregate. A nearby mine serves up iron ore to a cement mill in Hermosillo, employing a dozen or so residents and periodically sending rumbling dump trucks shuddering through the town's narrow streets. Other than that, Mátape relies on the ubiquitous cow for its livelihood. Studies done a couple of decades ago indicate that some of its inhabitants were Opata, but if that is still the case, they're not telling.

The Río Mátape is a bit of a joke as rivers go. Its waters are negligible. Flows reach the Gulf of California only in times of heavy flooding on the river. Most of the year the majority of the Mátape Basin lies bone-dry. Still, the valley looms heavily in Sonoran history. On maps you may search long and hard for Mátape and not find it. Supposedly Mátapeans early in the century petitioned the Sonoran government to change the village's name to Villa Pesqueira in honor of General Ignacio Pesqueira, who fought tirelessly for democracy in Sonora and later became governor many times over. Maps may show the name change, but residents and locals still refer to the village as Mátape.

In 1767 all the Jesuit missionaries in Sonora were summoned to Mátape. It had been the scene ten years earlier of a fierce raid by Seris who, according to a Jesuit report, "stole cattle and horses [and] also killed stock in the corrals with poisoned arrows." The gathering fathers may have imagined there would be discussions of these ever-increasing raids and those of Apaches as well. Instead they were informed of the edict of Charles III of Spain that they were to be expelled. The priests were placed under arrest and forced to march to Guaymas, nearly 150 kilometers away. It must have been a heart-rending journey, for Mátape somehow gathers the essence of Sonora as much as any other village in the state. The Jesuits knew the plants and animals almost as well as they knew the topography, the rolling, high hills and mountains they crossed innumerable times to serve their Indian converts. On that terrible day the desert must have been alive with organ pipes and saguaros, even an occasional *etcho* cactus. *Palo verdes, guayacanes,* ironwoods, mesquites, and cottonwoods would have lined the arroyos. Quail and doves would have darted from the thickets, hawks and vultures soared, roadrunners bounded. As they marched, on foot, it seems, the mountain ranges with their oaks, junipers, and pines must have said a sad farewell to the men who by their faith alone transformed Sonora forever. They had to have known they faced mandatory transfer to Europe and would never again have the experience of Sonoran rains, summer *chubascos*, or winter *equipatas*. There would be no more glimpses of vast wildernesses, some of which only they could comprehend.

No trace remains of the Jesuit *colegium* where aspiring priests could come to study, nor of the splendid church that was the pride of the *Aivono* district, the valley of the Mátape River and environs. Instead, there is a handsome small church with a bright red municipal water tower so close by it looks as though it is growing out of the church's nave.

CHAPTER 28

Batuc and Other River Towns

I'd read in various places about the mission town of Batuc, northeast of Mátape. I had learned of its history, how it was founded by Jesuits, learned of its palm weaving industry, and of its pretty church, but, come to think of it, I never found it on road maps. How could a town mentioned so often in early Sonoran history be so absent from maps? It was located on the Río Moctezuma, I knew, not far above where it joined the Río Yaqui.

One day, while I was looking at an old map, I found it and immediately realized why I hadn't located it on modern maps: it had been inundated by the waters of Lake Novillo, constructed in the late 1960s on the Río Yaqui. Current maps don't show Batuc because it has ceased to exist. As the waters rose, drowning the village, the University of Sonora organized a group of students who with great labor dismantled the church's facade, carefully numbering each stone block, and moved it to Hermosillo where they reconstructed it as a monument to Batuc and two other pueblos (Suaqui Chico and Tepupa) that had also been flooded out. I'd seen the monument in the Villa de Seris on the south side of Hermosillo.

I had to see for myself what had become of the village. What's left carries on a ghostly existence near the edge of Lake Novillo not far from the village of San José de Batuc, an hour northeast of Mátape. It's a mountainous ride as the road works slowly up the north end of the Mátape Valley and finally crosses a pass that overlooks the valley of the Río Moctezuma, now an arm of Lake Novillo. Reservoirs are our most accurate revealer of topography. When seen from the high pass twenty kilometers away the stored waters of the lake reveal the former valley of the Moctezuma to be only a finger of the Yaqui Valley. The water kills all vegetation except for the grasses, which survive when the level drops. Then the lake creates a wasteland.

Around the pass, the vegetation changes gradually from the scattered bushes and trees of the Sonoran Desert to the exotic aspect of dense thickets of the thorn scrub as the twisting dirt road descends abruptly to the lake. Just before the road reaches the edge of the lake, remnants of the old town come into view, a surrealistic landscape shimmering in the heat waves over the lake. A ragged bell tower, eroded by the rising and falling of the lapping waters, stands as a mute witness to the lake's onslaught. Fifty yards away a crumbling nave, its massive arches and walls intact but doomed, rises from the blue-gray waters, a seeming mirage. Once the lake's level has fallen low enough, baring the denuded sides of a once densely vegetated canyon, metal crosses mounted atop funeral crypts protrude from the surface like the great blue herons that stand patiently in the nearby shallow waters.

Batuc must have been a charming beautiful village, its church the crowning glory of the region. As I stared over the barren, exposed shores of the lake, drawn down to generate electricity for the air conditioners of Hermosillo, I tried to imagine how the homes of Batuc's habitants would have fit into these gentle knolls, now submerged or revealed until the next time of high water. I tried to envision the paths from the river, the village plaza, the shady trees, and the quiet, narrow streets. What stories could the fading, doomed church tell of birth, life, and death? When the bell tolled, summoning the faithful to mass, could I have heard the reverberating metal from where I sat staring over the calm indifferent water? In the cemetery, did the dead take consolation from the refreshing waters that poured over their remains? It was almost more than I could bear, almost as I felt when I saw the rising waters of Lake Powell bury forever the quiet, delicate walls of Glen Canyon. I took a last look, shook my head in finality, and returned to Mátape where the living tradition continues unbroken.

As for the inhabitants of the late village Batuc, I'm told that most of them were relocated in a new village with the clever name of San Francisco de Batuc, twenty miles or so upstream from Hermosillo on the Río Sonora, some seventy miles from their ancestral home. How successful the relocation was in terms of the lives of former Batucans I have not been able to determine. In the summer of 1991, however, I stumbled on some information about them when I was discussing their old village with social scientist, Professor José Luis Moreno of El Colegio de Sonora, a young man with an energetic earnest face and a brilliant encyclopedic mind. We sat in the comfort of his air-conditioned office, an oasis from the fiery heat of an Hermosillo July.

"Oh yes, Batuc," he told me sadly. "Those folks were all moved out, and the facade of their church was transferred to Hermosillo." I nodded in agreement and told him I knew of the monument. "Have you heard the latest?" he asked, a note of irony in his eyes. I hadn't. "The government's going to build another dam. The reservoir is going to flood their homes and they'll have to move again."

"My God!" I exclaimed. "Again?"

"Yes," he said, shaking his head sadly. "The government's decided there's a need for more flood storage, so people living downstream from the *presa* in Hermosillo can be guaranteed they won't be flooded. A lot of expensive real estate there."

Some things never change, I told myself. I shook my head in disbelief, and our conversation moved on to other topics less tinged with sadness.

The new dam was completed in 1993. On the Río Yaqui, below the dam on Lake Novillo, lies Tónichi, where the ancient Camino Real crossed the deep current. It was an Opata town, situated on a bluff overlooking the surging waters of the great river. The poor town reeks of depression. The railroad that once brought commerce and jobs from Guaymas and other ports has long since been torn up, its iron rails flooded in the late 1940s by the dammed waters of Lake Oviachic downstream on the Yaqui River. The mines that formerly gave up ore to be carried out on the railroad are asleep, their once-active mills scrapped for their junk value. Scarcely a newly painted building is to be seen in the town. Many structures are empty or used only to shelter live-stock, a far cry from when I first visited twenty-five years ago.

At that time no paved highway existed to transport goods across the middle of the state, and all traffic had to pass through Tónichi. A cable ferry provided a crossing of the Río Yaqui. Truckers could find a meal at any of several places and a room for the night if necessary. Now that two highway bridges cross the Yaqui—one to the north, one to the south—the need for such services is gone. For food, sleep, and love they go to Hermosillo, Obregón, or Chihuahua. The great cable piers have crumbled; the cable lies twisted and rusty. Tónichi waits patiently for something to happen. Only a few houses looked occupied, bursts of flowers hiding the ultimate decay.

Two dark-skinned fellows in their fifties were mixing concrete for a sidewalk on the run-down plaza. I asked them what had happened to the ferry. They looked up, tired and sweaty, breathed a laconic response. They said that the ferry was gone. They sat down to rest. "You from Hermosillo or Obregón?" one of them asked. I told them neither, and they showed no more curiosity.

At Soyopa, another Opata town fifteen miles upstream, the ferry across the Yaqui still operates, even though the north-south road on the west side of the river is much faster than the older road on the east side. The raft was nearly new when I first crossed the Yaqui in 1967. It hasn't been replaced since then. Bermuda grass grows in cracks on the surface. A wispy old man lives alone at the water's edge on the east bank. His job is to ferry vehicles and passengers across the fabulously deep river for five pesos. The boat is held fast at the banks by strong ropes, its path controlled by a cable. The old man slowly, painfully switched the position of a rudder to make the craft move. He asked me to help as he lowered a moveable ramp. I drove on, and in five minutes I was on the other side.

Business isn't great nowadays, he says. Until recently trucks from a mine a few kilometers from the east bank needed to be shuttled back and forth. Now the mining has dwindled, and days go by without a single customer. Only a few trucks carrying calves to the market in Hermosillo break the monotony. On some holidays a few tourists trickle in from Hermosillo, but they're not interested in much and don't stay around. Fishing in the Yaqui isn't what it used to be, either, the present-day Charon laments. He still lands a catfish from time to time, sometimes a bass or bluegill, but since the dam was built upstream, fishing isn't much good. The old man coughed painfully as he talked to me. I sensed that he will not be around long. The surging river endures, its powerful currents little by little undermining the pathetic attempts to defy it. The crossing at Soyopa will fade into history along with the other old villages along the rivers as they lose their weary battles and fall sleepily into oblivion. The new highways have left them to rot. New transportation and commerce centers will grow along the high-speed corridors. The weak, remote villages will perish. Batuc was killed by floods; the others will be killed by neglect and indifference.

Epilogue

More than thirty years after my first trip, after most of this book was written, I drove south from Tucson, thinking back on the Sonora I had first seen from my Cushman motor scooter. Now I drove in an air-conditioned pickup. I was familiar with Sonoran geography. I had a clear destination in mind. The route was as familiar to me as any road I drive.

The rest of the state is much changed. Parts of it are hardly recognizable. Nogales is very big now, swollen with new growth. Shantytowns leapfrog up the steep hillsides, while modern luxury hotels slowly take shape in the canyon bottom. The crush of people and traffic is far greater than before. The noise is more penetrating. The customs building in Nogales was replaced twenty years ago with a new, modernistic structure where for decades the same two agents sat pecking on the same old typewriters in a cavernous room. Another crossing has been added a few miles west of the old one. Produce trucks line up there, sometimes backing up for a mile awaiting permission to bring their cargos to United States and Canadian customers. Sonora's cities have exploded. The state has grown faster than rapid-growth Arizona. Nogales has spurted from 25,000 inhabitants to over 100,000, according to the government, 300,000, according to those who know. The hills in which it was nestled are now covered with homes, many filled with shacks of desperate squatters.

Hermosillo has mushroomed from some 60,000 people to nine times that number. Santa Ana has 20,000 inhabitants. Ciudad Obregón and Guaymas are metropolises. Of the major cities, only Guaymas, named after a band of Seri Indians who once lived in the area, even existed two hundred years ago. The number of people in the cities is staggering; yet still more come from the south because the south of Mexico is very poor, and people hear of jobs in *El Norte* and somehow make their way to Sonora. In addition to the astonishing numbers in the cities one is struck by the youthfulness of the population.

Driving is easier, faster, and expensive. Highway 15 is now a fast, four-lane freeway. A toll expressway bypasses Magdalena; a booth extorts exorbitant payment north of Hermosillo; another skirts Guaymas; a fourth and fifth join Ciudad Obregón and Navojoa. Around each toll station disgruntled drivers have fashioned bypasses to avoid the steep fees. One enterprising village maintains a dirt bypass, collecting donations in tin cans from the vehicles they assist, their partners in toll evasion. Paved highways head off in all directions. The peso is now worth less than one percent of its previous value against the dollar. Droves of Mexicans descend on Nogales and Agua Prieta, hoping to find work.

Travel is easier. Getting a visa is a sixty-second operation. Long lines are unusual. However, getting a car permit is a bureaucratic nightmare. Lines are interminable. Gasoline, including the unleaded variety, is plentiful but fifty percent higher in price than in the United States. Motels have cropped up all along the highways, extracting outrageous prices. Hermosillo sports a Holiday Inn; San Carlos Bay, near Guaymas, a Club Med and Howard Johnson's. New tourist facilities seem to materialize from nothing. Rest stops on the freeway have toilets that work and toilet paper.

What I saw proved what I had read: commerce is booming. Affluent Mexicans crowd the border, speeding in new cars north to Tucson to fill shopping carts with North American goods unavailable in their country. Americans flock in dwindling numbers to the beaches, the condominiums, and the resort hotels of the Sea of Cortés. Mexicans buy into condominiums in Phoenix, while Americans invest in beach resorts in San Carlos. Stampedes of semi-trucks hurtle northwards crammed with produce for American tables. American-packaged foods stock the shelves of Sonoran supermarkets.

The Mexican border operation is more efficient, even though permit procedures for travel south change with confusing regularity. I went to the visa desk. The agent looked at me and thrust a blank form with a pen in front of me. He seemed indifferent to the information I wrote down. There was no longer a space for me to indicate my religion. No one asked to see my wallet. Inspection of my citizenship documents was at best cursory. It hardly seemed to matter whether I filled in the blanks or not, for when I returned the document with the blanks filled, the agent hurriedly signed it, stamped it, and sent me on my way to the car permit section.

In the fall of 1991 Mexico announced a plan to crack down on the illegal importation of foreign vehicles: a computerized registration system for all vehicles entering the country would be put into operation. The government expressed concern about the huge number of foreign-licensed vehicles entering the country and being sold to Mexicans, thus bypassing the high duties and undercutting the domestic car industry. From the looks of towns like Sahuaripa and Ures where American license plates abound, the bulk of the cars come from the United States, although they are driven by what appeared to be locals.

I joined the long queue in the grim barracks that dispenses the permits, muttering to myself that a crackdown on police corruption would work better than this harassment of tourists. The process took two hours. Most of the people in line were Hispanics from the United States visiting relatives in the interior of Mexico, a change from thirty years ago when most of the tourists were Caucasians on vacations. So many Mexicans work in the United States that movement back and forth comprises a large proportion of migration processing for both countries. It's another sign of the intertwining of the economies of the two nations. After an interminable wait, I got my window decal. I never wanted to visit Mexico again.

South of the border city, cowboys are fewer now. Pickups are more numerous. The once-quiet valley leading south now vibrates with the unending roar of traffic. Tiny hamlets have been leveled to make way for the freeway. A tiny roadside chapel lies flung on its side by the bulldozer clearing ground for the new freeway. Ranch houses that had once nestled against the bluffs rising from the valley are empty, crumbling, their inhabitants gone. In Imuris, Magdalena, Santa Ana, and Hermosillo I saw more affluent people, and new full-sized Fords, Nissans, and Chryslers. I also saw more poor people, many more. They were on foot, waiting, waiting.

As I drove south toward the capital, I passed the place where only a year ago *federales* set up a checkpoint and harassed travelers, especially North Americans. The checkpoint was abolished as a result of widespread protest of the violations of civil liberties. While their boss, Mexico's Attorney General, announced in mid-1991 a crackdown on these shock troops, the federal judicial police, they're still carrying on as they have for decades. They're almost universally despised in Sonora for their ruthlessness and violent arrogance. I've been harassed by them on numerous occasions. Once in the back roads of the Gran Desierto I ran into one of their road-blocks. While machine-gun-toting youths stood scowling in the background, the commanders ordered me from my vehicle and proceeded to remove all the contents, even the panels from the doors, which they never adequately replaced. While I watched, they helped themselves to beer they found in my ice chest. Having satisfied themselves that another gringo had gotten the message, they let me go on my way.

Even worse was the experience Virgil and I had while eating lunch near Mexico Route 15 while traffic whizzed by. Virgil was adding our last five-gallon can of unleaded fuel to his gas tank when we found ourselves surrounded by a band of malevolent fully armed *federales*, driving brand new vehicles—a United States–made Chevrolet Suburban and a Jeep Cherokee. Without a word of explanation, one of them (there were nine, all dressed in black T-shirts) pulled down the truck's tailgate, climbed inside and began rummaging through our belongings. Another climbed into the cab and rifled through everything he could find. One of their number demanded to know where we were coming from. When I told him it was Hermosillo, he demanded to know why we were carrying five-gallon gasoline cans. "Well," I replied, "we always carry a supply because supplies of unleaded fuel in Mexico are uncertain." He didn't respond but was not placated. He then demanded to know our occupation and where we were heading, and what we happened to be doing right there. My reply that we thought it might be a nice spot to eat lunch didn't seem to assuage his curiosity.

One of their number, a hostile-looking young man of perhaps nineteen, kept guard over us with an automatic rifle. The others swaggered with .45s strapped to their hips. Twice they yanked open the ice chest and rummaged inside, disappointed to find only a small, mostly melted block of ice and some rapidly aging luncheon meat. Finally, their mission of terrorizing accomplished, they drove off without a word, leaving us with a ravaged vehicle and an enhanced hostility to Mexico's ranging bands of federally commissioned thugs.

I related the incident to a Mexican friend of mine. I expected some sympathy, since *federales* routinely harass Mexicans as well as United States citizens. "Well, David," she said, serious but insufficiently sympathetic for my taste, "now you know what it's like."

It took a few moments for the import of her words to sink in. I thought of the innumerable accounts of how Mexican citizens legally in the United States were harassed in a similar fashion by United States Border Patrol, Highway Patrol, Bureau of Alcohol, Tobacco and Firearms, sheriffs, police, FBI, and Treasury Police. Now I was getting a taste, Mexican-style, of the very treatment Mexicans have been complaining about in my country for years. She had a point.

For all the anger and injustice they generate, I sense that the day of the *federales* has come and gone, that they will gradually disappear from the scene as the trade that binds our two nations renders them obsolete and only a temporary impediment to economic forces that will bowl them over.

Sonora is more dangerous now. I can no longer camp with impunity. Murders are more common, just as in the United States. More and more tourists are robbed, more of Sonora's wealthy are kidnapped. When I was robbed in 1993 I was one of an increasing number of foreign nationals assaulted. In 1994, Donaldo Colosio, the PRI nominee for president of the Republic, a popular Sonoran and a shoo-in for election, was assassinated in Tijuana.

As I drove south toward Hermosillo, I realized that the mountains to the east and west aren't unknown to me the way they once were. They've come alive with people, places, plants, animals, natural features, hot springs, *milpas*, rivers, canyons, *chiruzas*, and fiestas. My curiosity about what lay out *there* has been mostly satisfied, only to be replaced by a desire to know all those places in more detail, to chat with the people, and to see the cows, the plants, the wildlife, the historic buildings, and the new enterprises.

When I arrive in the busy city of Hermosillo I know friends are there, eager to offer Sonoran hospitality, to talk about everything under the sun, and to promote the greatness of their city and their state. I speak by phone to my friends. Can they get me such-and-such a book? Can they find out this and that for me?

They tell me to write down what I want and send it by fax. Business is carried on by fax, photocopying, and computer. Instant communications bind my home state and Sonora ever tighter.

Everywhere I go, I sense that Sonorans believe fervently, almost naively, that big things are about to happen, that a new era of trade will boost their prosperity. A friend in Hermosillo told me proudly that he had finally been able to visit Yécora. He spoke optimistically of the opportunities there for tourist investment. Others I spoke with mentioned investments in ranches, farms, and *maquiladoras.* These people for the most part speak English, visit the United States regularly, and work in circles close to the government. They exude hope, energy, and a passionate optimism. They are Sonora's modern voices, and although rural Sonora, with its *vaqueros, teguas, sombreros de palma, bacanora,* and *machaca,* with its thatched roofs, its adobe homes, and its timeless air of cyclical life still penetrates to the heart of the city, urban, forward-looking Sonorans seem intent on keeping these ancient ties as mere archetypes, nostalgic reminders of what Sonora once was but cannot continue to be.

I inspect a satellite photograph of Sonora, thinking of all the places I've visited and people I've chatted with, and remembering their stories, joys, and sorrows, their pasts, and the forces that control them. I wonder about their future, how the imminent, vast changes will affect them and will tie their fortunes into this remarkable state and its remarkable people. I think of Carolina, the Pima woman, struggling with her canyon farmland; of Chalillo, the Guarijío, traveling across the mountains on foot; of Martín, the engineering student hoping to help create a new Sonora; of Cruz, the fisherman, facing a depleted Sea of Cortés; of Santiago, my Seri friend struggling to defend his culture; of María weaving hats. I hope for them, hope fiercely that the future will be kinder to them than the past has been.

Not long ago I drove once again to Yécora, across buffeled plains, through deep canyons, past tiny towns, and up the twisted escarpment of the Sierra Madre. From among the pines at the summit I looked to the west. Much of Sonora opened up before me, range after range, misty valleys following, one after another. In the late afternoon the smog from Hermosillo far to the west turned the setting sun orange. I thought I spied the Gulf, 175 miles away. I marveled at Sonora's beauty, its wildness, the strange and wonderful contrasts in the people. There's so much to preserve here, I thought, so much to cherish. There are so many people with a profound sense of place and history.

I will continue to visit Sonora—six, eight times a year. I will camp in the tropical deciduous forest, sleep by the Sea of Cortés, watch chiruzas in Cucurpe, and sit in the plaza of Bacadéhuachi. I will chronicle the changes, the gains, the losses. I hope the people will be understanding of my attempts to describe them. I hope our common humanity unites us before technology and nationalism tear us apart.

BIBLIOGRAPHY

Almada, Francisco R. *Diccionario de Historia, Geografía y Biografía Sonorenses.* Chihuahua: Private printing, 1952.

———. *La Revolución en el Estado de Sonora.* Mexico City: Instituto Nacional de Estudios Históricos, 1971.

Bancroft, Hubert Howe. *North Mexican States and Texas,* 2 vols. San Francisco: The History Company, 1886.

Colegio de Sonora. *Sonora en la Decada de los Ochenta.* Hermosillo: Revista de El Colegio de Sonora, 1990.

Crumrine, N. Ross. "The Mayo of Southern Sonora," in *Themes of Indigenous Acculturation in Northwest Mexico.* Tucson: University of Arizona Press, 1981.

Cummings, Ronald G., *et al. Waterworks: Improving Irrigation in Mexican Agriculture.* World Resources Institute. WRI Paper 5, December 1989.

Dabdoub, Claudio. *Historia de El Valle del Yaqui.* Mexico: Libreria Manuel Porrua, 1964.

Dobie, J. Frank. *Apache Gold and Yaqui Silver.* Boston: Little Brown and Company, 1928.

Eckhart, George B. *Missions of Sonora.* Tucson: Private printing, 1961.

Felger, Richard, and Mary B. Moser. *People of the Desert and Sea.* Tucson: University of Arizona Press, 1985.

Fernandez, editores. *Enciclopedia Regional Ilustrada de Sonora.* Mexico City 1982.

Gentry, Howard Scott. *Agaves of Continental North America.* Tucson: University of Arizona Press, 1982.

———. "Caminos of San Bernardo." *The Michigan Alumnus Quarterly Review.* Winter, 1942.

———. *Río Mayo Plants.* Washington, D.C.: GPO, 1942.

———. *The Guarijío Indians of Sonora-Chihuahua: An Ethnographic Survey.* Anthropological Papers 65. Bureau of American Ethnology Bulletin 186, Washington, D.C.: GPO, 1963.

Hastings, J. Rodney, and Raymond M. Turner. *The Changing Mile.* Tucson: University of Arizona Press, 1964.

Healy, Ernesto Camou, ed. *Potreros, Vegas Y Mahuechis.* Hermosillo: Government of the State of Sonora, 1991.

Hinton, Thomas B. *A Survey of Indian Assimilation in Easter Sonora.* Tucson: University of Arizona Press, 1959.

Humphrey, Robert R. *The Boojum and Its Home.* Tucson: University of Arizona Press, 1974.

Janzen, Daniel H. "Tropical Dry Forests: The Most Endangered Major Tropical Ecosystem," in Wilson, E.O. *Biodiversity.* Cambridge: Harvard University Press, 1988, 130–37.

Lumholtz, Carl. *New Trails in Mexico.* Tucson: University of Arizona Press, 1990.

Manzo Taylor, Francisco Javier. *El Corrido de Obregón: Un Hecho Historico a la Luz de la Tradición Sonorense.* Unpublished.

Molina, Flavio Molina. *Nombres Geográficos Indígenas de Sonora.* Hermosillo: Flavio Molina Molina, 1986.

Moser, Edward. "Seri Basketry," *The Kiva* 38,3–4 (1973):105–40.

Nabhan, Gary Paul. *The Desert Smells Like Rain.* Flagstaff: Northpoint Press, 1979.

———. *Gathering the Desert.* Tucson: University of Arizona Press, 1986.

Nentvig, Juan. *Rudo Ensayo, A Description of Sonora and Arizona in 1764.* Tucson: University of Arizona Press, 1980.

Ortiz, Alfonso, ed. *Handbook of North American Indians: Southwest.* Washington: Smithsonian Institution, 1983.

Painter, Muriel Thayer. *A Yaqui Easter.* Tucson: University of Arizona Press, 1971.

Pfefferkorn, Ignaz. *Sonora: A Description of the Province.* Tucson: University of Arizona Press, 1989.

Polzer, Charles W. *Kino Guide II, His Missions—His Monuments.* Tucson: Southwestern Mission Research Center, 1982.

Riding, Alan. *Distant Neighbors: A Portrait of the Mexicans.* New York: Alfred A. Knopf, 1985.

Ruiz, Ramón Eduardo. *The People of Sonora and Yankee Capitalists.* Tucson: University of Arizona Press, 1988.

Sheridan, Tom. *Where the Dove Calls.* Tucson: University of Arizona Press, 1989.

Shreve, Forrest, and Ira Wiggins. *Vegetation of the Sonoran Desert.* Stanford: Stanford University Press, 1964.

Sobarzo, Horacio. *Episodios Históricos Sonorenses.* Mexico City: Editorial Porrúa, 1981.

———. *Vocabulario Sonorense.* Hermosillo: Gobierno del Estado de Sonora, 1984

Spicer, Edward H. *Cycles of Conquest.* Tucson: University of Arizona Press, 1962.

———. *Potam: A Yaqui Village in Sonora.* Memoirs of the American Anthropological Association 77. Menasha: Wisconsin, 1954.

———. *The Yaquis, A Cultural History.* Tucson: University of Arizona Press, 1985.

Steenbergh, Warren, and Charles H. Lowe, Jr. *Ecology of the Saguaro: II.* Washington, D.C.: GPO, 1977.

Turner, Ray. "Long-Term Vegetation Change at a Fully Protected Sonoran Desert Site, *Ecology* 71, 2 (1990).

Valdés, Sergio Calderón, ed. *Historia General de Sonora.* 5 vols. Hermosillo: Gobierno del Estado de Sonora, 1985.

West, Robert. *Sonora, Its Geographical Personality.* Austin: University of Texas Press, 1993.

Yetman, David. *Where the Desert Meets the Sea: A Trader in the Land of the Seri Indians.* Tucson: Pepper Publishing Co., 1988.

INDEX

240